THE TIMES BOOK OF
CLIFFORD LONGLEY

THE TIMES
BOOK OF
CLIFFORD LONGLEY

Edited by
Suzy Powling

Introduction by
Lord Rees-Mogg

HarperCollins*Religious*

HarperCollinsReligious
An Imprint of HarperCollins*Publishers*
77–85 Fulham Palace Road,
Hammersmith, London W6 8JB

Published by HarperCollinsReligious 1991
1   3   5   7   9   10   8   6   4   2

A catalogue record for this book
is available from the British Library

ISBN 0 00215 992 9

Phototypeset by Intype, London

Printed in Great Britain by
HarperCollinsManufacturing Glasgow

CONTENTS

INTRODUCTION

W hen I became Editor of *The Times* in the beginning of 1967 there was a senior member of the staff who had the magnificent by-line 'Our Ecclesiastical and Naval Correspondent'. That by-line summed up the attitude of *The Times* towards the coverage of religious affairs. *The Times* was interested in church matters, seen as part of the order of British society, and particularly in the church matters of the Church of England itself. *The Times* too saw itself as an establishment newspaper and saw the Church of England as an established church.

When I appointed Clifford Longley as Religious Affairs Correspondent in 1972 I remember that we had a discussion about his duties. He was somewhat hesitant about the definition of his work because he thought that *The Times* might expect him to continue to report religious affairs in the old tradition. I was anxious that he should bring to their coverage that sense of contemporary reality which was already evident in his work and in his way of thinking. When he realized that I wanted him to work in his own style and from his existing point of view he seemed very pleased to take the job, and he has done it now for nineteen years.

Few people reading Clifford Longley's work would know what his own religious views were, but they would realize that he was writing from a Christian point of view. I doubt myself if anyone can report on religious affairs satisfactorily without at the least a profound sympathy for religion, though I have known at least one correspondent who combined a deep sympathy for religion with a personal agnosticism. It is necessary for a good religious affairs correspondent to see religious matters from the inside, otherwise he will not be able to understand the motivations of religious people or the inner action of the churches. He will become purely a correspondent of externals. No one reading this book will find that Clifford Longley is merely an external writer. Again and again one comes across a particular insight which shows that he is not only able to report about ecclesiastical structures but also about the spiritual realities that those structures contain. The book as a whole is a testimony to the religious spirit and a work of sympathy to all those who are carrying out religious tasks in different traditions but from a spiritual point of view.

Clifford Longley has never been under illusions about the society in which modern religion has to work. It is a secular society and one which treats the churches as in some real sense second-class citizens. Clifford Longley writes about the 'identity crisis' of the Catholic priesthood, and he writes repeatedly about the difficulty of the modern position of the Church of England. Indeed he is particularly sympathetic to the Anglican communion because he understands particularly well the difficulty of that communion's relationship with the modern world, and the tensions inside the Anglican communion which the relationship with a secular society necessarily causes.

The message that one gets from Clifford Longley's coverage of what has actually been happening in religious affairs in Britain is that of his own commitment to a personal response. He sees the churches as groups of individuals trying to find their way forward in a period of difficulty and does not see them simply as abstractions. 'To filter out from Christianity that essential element that demands a personal response is to change its nature.' He is a gentle opponent but he is opposed to the attempt of a secular society to re-mould churches and religious beliefs to suit its own pattern of assumptions. In a secular society it is easy for religion to be tolerated but only on a secularized footing. This is the neutral point of view which is indeed tempting to journalists because they ought to be impartial observers of events, and it is a view which Clifford Longley has rejected. 'To be neutral is to refuse to respond: to refuse to respond is to deny that it (religion) is true. Without involvement, what remains is not an approximation that can be made good later but a quite false version.'

Apart from the late Gerald Priestland, I think there is no doubt that Clifford Longley has been the most influential religious affairs correspondent of his period. It is notable that many other newspapers have followed the example of *The Times* in appointing a correspondent with a similar remit and with a wide discretion to report on the changes in the spiritual affairs of the churches and not simply in their formal structures. When he started writing about religious affairs most newspapers regarded them as of only narrow interest, a specialist subject, like having a rowing correspondent to cover Henley. Since that time church attendance has continued to fall, and it would be natural for newspapers to have continued to regard religious affairs as of low news value.

The contrary has happened because editors have seen that good religious correspondents write copy that is interesting in itself and is talked about and discussed by readers. Gerald Priestland said that when he went from being a general correspondent of the BBC to being a religious broadcaster his postbag went up from being negligible to containing a significant number of letters every day. Clifford Longley must have been one of the correspondents who attracted the most readers to communicate both to him and to *The Times*. His example has been followed, he has made a change in journalism by showing what could be done and he has helped the churches to understand the shifting relationships of a secular period.

William Rees-Mogg
London, June 1991

PREFACE

S taff journalists are distinguished from almost every other kind of writer by having no control over length (which is never enough) or time (likewise), and not much over subject matter. On a daily newspaper writing is more part of an indus-trial production line than a free-flowing creative enterprise. While everybody involved in the production of a newspaper knows that quality counts, meeting the deadline is the priority.

Many of the items in this collection were written in that helter-skelter way. Maybe that shows, and maybe that is not a bad thing. Not every item is in instant reaction, but many of them are. In a newspaper you get one shot only; there is no dress rehearsal, and your first attempt is usually your last. The limitations of space demand a concise style of writing, for the next link in the production chain is a sub-editor who can spot unnecessary words at ten paces. There is always too much material for the space available on each page, and sub-editors, too, are under intense time-pressure.

This is all very different, therefore, from writing a book. The fast tempo and high adrenalin of the world of daily journalism are sometimes out of step with the pace at which events actually happen, and sometimes with the character of the events them-selves, and that is particularly true of religion. If a week is a long time in politics and a day is a long time in a newspaper office, a year is a short time in religion. So daily journalism and religion do not fit well together, which is no doubt part of the reason some newspapers are sometimes tempted to ignore it altogether.

Furthermore, having seen plenty of both, my suspicion is that professional journalists and professional religious people come from opposite ends of the personality spectrum. There is an impatience about journalism which attracts a certain sort. Religion is often a waiting game: the only view which makes sense is the long view. Newspapers are bound to be concerned with the ripples on the surface of life; religion is about the deep ocean currents which are often completely hidden and which move enormous masses of water over long distances very slowly. But we know, particularly in Britain astride the Gulf Stream, that deep ocean currents are crucial to the overall climate while making little difference to today's weather. That is a valid metaphor for changes in the social climate as a result of religious movements far below the surface ripples.

Hence daily newspaper journalism might seem a most inappropriate vehicle for recording and interpreting changes in the religious climate. That is the challenge. As Samuel Johnson said of a dog walking on hind legs, the wonder is not that the creature does it well, but that he does it at all.

I was made religious affairs correspondent of *The Times* by the then editor, William Rees-Mogg, in 1972. It was a new idea in British journalism. Until then, the affairs of the churches were reported, if at all, with a certain deference; it was not expected that journalists would comment candidly or critically on such pious subject matter. Nor had one correspondent attempted to cover not just the Anglican and Free churches, but Roman Catholicism, Islam, Judaism and any other faith which required attention, not forgetting atheism if that can be called a faith.

So in 1968 the then Times Churches Correspondent, Basil Gingell, wrote nothing about the row in the Roman Catholic Church over the papal encyclical on birth control, *Humanae Vitae*, because it was not considered part of his job. *The Times* had a little black book of freelances, and the entry under Catholicism gave the name of a writer on *The Universe*, the Catholic weekly. When we called the number, we found the contact had left some time ago. It was our attempt to improvise round that difficulty – I was on the home news desk at the time – which first gave me a taste for this whole curious subject, an interest heightened when I later covered Northern Ireland.

While I was being asked to report in a new way, with no more deference than journalists showed in any other area – and no 'no-go areas' – I was also invited by the editor to contribute a weekly commentary. He saw correctly that normal news coverage was unlikely to do justice to what was really happening in this field. A column can probe at greater depth. And most readers, particularly when reading about an area of religion which was not their own, would need considerable help in understanding what was happening and why.

Hence my weekly article, which has appeared in *The Times* for almost twenty years. The collection assembled for this book covers only the most recent couple of those years, and a lot has had to be left out. The selection and organization has been made with great understanding by Suzy Powling, the book's editor, to whom I must record my sincere thanks. It if reads well, that is her doing.

During the two years the book spans I at last gave up covering daily religious news for the paper – a new religious affairs correspondent was appointed in 1990 – and I transferred to other work as the assistant editor responsible for the *The Times'* leader department. My weekly column continues, however, as does my title – albeit now a little titular – of Religious Affairs Editor.

So does the pressure of time and space; and so does the challenge of negotiating weekly between two very different and almost incompatible interests. One should know them well after nearly twenty years, but readers continue to surprise me. Their reactions are unpredictable, which fortunately excuses me from any duty to take those reactions into account. It is common for an article to have a quite different effect from the one expected. What I also have begun to learn is that they do not necessarily want to read – where religion is concerned at least – what most journalists would expect them to want.

Journalism is easiest when it is concerned with institutions, and personalities within those institutions. Religious institutions have their share of quarrels about personality clashes, and these make good copy. But religion is essentially 'about' something else. Readers are eager to be told about that too. Many people find religious belief extraordinarily difficult in the modern world. That they do not give up the struggle suggests that religious questions have an abiding attraction, even if orthodox religious answers do not always satisfy.

There is manifestly an appetite 'out there' – as journalists say to each other, pointing to the office window – for anything which illuminates these questions and answers. Strictly speaking, this is hardly journalism at all. But I know from experience that if I can find a journalistic 'peg' which allows some reflections on prayer, mysticism, suffering, holiness, the relationship between man and God, then the quality of the incoming correspondence changes at once. It is warmer, more intense, more personal, and indeed more grateful. If this is still, in some sense, reporting, then it is reporting both on what I can scavenge from others, and on what I can find inside myself. But I must say it took me a while to realize that that might be a useful place to look. It may be part of the normal beat of the novelist or poet, but not of a Fleet Street journalist.

Yet the one thing a journalist cannot know is 'what God is doing'. That is true in the simplest sense, and I am not much help to those who write to me asking why some personal tragedy has occurred to them. It is also true within communities and societies, including churches.

For instance, I am a Roman Catholic. But I cannot afford to read history, either recent events or the far past, through that one lens. I do not know, and nor can anybody, whose side God was on at the time of the Reformation. Was the split which has divided western Christianity for nearly five centuries an evil, contrary to God's purposes? Did He 'allow' it out of respect for human free will? Did He in some sense even cause it, and therefore wish into existence some of the consequences? An old-fashioned Roman Catholic would have answers, but I do not.

A great deal of my work is with the Church of England, to

which I do not belong but with which I would claim to have as much sympathy as is possible short of actual membership. If that sympathy occasionally fails me, then that is a fault (though I observe that sympathy is also sometimes lacking in its own ranks). But I do not wish the Church of England out of existence, as a sort of usurper of the role of my own church. I like and respect it; I wish it well.

It is almost too obvious to need saying (though perhaps a Roman Catholic still has to do so) that God works His purposes within the Church of England no less than in any other. I do not therefore fall with relish on some point in the church's affairs which calls for criticism. Nor do I feel a corresponding sense of sorrow when the Roman Catholic Church offers such a target. It is a long time since the late Cardinal Heenan tried to appeal to my Roman Catholic loyalty to get me off his back. I am afraid we did not understand each other, though I think we were friends. But this measures the distance that has been covered in twenty years. In England, at least, the Roman Catholic Church has long ceased dismissing all who criticize it as either 'bad Catholics' or 'malicious Protestants'.

There is a similar open-minded willingness to listen to bad news in the Jewish community, and growing signs of it – very encouraging evidence of maturity – among leading Muslims. In the Church of England, perhaps because it is used to a high level of internal controversy, there is a long-standing habit of immunity to criticism, and often more interest in looking for axes being ground that in weighing what is being said at face value. In fact the best place for reporting the affairs of the Church of England fairly and objectively is from outside its ranks altogether. At least then one has no private motive for wishing to see Evangelicals advance at the expense of Anglo-Catholics or vice versa.

I have been accused of both, of course. And for all the good friendships I have been grateful for with leading members of the Anglican community, I can still detect that quizzical 'what is he really up to?' question in their attitude to me. The answer is above. Newspaper journalism is too busy a trade to have the time to be 'up to' anything.

There are three purposes to it: advancing the interests of one's newspaper; earning a living; and spreading some truth around. Telling members of the public what happened yesterday, and what it might signify, serves all three purposes. There is no fourth. And this means that 'the cause of Christianity', which I am sometimes praised for advancing or blamed for impeding, is not my business, except in so far as circulating news or ideas may broadly or generally do one or the other. I am the last person to convert anybody, though I did once meet somebody who informed me I had succeeded in his case.

This detachment is not an agnostic or atheist position. There is, I believe, a Good Providence at work in the affairs of men. The work of that supernatural influence is hindered by lies, misunderstandings, exaggerations, mischief-making; it is assisted by honesty, truth, clarity, objectivity. In that respect therefore good journalism serves a higher purpose. It is important, paradoxically, not to know what that purpose is. But it does no harm, occasionally, to make a guess.

One of the great issues of the day is the connection between public policy and personal morality. We can all be grateful to Margaret Thatcher's years as prime minister for the effect they had on the quality of public debate. Whatever lesser men might be up to, her politics were about principle rather than pragmatism; and she liked to state her principles abrasively.

While politicians outside her ranks accepted her challenge, so did churchmen and religious leaders. The 'Thatcher versus the Church', story was a constant theme of the 1980s. Here was a prime minister who not only quarrelled with many of the prevailing prejudices most of them took for granted, but was prepared to present her challenge in their language (or nearly). It is appropriate, therefore, that this selection should begin here. It is, in a way, already history. But the 1980s will go on being fertile material for analysts long after the 1970s, possibly even the 1990s, are forgotten.

The present decade will be incomprehensible unless we understand the previous one. Politicians may well stop trying to answer the questions which Thatcherism threw up, but that does not mean they were not good questions, only that the

quality of the politicians has declined. I am not of her persuasion, but she made me think. And faced with the demand
to fill my space each week, some of those thoughts found their
way onto paper. One cannot enter through that door, however,
unless prepared to encounter some of the most difficult (and
baffling) questions facing British society. Some of the threads
covered here occur elsewhere in the book, which is not just
because events kept bringing them to the fore. It also reflects
my own judgement that these issues are perennial ones. I am
not sure whether I wish the reader to finish this section less
baffled or more so.

That, I fear, is no less true of the section on Anglican
identity. There is a tendency in the Church of England, rather
like the British constitution, to leave well alone because it
seems to work. Illogical though it may seem, too many probing
questions are 'unhelpful'. But my twenty years' acquaintance
with that church have been years of its decline: clearly something is not working as it should, and maybe some questions
ought to be raised. It is strictly true that one cannot know what
Anglicanism is without being an Anglican. Nonetheless the
Church of England is now an island of religion in a sea of
unfaith, and must give some account of itself to those who do
not know it from the inside. People want to know what it stands
for.

In any event it is an odd feature of the Church of England
that we are all invited to share in responsibility for it, whatever
our personal convictions. The ultimate authority over the faith
and life of the Church of England lies with the British Parliament, and everybody who can vote for an MP may, if so
inclined, join in the argument. Personally I do not think that
should be so; but the Church of England likes it that way.

One of the more illuminating events in the life of that church
was the 1988 Lambeth Conference, when Anglican bishops
came to Canterbury from all over the world for three weeks of
deliberation on issues of Anglican identity (with a few moments
of relaxing Longley-bashing for entertainment, as one of the
articles describes). It is not enough that these fundamental

issues should be examined only once in ten years, which is why they are in this collection.

It is far too soon to begin to ask how this debate will end. But I will not be writing the obituary of the Church of England in my lifetime. One of the problems of a selection such as this is that one may look back with hindsight; and I look back at the article 'A Tolerant Church, Worthy of a Generous Obituary', aware that it was misunderstood (partly because of the heading, for which I was not responsible). The article lamented the decline of a particular kind of Anglicanism, once dominant; I was accused of declaring it dead. Let me add the necessary footnote here: it lives.

The ordination of women is a debate which has many attractions to a secular journalist, not least that everybody thinks they understand it and therefore can hold strong views. Or almost everybody – in spite of the extensive coverage I have given it, I still do not know what I think. My disadvantage is that I understand both sides, each of which has a conclusive case. The nearest I come to an opinion, therefore, is the principle: in case of doubt, do nothing. Timidly, I recommend that to the Church of England, confident that it is not listening. When it ends in tears, at least I can say 'I told you so'.

Thatcherism, the Lambeth Conference, the change of Archbishops of Canterbury, all find their way into this selection because they were important issues in religion in the period covered. So were relations between the Church of England and the Roman Catholic Church, though here I do believe I was genuinely writing an obituary

Archbishop Robert Runcie's visit to Pope John Paul II represented an end to any immediate hopes for a reconciliation between these two great churches in their lifetimes. Part of the reason was the inconclusive nature of the discussion at the Lambeth Conference on female ordination. Undoubtedly another reason was the whole character of this Pope's reign, whose merits are best appreciated from the safe distance of another church. The selection here, on the subject of the Vatican and the Roman Catholic faithful, needs to be read with the same qualification offered earlier concerning the Church of England: the only complete way of understanding the life of such institutions is from the inside. Any other perspective is a distortion.

Two faiths which know each other only too well from an outside distorting perspective are Christianity and Judaism. Here I am not neutral: where antisemitism is concerned, neutrality is a sin. Over twenty years I have often felt a duty to remind readers of the dreadful history of this relationship and its catastrophic consequences, and a few contributions of that sort are a necessary part of this collection.

This tragic mistake is fortunately not likely to be repeated, though it would be complacent to suppose that the presence in Britain of a substantial Muslim minority will take care of itself. The Salman Rushdie affair, and later the Gulf war, brought that uneasiness to the surface; but since then there has been healing. And just as other religions in Britain have come to terms with a tradition of critical religious journalism, not afraid to see their affairs laid, warts and all, before the public gaze, so Islam is learning to accept it too. Hinduism and Sikhism in Britain remain, so far, impenetrable to the exploratory techniques of secular journalism, but in time that too will change.

Many opinion-formers in church institutions misread the issues in the Gulf war and gave a false lead; but one of their constant concerns was to uphold intercommunal and international harmony. We have come a long way from the days of the religious patriotism and militarism of the First World War, of 'praise God and pass the ammunition'. The fact that Britain is gradually overcoming some potentially serious communal divisions between races and faiths is in no small measure due to the presence throughout the country, in every square mile of it, of men and women of enormous goodwill. A high proportion of the most dedicated of those are Christian priests and ministers.

Such an influential presence in society belies the image of Britain as totally secular. None the less there is no greater challenge facing organized and unorganized religious belief than secularism. Some of the articles selected for this book try to throw more light on this apparently simple, but in fact mysterious, phenomenon of secularism. It is not primarily about hostility to religion, but of indifference to it. Religion, as one journalist on *The Times* once said to me, is 'over'. We can make our own way now. That is not a true statement, of course, but it accurately describes the secular mind.

The perceived or assumed 'defeat' of religion by science is one of the dogmas of this faithless faith, the impression that somebody important, sometime in the past – Charles Darwin, Bertrand Russell, A. J. Ayer, it matters not – has finally 'disproved' the possibility of an intelligent person having faith in God. Those who have that impression cannot actually reproduce any of the supposed arguments that went into that supposed demolition. Hence this is more a fashion than a philosophical opinion. But it is very common. In fact the issue is by no means closed, as I hope some of the items in this collection on science and religion may show.

None of these articles can claim to be more than snap-shots, taken hastily. Even added together they amount to no more than a wider snap-shot, albeit one composed in less of an almighty rush. They are not a personal testimony, and many of the things I privately believe are not echoed here at all. It surprises me, in fact, that these articles might have a longer life than the mere twenty-four hours which elapses between one edition of the paper and the next. Maybe journalists take themselves far too seriously in the short run, but not seriously enough in the long.

Part One

CHURCH

AND

STATE

WHEN CHURCH AND STATE DIFFER
Margaret Thatcher

6 June 1988

In May 1988 Mrs Margaret Thatcher, then Prime Minister, had made a speech to the Church of Scotland affirming her "Christian principles" in which she claimed that the needs of the poor could be met by acts of individual charity, and went on to emphasize the importance of wealth creation. The General Synod of the Church of England's Board for Social Responsibility quickly responded with a letter warning the Prime Minister that social harmony was threatened by "deep divisions and injustices" in society. The letter also stated that governments have clear social and moral obligations to "pursue policies which . . . encourage that sense of community and mutuality which are the hallmarks of a complete human life".

*

The relationship between church and state remains one of the most difficult controversies of public life, as recent events have proved once more. It has been a constant theme of the administration of Mrs Margaret Thatcher, by all accounts the most theologically minded Prime Minister this century, and her recent actions have made the issue even more prominent. But it is a controversy which refuses to settle into manageable shape: for even the terms of the argument are part of the disagreement.

No one can really suggest, for instance, that the cleavage between the spiritual and temporal realms should be absolute, the view sometimes naively summed up by saying that the church should "stay in the sanctuary". Mrs Thatcher herself certainly believes no such thing. And a constitution which puts two dozen bishops in the upper chamber of the legislature, bishops the Prime Minister helps to appoint, gives no warrant for such a radical separation either. No one suggests, on the other hand, that the church has any inspired means of knowing what should be the present level of the public sector borrowing requirement, for instance.

The argument falls within these two extremes, and it is not even clear whom the argument is between. "The church" of popular or political speech seems to mean the senior clergy, bishops especially, but they would be the first to disown such an exclusive label. Mrs Thatcher is as much a member of the Church of England as the Bishop of Gloucester, the latest prelate to challenge her publicly; and he would not deny it. One of the major complications, therefore, is that the controversy is only partly between the church and the Government; it is also partly an argument within the church itself.

The substance of the argument is about the practical application of Christian teaching in the organization of national affairs, particularly social and economic policy. But there are not even common ground rules as to the theoretical basis of the debate. It is easy to quote the Bible, easiest if one is fairly ignorant of it as a whole; but for almost every text in Scripture which can be offered on one side, there will be another saying the opposite, and a third mocking the conceit of the whole exercise. Thus Mr Kinnock's "more Christian than you" gibe at the Prime Minister last month founders on the parable of the Pharisee and the tax collector (traditionally, the "publican"). The Pharisee stood up boldly and thanked God that he was not grasping and unjust, unlike the tax collector he saw hiding at the back of the temple. The other simply prayed "God, be merciful to me, a sinner." But he had God's approval; the Pharisee did not, and Mr Kinnock was unwittingly bracketing himself with the Pharisee.

Mrs Thatcher's boast in reply that she voluntarily relinquishes part of her salary sounds like the advertisement of a good deed to gain public approval: which may sound disapproving, but why else did she do it? Of such people Jesus coldly remarked "They have had their reward," adding that the doing of good works and the giving of alms should be so little publicized that even the right hand should not know what the left hand is doing.

The Bible has a way of biting the hand that quotes it, and all politicians must stand under the judgement of the Magnificat: "He hath put down the mighty from their seats, and exalted them of low degree." But the daily political debate necessarily involves countless small acts of pride, and humble politicians just do not get elected. The meek may be otherwise blessed, but they do not perform well at the Dispatch Box.

Nor is the Bible useful as a text book of economics either. Selling everything to give to the poor is not exactly a text in favour of wealth creation; nor is paying the labourer the same for one hour as others received for a whole day, socialism: it is more a text for "management's right to manage" badly, perhaps.

So it might seem safer to rely on three other sources from which religious teaching may be drawn: tradition, what the church has consistently said down the ages; the *sensus fidelium*, the agreed mind of the church today; and theology, what the religious experts have to say. But if it is impossible to find in the Christian tradition evidence in support of something as fundamental as democracy, there is not much point in searching it for clues concerning the right balance of powers between national government and local education authorities, on which churchmen have recently stated strong views. The *sensus fidelium*, on the other hand, is a neat theory but a dangerous concept in practice. If articles of faith cannot be decided by majority votes, and no one in the church thinks they can be, then why should the application of the faith in specific cases be so decided? What a majority of members of the General Synod of the Church of England vote for cannot have much more authority than a straw poll of a rather peculiar sample of the total population. It might or might not be sensible; but it certainly cannot claim to be the Word of God.

Theologians, on the other hand, tend to think they really do know some of the answers. The problem in Britain is that the development of social theology is weak and neglected, and what passes for it is often not much more than a sprinkling of holy water over what are essentially secular political prejudices. The famous 1985 report *Faith in the City*, for instance, was written by an Archbishop's Commission which was emphatically weighted towards sociology, with hardly a theologian in sight; and the report itself was at its least convincing in its theological section (as the Church of England has subsequently come to realize).

When an earlier commission was set up to write the report *The Church and the Bomb*, the Church of England invited on to it a distinguished Roman Catholic moral theologian to give it theological weight; when a later committee was asked to study "values in British society" the Church of England borrowed a Jesuit for the same purpose. These were implicit admissions of weakness in this area of Anglican theology. And this strongly suggests that the Church of England is not quite at home even on its own territory, and needs to be very much more careful than it has been so far in challenging Mrs Thatcher's theology as incompetent. It certainly has no right to patronize her.

WEALTH AND SPIRITUAL HEALTH

13 June 1988

There is currently a deep suspicion of wealth in British Christianity; wealth has taken over from sex as something about which churchmen feel they can safely be self-righteous. It is a kind of puritanism which runs through all denominations, and it largely explains the instinctive dislike most church leaders feel towards the present Government.

In fact the gap between rich and poor in British society is a good deal less blatant than it was up to the Second World War, when the churches made a good deal less fuss about it.

14

This change of mood is therefore not easy to explain: it may be a complicated kind of middle-class guilt, or it could even be that the churches are living closer to the true values of the Gospel than ever before.

Those who prefer the latter view are entitled to count on their side a very considerable quantity of New Testament teaching concerning the perils of wealth, much more than on the perils of sexual licence. It is notable, however, that this contemporary Christian hostility to wealth does not show itself in the development of new forms of personal asceticism; it shows itself as a posture of disapproval towards a certain kind of political philosophy. Wealth is offensive because its existence is seen to contradict ideals of economic equality and social justice, rather than because the wealthy as such are spiritually impaired.

It is rather characteristic of modern Christianity to place the emphasis on social morality rather than on personal spirituality, on this world rather than the next. That way it can establish a bridge with the secular world, albeit at a considerable risk of distorting the Gospel's own priorities. For on its own terms Christianity is not a blueprint for putting the world to rights but the pathway to heaven. It is a religion, not a set of moral and political beliefs.

There is no doubt the New Testament prefers the poor to the rich, as being nearer to heaven. It does not treat poverty as morally scandalous, a condition to be cured: it says it is blessed. Those who are wealthy are warned, and those whose main aim in life is to become so, are contemptuously condemned. These are very awkward texts both for the economic egalitarians and for the prophets of wealth creation.

It is the major flaw in Mrs Thatcher's theological defence of Thatcherism, that she speaks as if Jesus never said an ill word against the wealthy. But it is also a major flaw in the theological critique of Thatcherism, as so far presented, that it seeks the wider distribution of wealth while ignoring no less than she does the warning on the wrapping: "Wealth is bad for your spiritual health."

Jesus did not treat wealth only, or even mainly, as a moral

problem, concerned with relations between people: he treated it as a spiritual one, concerned with the state of a man's soul. In the same way his remark "If thine eye offend thee, pluck it out" is not a statement of a principle of medical ethics, nor is his demand that those who follow him must "hate" their father and mother, a prescription for the moral basis of Christian family life. He was talking about spiritual renunciation as a necessary condition for entry into the kingdom of heaven. All "attachments", whether to money, to parts of the body, to members of one's family, and to life itself, are barriers to the life of the spirit that he preached. One of the most famous examples of this preaching, thrown at Mrs Thatcher by the Bishop of Gloucester recently, was the challenge to the rich young man to give all he possessed to the poor, because it was "easier for a camel to pass through the eye of a needle" than for the rich to enter heaven.

But spiritually it is possession that is relevant, not what is possessed. The bishop treated this teaching as meaning that the rich are condemned because of how they treat the poor, implying if there were no poor, the rich could keep their riches. But the point of the renunciation of attachments and possessions is not the benefit to some recipient – Jesus did not say "If you see a blind man, pluck out your eye and give it to him" – but the spiritual condition which makes renunciation possible. It is the willingness to let go, not the letting go itself, which counts.

The challenge to the rich young man was only incidentally a financial one, therefore. In its spiritual meaning it corresponds exactly to the challenge to Abraham to sacrifice his beloved son Isaac, to give up what was most precious in his life. And Abraham's mental act of renunciation, his willingness to obey, was the end of the test – he was not obliged to carry it through. Similarly there would have been no need for Jesus to insist on the young man actually disposing of anything, if he was genuinely ready to get rid of everything.

This spiritual teaching is by no means confined to Jesus or to Christianity; it is equally present in Judaism, Islam, Buddhism and Hinduism, often with very similar images. The

16

wisdom of all these religions is that the man who defines himself by his possessions and attachments is controlled by them; he is not free to love, to serve God, or to die. The one who may safely own a million pounds, without risk to his eternal salvation, is the one who could not care less whether he does or not. But it is a fact of life that most people with a million pounds care very much, and want a million more.

GOVERNING IN THE SHADOW OF THE GOOD SAMARITAN

3 September 1988

The Thatcher Government has left itself wide open to the criticism that it has no theory of society; and one of the Prime Minister's most notorious utterances, that there was "no such thing as society", suggests she thinks the lack of such a theory to be a virtue rather than a vice. Whatever she really meant by that remark, modern Conservatism is manifestly more interested in economics than in social philosophy, which goes a long way to explain the cross purposes, occasionally erupting in periods of friction, which exist between it and the Christian churches. Their priorities are the other way round. They, like the Labour Party, have tended to start from the question, "What sort of society do we want?" treating economics as a means by which those ends may be pursued. Conservative politics under Mrs Thatcher has started from the question "What sort of economy do we want?" leaving it to society to shape itself accordingly.

Critics dismiss this as an amoral approach, and have failed to take seriously the radical Conservative reply that the free market is itself a primary ethical principle. It seems there is not much room, therefore, for philosophical or theological dia-

17

logue with the Government on the part of those who do not share this ethical premise, and who may well regard the free market, if it is a moral force at all, as a malign influence.

But there is another route by which the Government could be brought to engage in moral debate with its critics, which begs no questions about "society", which has good Christian credentials, and which could ring bells in Conservative think-tanks and elsewhere once the implications are understood. There are signs that some Conservative theorists have begun to hear them ringing already.

The Government has shown itself eclectic enough to take good ideas wherever it finds them, which may be fortunate in this case as the source could hardly sound more unfamiliar to most Conservative ears: Roman Catholic social teaching. The two principles on which it builds, claiming to find them at least implicitly in the Scriptures and in Natural Law, are subsidiarity and solidarity. They have been variously defined: almost every Pope this century has had a go. The first can be sufficiently expressed as the principle that society in general is there to serve the good of individual persons, particularly when grouped in the basic natural community, the family. So society should seek to support and promote activity at the personal and familial level, not supplant or suppress it.

One facet of the principle of subsidiarity is that decisions affecting individuals and families should wherever possible be made by them themselves, not by others on behalf of "society"; and the implication for social organization is that a small and local administrative structure is better than a large central one. So decisions should be made as far down the chain of adminis-tration as possible, as close to the personal level as possible. And "small is beautiful" is, in fact, a slogan which owes its origins to the principle of subsidiarity in Catholic social teaching.

Solidarity was not a word invented by Polish trades union-ists, for they too know Catholic social teaching. It is the political expression of the parable of the Good Samaritan, which simul-taneously answered the questions "Who is my neighbour?" and "What is my duty to him?" It gave an enlarging answer to both questions: one's neighbour is potentially every other member of the human race, transcending race, class and nationality; one's duty is unlimited.

It is this solidarity which constitutes the moral basis for society, being a collection of persons who acknowledge their mutual responsibilities. In that sense society cannot and does not exist independently of the individuals who make it up, or of the responsibilities they accept for each other. The focus is on "persons in community"; but the community exists for persons, not the other way round. Solidarity and subsidiarity are thus closely related concepts. Where they may answer the present need for a new sort of language for discussing political philosophy is that neither of them magnify the state.

Solidarity and subsidiarity apply even where there is no state at all, and apply in spheres – such as non-state voluntary or religious organizations – which are not the business of the state. They apply internationally. They also apply particularly to families and things which touch family life. They emphasize what people can do for themselves and each other, rather than what should be done for them by "society". And towards economic policy they are neutral: in some respects they support the theory of the free market, in some respects not. But without the choices that the market makes available, it appears that neither solidarity nor subsidiarity have the scope they need.

"Rolling back Government" and "handing power back to the people", two ideas which have dominated the political rhetoric of Mrs Thatcher's Government, are not so dissimilar to the principle of subsidiarity. But on its own, without solidarity, subsidiarity can deteriorate into selfish individualism, materialism and "devil take the hindmost".

The Government has not been so good at enhancing solidarity (and in practice not always a consistent friend of subsidiarity either) and has gone out of its way to weaken one of the most powerful instances of the solidarity principle at work, through its assault on trades unionism. The Welfare State, equally, has a strong element of solidarity in its title deeds, though it has not been too careful of subsidiarity. Recognition of the profound coupling between these two moral principles would tell the Government that both those institutions need more of the subsidiarity principle, not less of the solidarity principle, to make them more human, more healthy – and more Christian. And the same may apply to the Government itself.

CHANGING VIEW OF THATCHERISM

22 October 1988

The churches have been at loggerheads with Mrs Margaret Thatcher almost from the day she was elected nine years ago, although they were sparring not so much with the lady herself but with what her opponents and now even some of her supporters call Thatcherism.

It has been an infinitely frustrating contest on both sides, however, because there is no precise political creed of that name, and its enemies define it differently from its friends. But because it is undefined it is also mutable; and church critics of the Government are entitled to take some comfort from certain recent shifts reported by political commentators. Thatcherism in late 1988 appears to have taken on board some of the things that were being said by its critics, ecclesiastical as well as political.

The argument has also been frustrating because Thatcherism has its own views on the proper role in society for institutions such as churches, which do not fit well with how they see themselves, confounding the cross purposes. As in economic Thatcherism, this is an individualistic conception, summed up by the Thatcherist writer Rachel Tingle, in her recent pamphlet *Another Gospel*, as the business of extending the Kingdom of God by "individuals becoming Christians ... The way the churches can help usher in the Kingdom is through personal evangelism."

This was once the standard line among Evangelicals,

though it has largely been repudiated, according to the Rev. Pat Dearnley, director of the Church Urban Fund. Writing in the latest edition of *Third Way*, an Evangelical monthly, he states that Anglican Evangelicals are now on the left of the political spectrum, emphasizing the communal and collective dimension rather than individual activity, "for the sake of the Kingdom".

This politicization of the Evangelical Movement has been one of the most significant in church-government relations, for it has withdrawn from Thatcherism what could have been a large constituency of support in the Church of England. For they were once more or less entirely apolitical or right-wing, almost an early version of the American "moral majority" and therefore natural Thatcherites. Instead, without any significant strand of church opinion on her side, Mrs Thatcher has been faced with an almost united front of church criticism, distrust and incomprehension. Undoubtedly one of the difficulties has been that even among those senior Conservatives who have wanted to engage with the churches, few of them are theologically literate, and their understanding of Christianity has sometimes been stated simplistically.

In the July edition of *New Blackfriars*, the journal of the English province of the Dominican Order, Dr Nicholas Boyle, fellow of Magdalene College, Cambridge, declared: "In recent months there have been signs that the hypnotic spell of Thatcherism is waning, and that a new and more fundamental debate is beginning, within, between, and outside the political parties . . . It is no accident that the churches have been prominent in bringing about the present discussion." Though a Roman Catholic, he gives most of the credit to the Church of England, which he says has been willing to risk disestablishment while his own church was still pursuing respectability and still scared of the suspicion of treason.

His thesis is that Thatcherism is essentially about the radical modernization of the British state along Continental lines, discarding customs and traditions – including the concept of the national community as a moral entity – that do not fit. He cites Napoleonism, Leninism and contemporary Eastern

21

European socialism as models for such a "modern" state. In the process citizenship is being reduced, as Marx reduced it, to narrow economic terms, either as producer or consumer; and so there is no longer any higher idea of what "being British" is about. Britain's role in the Empire once answered such questions, and the end of empire left an absence of vision into which Thatcherism has moved.

Dr Boyle's analysis suggests the very inevitability of the revolution called Thatcherism that the Prime Minister herself claims for it. It also explains why in the earlier phase of the church-government argument the churches got the worst of it, for they were defending a pre-1979 social and political consensus in support of a world-view that was both fundamentally unstable and obsolete.

The Prime Minister's conversation with bishops at Chequers last year, and several subsequent attempts at dialogue with the churches, can be seen as a sign of recognition that what Dr Boyle says about the materialism and hollowness of the first edition of Thatcherism is felt to be true; and that it therefore needs modification. The Home Secretary's concept of the "active citizen", and some features of the Prime Minister's recent address to her party conference, both imply that life ought to be about something other than the satisfaction of economic needs, as the churches have said all along.

But who is to decide what it is about if not that? In spite of the left-wing perception of her as a budding ideological dictator, Mrs Thatcher herself eschews such a role. The basic complaint of the Government against the churches is that they have not given a strong enough lead in these directions; but that is not very different from the basic complaint in the other direction. Mrs Thatcher said in a interview last year: "Parliament isn't the great institution of life. Churches are your great institutions, as are your great voluntary associations . . . ". Yet the churches have contributed to the view, which Mrs Thatcher seems to regard as a myth, that Parliament is somehow "the nation in council", the supreme and symbolic representative body of the community in all its aspects, to which the nation can look for every variety of leadership, moral, political, social,

22

even spiritual. But it is part of an integrationist model of a Christian state, a powerful symbolic component of which is the concept of an Established Church. Thatcherism is a movement away from such a vision: a modern state is a secular state.

The most significant proposal made by Dr Boyle in his analysis is that the nation now needs what all other modern states have found they needed, a written constitution and a Bill of Rights, in which the British people can declare "who they are and how they wish to arrange their lives". But it had better be done before they forget who they were.

A SUCCESSOR TO ECUMENISM
A search for communion

------◆------

11 March 1989

The Government needs better theology if it is to hold its own in argument with the churches. In particular it needs a grasp of ecclesiology. This is the branch of theology which deals with the church itself, where it has blossomed in the past decade apparently unnoticed by the Government and its advisers.

This neglect is not surprising, for four reasons. The first is that most of those in and around Government with some theological literacy are likely to have completed their theological intake in their teens – 30 or more years ago – and not to have kept abreast of trends since. They may not even fully realize that theology is a moving thing, and it is not where it was.

The second is that there is a leaning towards an old style Evangelical or Low Church version of Christianity in such circles, where a church is a church is a church and there is nothing much more to it. The third is that ecclesiology is difficult, a matter more for experts than for amateurs. Hence it operates with a great deal of professional shorthand, which is hard for outsiders to penetrate.

The fourth is that ecclesiology in Britain cannot escape from the fact of legal establishment, which not only defines a certain relationship between church and society in the two cases to which it applies, but also shapes, and complicates, the ecclesiological self-understanding of the non-established churches. It is even open to question whether the Church of England, in particular, has an ecclesiology of its own, independent of its established status. There is much interesting confusion generated when the Church of England tries to recognize itself as part of the Anglican Communion, whose ecclesiology is really rather different.

No Government criticism of a church, for not doing what it is supposed to, is going to cut much ice if it extends no further than tautology: a church has to do what a church has to do. There is no obvious answer to what a church has to do – as churchmen, who wrestle with this all the time, know only too well. To single out one individual strand, as for instance in the Prime Minister's insistence to the Church of Scotland that it must support the family, is simply to tempt contradiction. The church in theory regards itself as one enormous family already, without regard for kith and kin – for if in Christ there is even neither Jew nor Greek, there is certainly neither Smith nor Jones.

When the General Synod hears the Home Secretary, Mr Douglas Hurd, tell it that what the church has to do is to help the Government defeat crime; or when it hears the Education Secretary, Mr Kenneth Baker, tell it that it has leant too far towards the Catholic (supposedly collectivist) rather than the Evangelical or Protestant (supposedly individualistic) strain in its tradition, the politest comment it can make is: "Up to a point, Lord Copper."

For instance, that great apostle of collectivism the Bishop of Durham, the Right Rev. David Jenkins – certainly no Catholic, he – has had much support from the Evangelicals of his diocese precisely because of his social concern of a pinkish hue; they are even prepared to put up with his doctrinal devi-

24

ations because of it. Cabinet ministers should bring with them to synod something better than the theological understanding of an average Any Questions panel if they want to be taken seriously.

As it prays, so it believes, is an old principle of ecclesiology. It being Lent, the churches and their members are currently praying for repentance and sorrow for sin; and as Good Friday approaches, they are preparing to face the suffering and death of themselves and their God. It is a journey inwards to cleanse the self, the phase of spiritual individualism in the annual cycle of the liturgy. Personal renewal and spiritual rebirth come with Easter; but the seasonal flavour changes gradually from the individual to the collective with the approach of Pentecost, the birthday of the church. It is significant that it is during the almost endless "Sundays after Pentecost" that the church stays on a liturgical plateau, as if the collectivism of Pentecost is normative, the individualism of Lent and Easter interruptive. But there would be no Christianity without Good Friday and Easter.

It could almost be said that the answer to "What is the church for?" changes with the date. There is a profound human logic to the progress of the liturgical season, which if lived closely enough induces transitions of mood and levels of introspection almost as if one were following a course of psychoanalysis. In his famous *Spiritual Exercises*, St Ignatius virtually brought the two ideas together, though he does not wait for the calendar. But clearly the phrase "the Gospel" does not refer to one tidy thing; it is more like a jewel which changes shape and colour when rotated in the light.

Ecclesiology's business is trying to sort out the relationship between the parts and the whole, between the individual, the small group, the local church, the whole visible institution, the mystical and undivided Body of Christ, and the entire human race. In this respect it has virtually taken over from ecumenism, which is becoming yesterday's word. It is no longer a search for unity but for communion. This is where the Church of England's ecclesiology comes into its own, for it speaks of the noble possibility of a whole nation being a communion; and it

25

is also where it feels its limitations, for nations do distinguish between Jew and Greek, between those who belong and those who are strangers. "National Catholicism" is a contradiction in terms; and so the Church of England needs the Anglican Communion (and perhaps the Roman Catholic Church too) to lift its eyes to the horizon.

A politician who joined that debate would be connecting with thought processes already engaged; and would do well to offer a philosophy of equally visionary scope, as the context for attention to the detail he wants to pursue. "What is the Government for?" is the best reply to a Government which presumes to tell a church what a church is for.

MORAL MARKET FORCES

15 July 1989

People with an appetite for omens would have been given food for thought had they noticed a very senior member of the Jesuit order making for a seminar on business ethics in the City of London two weeks ago, convened by a top London banker, a practising Anglican.

The concern of theologians with the philosophy of big business is one of several signs of a new interest in the inter-space between morality and finance, an interest which seems to be growing equally on both sides. It appears that there are many top businessmen in Britain who admit that the success of the British economy in responding to the stimulus of free competition has exposed an ethical gap. As a subject for debate, it is becoming a growth industry.

This interest in the search for a new moral basis for the business of capitalism has been well documented by David Walker of *The Times*. After talking to a good handful of reflective doers and active thinkers, top financiers, bankers, economists and sociologists, he presented a persuasive case that even among those totally dedicated to market forces, market forces are not felt to be enough. And the need is not just for a surface coating of practical ethics, to tell them whether or when they can bribe a bent foreigner. They feel the need for an underlying moral philosophy to the whole operation.

Many businessmen hold religious beliefs, often of a fairly simple and straightforward middle-Anglican kind. So their search for a moral philosophy starts naturally enough with those beliefs, though unless they are very lucky they may quickly discover that the professionals in religion regard them simply as Mammon worshippers, of not much interest except as future targets for fund raising. The ethical case for free market economics, at the beginning of the Thatcher era, was argued on the basis of personal liberty in opposition to an alternative model of social and economic order described by concepts like collectivism or socialism, regarded as a threat to personal freedom. Somehow that argument seems to have died, perhaps because of a new political consensus in Britain that the move away from the collectivist climate of the seventies had become irreversible.

For the unfree, freedom is goal enough; but once free, the next question is harder: what is to be done with that new freedom; what is it for? The engine of an enterprise economy may be driven well enough by simple greed; but wealth increases freedom further, merely posing the same question more sharply. Freedom to get wealthier still is not an answer that will appeal to every temperament. And while freedom is easily recognized as a good, wealth is spiritually problematical.

Christianity has an ethic of asceticism and self-denial, and avarice is not among the cardinal virtues. Jesus said it is impossible to worship both God and Mammon, that the poor are blessed, and that it is easier for a camel to pass through the eye of a needle than for a rich man to get into heaven. It is not obvious that the ethical circle can be made square simply by individual or corporate donations to good causes, however desirable. And the wish to be rich enough to make generous donations to charity is a somewhat feeble idea as a sole motivation for a lifetime of stress and struggle towards success in business. There must be something more, something that will give moral value to such a life for its own sake.

The reflex response from religious sources, until recently, has been to direct attention to the poor, and the duty of the non-poor towards them as the primary measure of their virtue. And it cannot be doubted that there is an absolute moral obligation towards the hungry, the homeless, and the sick. But poverty, in Britain at least, is now largely relative; and the statement "the poor are always with us" has become little more than a tautology, just another form of the statistical truism "there will always be a bottom quartile". What the average income of that sector ought to be, as a proportion of the average of the whole, is a nice point but largely a socio-political one, because a unified culture with a common mass media will require a higher degree of equality than one where the social classes are more culturally segregated. So there can be no absolute moral obligation on that score.

Businessmen handle money. And it may well be that the practical amorality of their trade, about which they seem increasingly uneasy, derives from the theoretical amorality of the concept of money itself. It is a token of the value of real things. But real things have real uses, and moral responsibility for such use cannot be disowned. One who hands over a gun shares in moral responsibility if there is a shooting; one who hands over fifty pounds has let go of that responsibility and abandoned all control over its use unless there are strings attached.

But the complexity of big business renders money anonymous and impersonal, and takes away its moral character. It is very difficult to imagine a moral string attached by an individual to a monthly payment into a pension fund, for instance, in such a way that that string will remain attached, following it through all the intermediate processes of banking and investment, and emerge still intact at the end of its journey.

If there are to be such moral strings at all, they will have to be applied by proxy, at the point at which the money is delivered to its end purpose. And it is the business of a businessman to get that money to its end purpose. The inability of the initial saver or investor to hold on to any ethical responsibility for the way his money is used, because of the complexity of the intermediate transactions, may point to the conclusion that it is the duty of a businessman to act as an ethical agent in his place, for in practice only he can do so. That would mean that all business decisions were primarily moral decisions (and refusing to treat them as such would be no less a moral decision). Then every business would have to learn the skills of the casuists in the true and honourable sense and the vocation of businessman would have become a very high calling indeed, needing no apology whatsoever.

ONE PARLIAMENT, ONE PEOPLE

22 July 1989

There is a profound but profoundly questionable conviction among some Anglican Members of Parliament that the establishment of the Church of England gives them the moral as well as the legal right to regulate the doctrines of the Church of England. They demonstrated their belief in the debate in the House of Commons on Tuesday morning when a majority of the hundred or so MPs present narrowly defeated the Clergy (Ordination) Measure, which is concerned with the ordination in the Church of England of those who have been divorced and remarried. Though some members also raised constitutional questions concerning the correctness of the procedures in the General Synod when the measure was before it, the victorious majority clearly believed above all that the synod had erred in a matter of faith and morals, and therefore Parliament had a right and duty to intervene.

Many of these MPs are also implacably opposed to the Ordination of Women measure now before the synod, and their recent campaign has been something of a rehearsal for that more major matter. But while few in the church are greatly excited by the prospect of disestablishment at present, and the ordination of a handful of extra clergy is not the issue to rouse them, there can be no doubt that a Parliamentary block on the women priests measure, once the General Synod had approved it, would bring converts to disestablishment in droves.

The key difference between the two measures is not necessarily the relative seriousness of the issues involved, for some would say that divorce was no less important than female ordination. It is that the women priests measure would have gone before all 43 diocesan synods for a majority decision, with debates down to deanery synod level, and that that degree of endorsement would amount to a democratic mandate much superior to the entitlement of MPs to decide on such an issue. It is doubtful whether many of them have offered themselves to their electorates on the basis of their theological opinions, and can therefore claim that they are representing the will of their constituents. It is some while, in any case, since the Parliamentary franchise was restricted to communicating Anglicans, and since Anglicanism was legally established in Scotland, Ireland and Wales. It is some while since the repeal of the Test Acts too.

This is the fundamental flaw in the concept of Parliament as the governing body of the Church of England. It is based on the theory called Erastianism, and the fiction that legally established Anglicanism is the uniform religion of all the people. But Parliament has members from Wales and Northern Ireland, where no church is established. It has members from Scotland, where a different church is established. It has numerous Jewish, Roman Catholic, Methodist, Baptist and Presbyterian members, and it ought to have Muslim, Hindu, Sikh and Black Pentecostal members. Quite a number of members will be disbelievers in any religion.

So far the convention has been maintained that non-Anglican MPs should distance themselves from Parliamentary business concerning the Church of England, so that those who do interest themselves in such business virtually constitute a "parliament-within-a-parliament". That was the body which seemed to have taken over the chamber of the House of Commons last Tuesday morning. To accept its credentials as a proper Parliament, however, is to say something which is quite offensive to all those many Parliamentary electors who are Scottish, Irish, Welsh, Jews, Catholics, Methodists, Baptists, Presbyterians, unbelievers, Muslims, Hindus, Sikhs and Black Pentecostalists, and probably not a few Anglicans too. It tells them that there are two classes of citizenship in Britain, and they belong to the lesser class. It also tells them that they had better shut up about it.

But Parliament is the voice of all the people. Every time there is a general election, the entire people speak. Every time there is a division in Parliament, the proxies of the people, who were elected by the people at a general election, speak for them. Non-Anglican electors are full citizens, no less fully entitled to have their views represented in Parliament than Anglican electors. The doctrine that they are not entitled to have their views represented on religious matters, however, so that non-Anglican MPs are expected to sit in silence or leave the chamber and Anglican MPs to ignore the views of all but their Anglican electors, is to drive a coach and horses through the notion of Parliamentary democracy. Or it is the mark of a sectarian state?

The history of religious dissent in England has produced a warped political consciousness among dissenters, who are more relieved to be allowed as close to the top table as they have got, than indignant that such a top table exists at all. But it is of little more merit than the respect and gratitude of a victim towards a bully when he stops his bullying. In no way is this the fault of present members of the Church of England, who are much too nice to bully anyone; it is the fault of the dissenters themselves, who have failed to push their claim to full citizenship to its proper limit.

That claim is quite incompatible with Anglican establishment, in its present form, because of the exclusion of non-Anglicans from the Parliamentary process both as members and as electors when Church of England business is on the

31

order paper. And it is not enough that they should consent to be excluded, for no one should be allowed to consent to second class citizenship. So long as Parliament confined its interest in church business to making sure the formalities were in order, this was no more than a somewhat anomalous regulatory and quasi-judicial function. But once Parliament, or sufficient of its members to constitute a late-night quorum, decides to exercise power over Anglican faith and morals, the nature of the case has changed. It divides the nation in two: those who are represented in Parliament on everything, for whom Parliament is "our" Parliament, and those who are represented in Parliament only on some matters, for whom Parliament, on other matters, is someone else's – "their" – Parliament. For Parliament's own sake, it needs to be reclaimed as the Parliament of all the people, non-Anglicans included.

The conscience of the Church of England is increasingly troubled by anything which produces two ranks of citizenship in Britain, particularly on the basis of race, culture or national origin. Now it can add religion to its list.

MANACLED TO A SPIRITUAL CORPSE

———————•◆•———————

2 December 1989

The news that England is now among the most secularized nations of Europe, measured by religious observance, demands an explanation, even a calling to account. From the point of view of the Church of England something must have gone dreadfully wrong with the master-plan, notwithstanding that it is difficult to detect any hint of crisis among the Anglican church's national leadership.

Nowhere else in Europe does a religion by law established enjoy anything like the privileges the Church of England enjoys here. A totalitarian regime wishing to indoctrinate the population with its beliefs could hardly ask for more: favoured time on radio and television, a guaranteed unique role in the law and constitution, reserved places in the upper House of Parliament, the exclusive religion of the head of state, a special protected status in the school curriculum, the right to the leading role on occasions of national solemnity, and a vast tax-free income.

All these things are taken for granted. Only in Eastern Europe has one system of belief enjoyed anything like the same privileges. Yet the official Marxist-Leninist faith "by law established" in Eastern Europe is visibly collapsing in a mood of deep cynical alienation, having gained nothing by its former predominance. The Communist Parties there are now queuing to give up their protected status and to take their place in a plural democracy where they will have to fight the others on equal terms. The comparison is not exact, and is a little unfair to the Church of England, but it does invite the drawing of certain parallels. It suggests that the English have withdrawn their consent to the establishment of the Church of England already, not by crowding into the cold streets to shout but by not crowding into its cold churches to sing and pray.

Anglican church attendance is now about 2.5 per cent of the total population, and the only reason that is not a shocking figure is that it is all too familiar. It is a massive demonstration of consumer choice and market force: the great bulk of the English population, 97.5 per cent, are now religious refugees. They have exiled themselves from the national church, and gone elsewhere or nowhere.

Disestablishment is usually argued as the last escape route for the Church of England should Parliament, perhaps in the late-night grip of a minority of obscurantist Erastians, ever decide to intervene seriously in internal Anglican decision-making. Until that happens establishment is counted a blessing, an "opportunity", even a duty: it is rarely seen as a curse, and never as one of the basic reasons for the deep and wide alienation of the English from organized religion. People and institutions with privilege hardly ever give it up voluntarily, even if they are Christian and ought to know better. They rationalize the dependence it brings, as a burden to be dutifully borne in the name of virtue. Yet the quality of its membership is good and growing, and there must be some deeper reason why this does not show forth in greater success. To treat its established status as the Church of England's greatest handicap may reassuringly suggest its poor showing is not the fault of individuals, and it would explain the apparent paradox that an enormous amount of dedicated effort is spent trying to turn the inexorable tide, to so little effect.

Establishment may even be a gentle brake on the rate of decline, though it makes a hopeless springboard for recovery. One of the most extraordinary features of the Church of England at present is the conspicuous absence of any strategy, or even any serious desire, to bring about that recovery. It has already accepted quiet defeat, and called it something else. A legally established religion is evidently no longer what people are looking for: religion now belongs firmly in the realm of the private, the unofficial, the part of life reserved and withheld from state and national power.

When once the British constitutional system had a kind of magic about it – the mysticism of the Christian state – the Church of England benefited from its central sacred role and drew weight, mystique and authority from its closeness to such majesty. At the height of Empire it was still possible for thoughtful people to believe that this one small island off the north coast of Europe really was the closest of all to heaven, for the God of Battles had put it in charge of history and awarded it the prize of world leadership. That game was up some generations ago. The idea of a nation-state especially blessed by God has been fully drained of meaning; and a church which insists on being tied to such a nation-state just makes itself look provincial and sectarian. Even the present government actively campaigns to cut state power down to size, belittling it as the plaything of centralized bureaucracy and telling individuals as far as possible to run their own lives; and it was a trend already well in place before they made a virtue of it. But in a Thatcherite or post-Thatcherite Britain an established Church of England will look increasingly anomalous, a throwback to ideas no one can quite remember ever having had.

So the idea of a state religion is rapidly becoming incomprehensible to the public at large, no less so than state music, state art, state literature, and state science ever was. The only way to deal with it, short of abolishing it, will be to treat it as the custodian of an archaeological remnant, with the Church of England just a branch of English Heritage. Already the one thing it still does bravely well is to look after its ancient buildings, sometimes even now with English Heritage money and advice.

It is also still one of the places, though no longer the majority place, where people can feel the full heat of the Christian Gospel and be transformed and uplifted by it. What the Church of England has failed to see, however, is that it looks from the outside to be a most unlikely spot to find such treasure. It seems to exist for other purposes, or no other purpose than its own existence. It is bedevilled by internal rivalries and conflicts, even concerning its basic message. Half the Church of England seems to think that the only thing wrong is the presence of the other half. It has become, in short, all too transparently and quarrelsomely human, and not the least bit mysterious, holy, or necessary for salvation.

Its best hope, and not a very happy hope, is that the Evangelicals will take it over before it is too late, and extract something from the wreckage which that figure of 2.5 per cent must stand for. They will be among the first to see that the church's legal establishment, requiring a submissive relationship with a non-Christian Parliament and a dependent relationship with a non-Christian society, is part of the problem and not part of the solution. Any Christian Church which still needs official state privilege for support in 1989 has chosen to manacle itself to a spiritual corpse. In their hearts, everybody knows it; but no one will admit it.

WHAT HOPE FOR WEALTH CREATORS?

3 March 1990

The new director general of the Institute of Directors, Mr Peter Morgan, was venting a widely spread sense of frustration in business circles when he included the church in his list of those establishment institutions which were hostile to the enterprise culture of wealth creation. In his keynote speech to the institute's annual convention this week, he recalled some remarks of the Bishop of Peterborough, the Right Rev. William Westwood, who had said that the church had "no message" for those who were successful because it was too preoccupied with the poor. The church and other pillars of middle class establishment values, Mr Morgan said, regarded the creation of wealth as "mucky and squalid".

The commitment of the church in Britain to the poor is rather more apparent than real, as the Bishop of Peterborough well knows. The Church Commissioners possess an enormous treasury of inherited wealth, from which the clergy are paid. Church of England church-goers are among the more prosperous members of the community; and bishops often live in palaces which would be eagerly coveted by multi-millionaires.

The preoccupation the bishop was referring to is a complex and ambivalent phenomenon, therefore. On the one hand church ministers are aware of economic distress, and they universally report that recent changes in social security arrangements, including the Social Fund loans scheme, have bitten deeply and painfully into the lives of the less well-off. On the other hand they are impressed by, and even envious of, the exciting engagement with radical politics associated with the theology of liberation in Latin America. They tie the two together, and deduce that poverty is the fault of wealth, to be rich is to be guilty, and the poor are more sinned against than sinning. They want to take an "option to the poor", in the Latin American terminology, but they are too firmly rooted in the property-owning middle classes to do so drastically. The result is that it inevitably becomes more a sentimental than a real "option to the poor". There is no talk of giving away the assets of the Church Commissioners, for instance, nor of bishops moving into council houses.

This confused attitude has become thoroughly mixed up with a whole bundle of older cultural and class prejudices towards business and industry, represented by the view that "trade" was no fit occupation for a gentleman. Given that those in trade are generally interested in the creation of wealth – wealth for themselves in particular – it is, the Church of England seems to have concluded, no fit occupation for a Christian either.

The confusion is made worse by a disregard for the Old Testament and a selective reading of the New – the poor are blessed, the rich cannot pass through the eye of a needle, and no one can worship God and Mammon. First-century Jewish society was by no means hostile to what is now called wealth creation, however, nor to the possession of it; and it cannot be shown that Jesus repudiated that in principle. He warned of the spiritual dangers, just as he warned of the dangers of virtually every other condition of life.

The Christian "message to the successful" that the Bishop of Peterborough would like to see, if Mr Morgan has interpreted him correctly, would be a message of congratulation, of "well done, thou good and faithful servant". In so far as there is any implied message from the Church of England in fact, it is of the opposite kind: that if one must have wealth at all it is better to have inherited it than to have made it oneself, and success in business is slightly indecent, as if every pound in a businessman's pocket might have been snatched from a single mother's meagre grocery purse.

Neither approach meets the need. Businessmen and industrialists are necessary, and the church must have a message for them better than "go to hell". Congratulations, on the other hand, are hardly what the Gospel is about, in this or any other connection. Neither approach has any spiritual depth to it. A Christian attitude to wealth can only flow from a Christian attitude to life, which in turn can only flow from a Christian attitude to death. The metaphor of dying "to self" is used repeatedly in the Gospels, coupled with rising again, "to new life". It refers not only to the moment of actual death, but to the spiritual turning points in life. Prior to this dying and rising transformation experience, the soul was in bondage to sin; afterwards, it is free. Each of those states has a characteristic attitude to possessions. Before, they dominated life; after, they are merely useful. Before, a man would do almost anything to hold on to what is his; after, he can take it or leave it. In this sense, therefore, before he worshipped Mammon; after he worships God. But it does not follow that his bank manager would notice anything different, before and after. The famous challenge to the rich young man to give away all he possessed would have had no point to it if he cared little whether he did or not. Jesus perceived a man with a fanatical attachment to what was his.

A man should be able to give everything away and think nothing of it: but it does not follow that he is obliged to do so. The necessity applies only in the particular case where that action distinctly marks the "death to self" which the Gospel demands. In other cases the action could be different because the fatal attachment could be different – willingness to abandon an agreeable career, willingness (in the case of celibacy) to forego sex, willingness to lose the approval of family and friends: even, conceivably, the willingness to give up a state of poverty. Each potential moment of loss is a potential spiritual death, with the potential for liberation. It is an act of letting go, and then freedom follows. Real death involves the loss of everything, and all these forms of spiritual death are rehearsals for it. And so an unencumbered soul may slide peacefully from this world to the next.

None of these things is bad in itself, nor are possessions bad in themselves. But someone who is possessed by his possessions, and compelled to seek ever more of them, is in bad spiritual trouble. He has fallen victim to a kind of addiction or dependency; and he is also a danger to others for he has power over others. A spirituality of wealth creation, therefore, would have to start from the particular spiritual risks of that activity.

Creating wealth is no sin, provided there is no sin in the means of creating of it; nor is enjoying it, provided there is no sin in the means of enjoying of it. Falling under its spell, however, is when the gates of hell begin to beckon. So those who create wealth need and deserve a rather special kind of spiritual care, to keep them safe from being ensnared by it. That would make rather a welcome message from the church to the enterprise culture, but it may not be quite what the Institute of Directors was hoping to hear, nor what the bishop was offering.

FAITH IN THE MARKET

5 May 1990

Free-market economists have tended not to waste much time on theology, particularly if they are British: the dismal science finds the queen of sciences a tiresome irrelevance. But this may only be because most theologians are on the left: a theologian who announces his conversion to the right is a precious rarity. When one such turned up in London this week, the Institute of Economic Affairs had to move his lecture to a larger hall to meet the demand for tickets. The star turn was Professor Michael Novak, a minor American guru of the left who is rapidly becoming a major American guru of the right; and his backing and blessing was provided by no less than Professor Brian Griffiths of 10 Downing Street, who, it is said, guides the Prime Minister's hand on her occasional and invariably stormy excursions into theology's deep and chilly waters.

Griffiths is only an economist with theological leanings, however: Novak is the real thing. All he lacked was a dog collar, which he missed by switching his vocation just before completing twelve years of study for the priesthood. So he became a professor of religion instead, and professed to all who would listen that capitalism and Christianity are mutually exclusive. Then he woke up.

What he saw around him, once he had adjusted his consciousness, was American capitalism's vibrant world of wealth creation and human achievement which was bringing about by accident the very objective that socialism was failing to do by design: improving the lot of the people.

Novak, of Czech origin and on his way back to Czechoslovakia after London, is the ideal man to celebrate the collapse of Soviet and Eastern European socialism. In the event, his IEA performance was surprisingly untheological. His main thesis was that Christianity, capitalism and the American ideal of civil society are exceptionally well suited to each other, which is why they have thrived together. America, thanks to its political and moral culture, liberated the creativity of its people and set them to productive effort. Much of the credit, he felt, had to go to the Scotsman Adam Smith, and to the American founding fathers who seized and digested his point while they were still building the foundations of their nation.

National wealth is built on creative intelligence, and once a society makes that its guiding economic first principle, the future will take care of itself. Or almost. The moral basis of society, said Novak, still has to come from outside the economic system, from the diversity of beliefs encompassed by the phrase Judaeo-Christian. He is definitely not a free marketeer in morals, not a trendy libertarian.

Professor Novak knows little of Britain, and admitted as much. His advice to scrap the native constitution and replace it with the American one was interesting but not very practical. But his key idea, which cannot be dismissed in a British context, is that economic progress is not purely a matter of economics. First, the constitutional structure, social culture, politics, the law, religion – he would even say that was primary – have to be right. Only then will creative intelligence find the freedom and encouragement it needs. He calls this democratic capitalism, but more to rub the noses of his former socialist friends in the dirt than as a precise definition; his ideas have more to do with small people making good than with big people making better.

Britain is a far more secular society than America, where religion is still a key element of the national ethos. A bedrock of explicit Judaeo-Christian morality was not, he thought, entirely necessary to capitalist success – witness Japan – but the question arose whether democratic capitalism was ultimately self-sustaining, or whether it needed a long-term input of Judaeo-Christian beliefs and moral ideals. He strongly held the latter view; the Judaeo-Christian insistence on justice and charity was an indispensable corrective, and would, in due course, correct the remaining injustices in America.

Christianity is secure in the United States, and still a major dynamic force, though gradually becoming more Catholic than Protestant. But Christianity is very unsure of itself in Britain, and many see the nation as in the process of casting it off entirely. Democratic capitalism moderated by entrenched Christian values is a very different thing from capitalism red in tooth and claw, tempered by nothing. That is one reason capitalism is feared by so many people in Britain and the very word is out of favour, even on the right. And it is therefore one of the reasons that collectivism still has its supporters in Britain, who vote for socialism to defend them against a possible tyranny of the rich and powerful.

Christian America is an open, generous and gregarious community; secular Britain is becoming a closed, insular and selfish one. Americans believe that Uncle Sam has sent a personal invitation to every one of them to join the ranks of the rich and powerful. It is this universal opportunity, more than anything else, which makes America a fundamentally fair society. The British believe, on the contrary, that the rich still belong to the ultimate closed shop. Visiting American theologians need to note this difference; then, perhaps they could tell us what to do about it.

TODAY'S JUST SAMARITAN

25 August 1990

The parable of the Good Samaritan has been much abused in political debate. Mrs Thatcher has used it to make the point that, to be charitable, the Samaritan first had to have money in his pocket. On the other hand, the parable is often cited as the moral basis of the welfare state. It is a pity that one of the cleverest stories in the New Testament has lost most of its meaning by being reduced to a platitude about helping the less fortunate.

Whether there is such a thing as social justice is increasingly controversial in political debate in Britain and America. The failure to make society fairer is said on the left to be the principal moral defect of free-market capitalism, while on the right, socialism is attacked as the vain pursuit of equality in the name of social justice. Dr David G. Green, director of the health and welfare unit of the Institute of Economic Affairs, has just published a pamphlet, *Equalizing People*, which argues the second view. He advocates "personal moral responsibility" and benevolence, but voluntarily, and opposes use of the state as an instrument for economic levelling, which in his opinion is impossible.

Justice, at its simplest, is giving someone what they are entitled to. Among Jews, long before Christ, the word came to refer specifically to alms-giving, which implies not only that the giver of alms had a duty to give, but that the receiver of alms had a proper claim on the giver. This understanding was assimilated by Christian thought, and later enriched by Greek philosophical notions of justice, especially those of Aristotle.

The audience to which Christ preached was, like him, Jewish. Steeped in the teachings of the prophets, they did not need to be told that a Jew had a personal obligation to help a fellow Jew. Had one of the two Jewish passers-by-on-the-other-side stopped to help the man fallen among thieves, the story would only have made a point they already accepted. Had the victim not been Jewish, the story would have reminded them that their charity could extend even to helping Gentiles.

In modern popular culture, a Good Samaritan is someone who helps a stranger in need – an upright citizen who helps a drunk across the road, for instance – but in the original parable, it is the drunk, as it were, who helps the upright citizen. For Samaritans were outcasts not bound by the teachings of the prophets, or so the Jews believed. Samaria was no place for a self-respecting person at all. A welfare state founded on the Good Samaritan parable would be manned by heroin addicts with AIDS, for the benefit of the respectable middle classes.

Christ had swapped texts with a Jewish lawyer, ending with the words of Leviticus: "Love your neighbour as yourself." The parable came in answer to the next trick question: "And who is my neighbour?", that is, to whom was a pious Jew bound to give alms? Christ never directly answered. The question was about the limits of social justice in Jewish teaching, and he replied that there should be no limits. For the Samaritan was not a "neighbour", because he received benevolence (as an object of pity), but because he was a giver (who was moved by pity). He proved himself the victim's neighbour. It was a trick answer, but it established that in Judaeo-Christian thought there can be no narrowing of the circle of those to whom the duty of alms-giving applies, and who therefore have a right to receive alms. (The Good Samaritan is not a specifically Christian tale, for it is clear Christ's wholly Jewish audience recognized that he was expounding Jewish scripture.) The story has other layers of meaning too, but its political force is relevant to Dr Green's blithe dismissal of social justice.

The claim of the new right is that the economic forces of the free market are natural and ineluctable. One may speak of their "victims" only as one might speak of the victims of an earthquake, and it would be absurd to speak of an earthquake as unjust. Such victims, therefore, have no right to claim remedy for their condition. They must wait upon charity. The more fortunate who escaped the earthquake or benefited from the free market may perfectly well help them if they wish, but this is voluntary.

The right opposes any coercion by the state in the name of social justice, for instance in the redistribution of wealth. And the essence of this dismissal is not that social justice is a disguised excuse for promoting equality (which is not part of Judaeo-Christian thought), but that the "victims" of capitalism are "owed" nothing. Whatever they may receive is purely *ex gratia*. The language of justice, on the other hand, speaks of paying a debt, receiving what is due. Ineluctably, according to the concept of social justice, capitalism creates its own creditors, the poor.

Was the man who fell among thieves entitled to demand the help of the Good Samaritan? He was certainly entitled to the help of the priest and Levite, for they were bound by the Jewish law and prophets. The parable makes social justice a universal obligation, part of the natural law by which all are bound. But obedience to natural law cannot be reduced to the status of a voluntary act, even if the law of the land does not compel it. Nor can obligations to pay what is due ever be *ex gratia*. So the question therefore is not about social justice but simply to what extent the state is the appropriate agent of its enforcement. But then if enforcement of justice is not the state's business, what is?

RIGHTS RATHER THAN RITUAL

6 October 1990

People are beginning to think that something fundamental is lacking in the British constitution. Lord Scarman raised the question again in last week's *New Statesman*, and the Institute of Economic Affairs has just published a pamphlet drawing similar conclusions. The Liberal Democrats said it at their party conference, and Tony Benn has been saying it much longer. There is a logic to this progression.

Britain has no written constitution or fundamental law, and no Bill of Rights, though it was careful to equip its former colonies with them at independence. It is widely supposed, though less widely as time goes on, that Britain does not need such things, that pragmatism alone will see us through. This British faith in common sense is remarkable, and ought to be alarming.

Most of the talk on this issue so far has come from lawyers and libertarians, who fear an overmighty British state (or in the IEA's case an overmighty EC superstate). It should also be the concern of moralists, philosophers and even churchmen, for at bottom the change in society that makes a written constitution gradually more desirable is moral and religious. Nowadays one can hardly reach a consensus on any moral issue, and any opinion can be countered by twenty opposing ones.

The necessary condition for a state to survive without a written constitution is general agreement about the moral foundations of society. Since the Elizabethan Settlement in the sixteenth century, that agreed basis, albeit an imposed one, was the state religion, Anglican Christianity. Dr Hugh Montefiore, former Bishop of Birmingham, rebuked the Liberal Democrats for voting in favour of the disestablishment of the church, saying: "There has to be a form of public religion: a state has to have values." He is right in the second respect, but his first point would have been better made had he said that a state which does not enshrine its values in a public religion must enshrine them elsewhere, and a written constitution is probably the only alternative. Perhaps it is no coincidence that none of the former colonies on which Britain bestowed written constitutions has a public religion or established church. The greatest of all written constitutions, the American, takes the logic to its conclusion by insisting on the separation of church and state.

The existing British constitution can be written down. It simply states that absolute national sovereignty subsists in "the Crown in Parliament". But there is no statement of values enshrined in the phrase "in Parliament". Democracy is in theory value-free, so a sense of common moral purpose must enter the national self-definition through the Crown. The Crown, therefore, is not neutral or value-free. The law establishes that the Crown must be Christian. Certainly it must enshrine some values, for otherwise there would be a vacuum where there should be a national heart and soul. Instead of a written constitution, the British have a coronation, a quasi-sacramental ceremony dedicating the head of state and hence all subjects to uphold a Christian moral basis for the state and for what goes on within it. This is a symbol, but in building the substance of statehood, such symbols are the primary material.

This explains the emotive power of royalty in Britain. Many Britons cannot conceive the state without it. Yet the role of the Crown is questioned, not by overt republicanism (of which there is little), but by the decline in Christian belief and practice. Instead of being universally acknowledged, the values symbolized by the Crown's official Christianity are disputed and disregarded by many, and the next generation has hardly heard of them.

Anglicanism is not the political theory it once was. Its understanding of the rights of citizens in relation to one another and to the state is undeveloped; its grasp of the concept of human rights is tentative and theologically controversial. So is the grasp of these concepts by the English legal system – which is no accident, for the common law system is rooted in medieval Christian teaching.

Unlike an American president at his inauguration, when the Queen swore at her coronation to uphold the Christian faith, she did not thereby recognize or concede any rights to her subjects. And the word "right" is accordingly rare in English common and statute law. Instead, reflecting its Christian, pre-Enlightenment basis, the law is full of duties.

In everyday moral language, the new idea of "rights" has begun to take over from the old idea of "sins". There has been a shift from a sin/duty moral code to a rights/justice code. Most items of the old code can be translated into the new – "thou shalt not kill" becomes a "right to life", for instance – but the order of moral priorities is different. This slow movement in moral consciousness takes society further away from the Christian foundation of the state, and an agreed statement of rights is needed to stop society and the state drifting apart to the point of mutual incomprehension.

Every coherent society must have civil dogmas if it does not have religious ones. States with written constitutions enshrine such dogmas in their foundation documents; those without enshrine them in their public religion. If the British no longer hold Christianity to be self-evident, its dogmas can no longer provide the moral foundations of the state. A fundamental flaw is appearing in our constitution as it empties of moral meaning for the majority of its citizens.

INTER-FAITH THE GREAT HEALER

21 July 1990

One of the last acts of the Polish parliament in 1939, as German guns thundered ever closer, was to elect the Blessed Virgin Mary to be Queen of Poland in perpetuity. There could be no more poignant demonstration of the intense relationship between religion and national pride.

In the same spirit Pope John Paul II insisted in 1978 that regardless of the rules of heraldry, he wanted a large M on his coat of arms, for Mary, Queen of Poland. Addressing Polish emigrés during his visit to Britain in 1982, he paid tribute to the Polish pilots who died in the Battle of Britain. He did not say they had died "defending Britain", but "for Poland". And that is how Poles had seen it; they had borrowed the British war to continue their own.

During Eastern Europe's years of communist rule, the West saw religion and national pride as a force threatening the cohesion of the Soviet empire, and hence as potentially pro-Western. But the end of that empire, at least outside the

Soviet Union itself, has changed the situation. The 1989 East European revolutions were as much a triumph of nationalism as of democracy, and Europe has yet to face up to the consequences.

Nationalism is seldom entirely secular, and seldom fits easily into secular political geography. Political maps tell us much less about the past, present and future of Europe than religious maps charting the frontiers of Protestantism and Catholicism, Catholicism and Orthodoxy, Orthodoxy and Islam. The reunification of Germany across the first of those lines is a triumph of nationalism over religious differences or perhaps, more truthfully, a triumph of decades of ecumenism, which is the one new force which may yet prevent the history of European tribal warfare repeating itself.

Within Russia and the Ukraine there is an invisible line between two sorts of Orthodoxy, one looking to Constantinople, the other to Moscow. And the Great Schism between Greek Orthodoxy and Catholicism, which formally dates from the eleventh century but in reality from five hundred years earlier, is now the cause of one of Mr Gorbachev's worst headaches, as growing Ukrainian nationalism finds a ready focus in Ukrainian Catholicism. There will be much agonized thought before the Pope is welcome in Kiev, in case he sets light to some very dry nationalist tinder (intentionally or otherwise). The election of a Polish pope in 1978 was crucial to the rise of the Solidarity movement and was one of the first signs of the East European nationalist avalanche.

The Russian Orthodox Church has sought to outmanoeuvre the rising religious force in Ukrainian nationalism by renaming its own Ukrainian religion the Ukrainian Orthodox Church, hijacking the title of the church now emerging from the shadows alongside the Catholics. But the Russian Orthodox Church is Soviet-orientated, even in its new Ukrainian disguise. The Ukrainian Orthodox Church and the Catholics were persecuted and driven underground during the years of Stalin's oppression because they were anti-Soviet; some Ukrainian churchmen even welcomed the arrival of Hitler's troops as liberators (before they realized their mistake). Yet thanks to ecumenism, the Russian Orthodox and Ukrainian Catholic churches and even the real Ukrainian Orthodox Church have been making great efforts to settle their differences peacefully.

In Europe and the Middle East, countries on the tide mark of the Ottoman Empire find themselves standing on the rim of a rumbling religious and racial volcano, where Christian (usually Orthodox) nationalism collides with an increasingly militant Islam. Elsewhere, however, there are grounds for hope. Since the war, the modern ecumenical movement has transformed Catholic-Protestant relationships almost everywhere except in Ireland, where its influence has largely been confined to the clergy. The success of ecumenism, the painstaking and often tedious building of understanding and co-operation brick by brick, explains why the religious dimension of German reunification has had a benign effect; why, for instance, Herr Kohl's mainly Catholic Christian Democrats feel confident they can cross the confessional divide into mainly Protestant Prussia without religious obstacles. And while political barriers were still in place, the tentacles of ecumenical friendship spread through the whole of Eastern Europe, with the churches beginning to be incorporated into a common European home before any other national institutions. A united Europe from the Urals to Gibraltar was a Christian hope and vision even in Brezhnev's day.

Though little noticed in Britain, the most vital of all ecumenical bridges may yet prove to be that between Catholicism and Orthodoxy, in which both sides have invested heavily over the last decade. Along with race and language, religious division has the potential to splinter Eastern Europe into dangerously sharp fragments; but ecumenical goodwill and co-operation may work to hold things together. The local clergy can either stand behind the stone-throwing crowds, condoning ethnic mayhem, or they can stand together, urging peace, making connections, cooling tempers. Thanks to ecumenism, they are now much more likely to do the latter. For years ecumenical dialogue was regarded as a hobby for the few, who often found themselves dismissed as "ecumaniacs", but now they may hold an important key to future peace in Europe.

FEEDING THE OLD ENMITY

12 May 1990

Archbishop Robert Eames of Armagh, Anglican primate of Ireland, was once asked if he thought of himself as an Irishman. There was a very long pause, followed by apologies for having no clear answer. A similar question to his neighbour, Cardinal Tomas O Fiaich, would have produced an instant explosion of Gaelic laughter at the absurdity of the question; O Fiaich was an Irishman to the core, and changed his name to prove it.

The Roman Catholic primate of Ireland's deepest wish was that people like Dr Eames could answer that way too, preferably in Gaelic. Those long seconds of the Protestant archbishop's silence and anguished thought contain the essence of Ireland's tragedy. It is not that Dr Eames was perversely refusing to acknowledge the obvious, but that the definition of Irishness has been hijacked, partly unconsciously, partly deliberately, by the Catholic Irish. Yet there can be no united Ireland until there is at least a united idea of the meaning of Irishness to which all Protestant primates particularly can subscribe. Cardinal O Fiaich died without ever having faced that fundamental challenge.

The Catholic character of Ireland goes much deeper than the occasional row about contraception or divorce. It is a symbiotic relationship with Protestant Britain, except that it has lost sight of the question of whether Britain is in any sense still Protestant or even Christian. The story of that relationship, a tangle of myth and fact which will never be unravelled, is central to Irish history.

It is to the credit of Cardinal O Fiaich that he devoted much of his life to the nurturing of Irish culture – Gaelic language, music and sport – that could have become the tokens of a national identity independent of Irish anti-Britishness.

The collective historical hatred would no longer be needed to identify what an Irishman was, and there could have emerged a society founded on being itself, rather than on not being something else.

Acrimony against individual Britons is alien to the Irish nature. But there is something in the Irish soul which distinguishes between Britons and Britain. It puzzles the Irish as much as it confuses the British. It is not about personality but about identity. So strong is the negative, rejecting element in Irish identity that even Gaelic language, music and sport have become subsumed into it; they, too, have become symbols of "not being British". It is the strong force in the national character, whereas the native culture is the weak force, almost a minority interest. The anti-British component in Irish identity is much deeper than, say, the Canadian insistence that they are not American. It is as deep as religion.

The British today have difficulty in understanding that the Protestant Reformation was only imposed on the British people of the sixteenth and seventeenth centuries against their will by considerable force over a long period. The people of Ireland were soon exposed to the same crushing pressure. In the long run the oppression nearly broke them, but it did not break their faith. It was an amazing example of courage and commitment through centuries of suffering under tyranny, which gives real truth to the phrase "the martyrdom of Ireland". The resistance was not just Catholic but also Presbyterian; anti-Catholic Presbyterianism was a later phenomenon and it consisted essentially in the refusal of allegiance to a Protestant English Crown and a Protestant Established Church, regardless of the consequences.

It is difficult to see what else Irish history could be about, if not about that. It was not one element in a complex story; it was the underlying theme of all the stories. Inevitably, and with good cause, there is now intense national pride in the survival of Catholic Ireland under the heel of Protestant England, and in its eventual brave liberation. Irish citizens have a right to be proud of their country, and of their single most important experience as a people – the long struggle to keep the faith, in the face of British contempt and cruelty, British hatred and bigotry, even British massacre and genocide.

Roman Catholicism became the central folk symbol of that long ordeal of defiance, for its destruction was, after all, the chief aim of British policy. The British sometimes like to congratulate themselves that by good sense and toleration they missed the worst of the European religious wars. But they did not; they merely transported theirs to Ireland. And while the rest of Europe now enjoys religious peace, the war continues in the north of Ireland, its original point forgotten, the British having long since grown indifferent to the nature of Irish faith.

The Irish Catholic Church, if true to the universality of its Catholic name, could have been the one institution in Ireland to rise above the enslavement of Irish identity to the historical anti-British experience. It could have said, for instance, that hatred was a grossly sinful basis for national pride, and that Christian duty demanded a profound and urgent reconciliation with Britain and the convergence, with pride, of the two histories, so that each was shared by both. Instead it has let the people nurse their grievances. It was the easy way to keep Ireland Roman Catholic. But it has nothing to do with making Ireland Christian.

Part Two

ANGLICAN IDENTITY

BATTLE TO RETAIN AN ANGLICAN IDENTITY

20 July 1988

This meeting of leaders of the Anglican Communion has already, after two days, been charged with adrenalin. The Archbishop of Canterbury, acting with other key people in the international Anglican world, has confronted them with the crisis around the corner. He has also put forward possible answers: but there will be a lot of hard talking before they agree with him.

Put five hundred bishops on to a university campus for three weeks, and they could simply talk about everything and nothing. That seemed to happen at the last Lambeth Conference 10 years ago. But in 1988 some furious thinking has to be done before the conference ends.

There is a battle going on, in world Anglicanism, between two tendencies. One, a fragmenting movement, arises from the way the twenty-seven provinces of the Anglican Communion have matured and taken charge of their own affairs. Not long ago many were mission territories, depending on the mother country for money, manpower, and motivation. Now more than half the bishops at Canterbury are black or Asian; and each part looks to its own resources, has its own ideas, and values its autonomy. In the process, the universal identity of Anglicanism is being lost.

The other tendency is towards unity, towards finding inter-

The 1988 Lambeth conference had just opened.

55

national structures for the Anglican Communion that will hold it together and give it some definition. The 1968 Lambeth Conference invented an Anglican Consultative Council, which was to meet every two or three years to keep track of the way things were moving. The 1978 Conference invented a Primates' Committee bringing together the top men from each province to discuss doctrinal developments and similar matters. But neither had any power. The 1988 Conference has been told that this is not enough: the fragmenting tendency is still winning. If each province continues to insist on independence, there might not be much of an Anglican Communion around in 1998 for another Lambeth Conference to worry about.

Some churches, such as the Anglican Church in New Zealand, want to let the fragmentation happen, and don't mind at all if there are no more Lambeth Conferences. Some, like the Church in Wales, want a much stronger primates' committee, and some tough rules (by Anglican standards) for all. If they had their way, the New Zealand church would soon be on its way out, and probably the American church too. American Episcopalians like to think the American Revolution was an ecclesiastical break from England as well as a political one.

Into the middle of all this, Dr Runcie has tossed the question of the Papacy. He says, in effect, that the church needs a personal focus of unity, a focus he supplies for Anglicanism. At the very least it needs someone to call Lambeth Conferences, and to decide whom to invite. It now seems also to need a central structure with authority, albeit a minimum structure, in deference to which the separate provinces will have to give up some independence.

But if a communion of 70 million, with a common recent history and culture, and still largely a common language, needs those things in order to hold it together, then any united church of the future, formed from Eastern Orthodoxy, Anglicanism, Roman Catholicism, and Protestantism or any combination thereof, probably amounting to a billion people or more, is going to need at least as much. If the Pope didn't exist, he seems to be saying, they would have to invent him.

RUNCIE'S FRAGMENTED FLOCK

23 July 1988

At the end of the first week, the real question facing the bishops attending the Lambeth Conference is not that posed by the Archbishop of Canterbury at the outset: do they really want the Anglican Communion to survive? It is, rather, does the Anglican Communion really exist? This seems to be a doubt shared by churchmen from all points of view and every part of the globe.

Most do not seem to recognize Dr Runcie's definition of a communion commitment to a common faith and life. One bishop conceded that they could, if they wished, try to bring such a thing into existence, but it is not there yet. He pointed out that even attendance at the daily act of worship was fast dropping off, as too many bishops decided it was not to their taste. Yet Anglicans have always prided themselves on being a church united and defined by the way they worship rather than by common declarations of what they believe.

Surprisingly, the two strongest endorsements so far of the belief that the Anglican Communion actually does exist have come from the Roman Catholic and Greek Orthodox delegations. But perhaps they have only Dr Runcie's definition of it to go by; and perhaps Anglican bishops themselves know differently. One New Zealand churchman, theologically liberal, morally permissive, and strongly in favour of women priests and bishops, said the only world body which fitted Dr Runcie's definition of an international communion was the Roman Catholic Church, and it was pointless to invent another.

None of the American bishops would appear to accept Dr Runcie's description at face value: the traditionalists among them see it as hopeful rather than accurate, and would move that way if only because the "modified autonomy" Dr Runcie has prescribed would be a good way of wringing the neck of

57

free-thinkers like Bishop John Spong of Newark, New Jersey. Liberal American bishops, on the other hand, consider they have already made their maximum concession, by voluntarily delaying the consecration of the first woman bishop until after the Lambeth Conference. Having thus "consulted" the rest of Anglicanism, they will shortly feel free to act as they choose.

New Zealanders explain patiently to whoever will listen that they will consecrate their first woman bishop some time after next May, regardless of whatever the Lambeth Conference might say beforehand, or whatever other parts of the Anglican world might do afterwards. They say they are running a multi-racial, multi-cultural church, and must be free to do whatever those conditions dictate. Yet this is the most pro-British, most royalist of dominions.

The Australians seem prepared to accept deeper and more thorough "consultation" between various Anglican provinces in future, but do not envisage any limitations to their local sovereignty. And the Church of England bishops have never even considered the possibility that one day the Anglican Communion might have authority over them. Parliament itself would have a pretty sharp reaction to that idea, said one of them.

In Dr Runcie's terms, the cement that holds a communion together is something called interdependence in English, *koinonia* in Greek, *communio* in Latin – as he says, commitment to a common faith and life. And it is this very commitment that seems lacking. All five hundred bishops are warmly attached to Dr Runcie personally, and he is reaping the harvest of his many overseas visits to them in their dioceses. But even the "first among equals" status of the Archbishop of Canterbury may not survive his retirement. A document circulating at the conference disputes the right of the British prime minister to nominate the Primate of All Anglicanism and suggests instead that either the primacy should rotate or the archbishop should be elected.

In the past, the Anglican version of *koinonia* has depended largely on personal friendships and a sense of common background. At past Lambeth conferences bishops from all over the world would greet each other as old friends and reminisce about their days at Oxford together. But the 1988 bishops do not seem to know each other at all. One group actually asked some journalists to try to find out for them what another group was thinking.

The way the conference has been structured has contributed to these feelings of isolation. The bishops meet in small groups, each allocated a special topic, and come together only to be addressed from the platform. There is therefore no scope for a group dynamic to develop or a common mind to emerge. A body this size (five hundred and twenty five bishops are officially accredited) would take months to weld into a real community at this rate.

There is a further fundamental flaw in the notion of a conference of Anglican bishops being able to decide anything at all as the voice of world Anglicanism. Each bishop, back home, shares authority in his local province with the clergy and laity. As in England, their General Synods have three Houses, and all three must agree before any important changes are made.

Dr Runcie suggested that Anglicanism could teach the Roman Catholic Church a thing or two about lay involvement in the machinery of government; but there are just as many laymen who are full members of the Lambeth Conference as there are of the Roman Catholic International Synod which meets every two or three years in Rome: precisely none. At local level, he was right; but the very absence of lay members of the Lambeth Conference means it cannot commit the twenty-seven provinces to anything, not even to greater consultation. It is an irony that the only matter on which it has any sort of mandate from the provinces concerns relations with the Roman Catholic Church, on which the provinces were carefully polled in advance.

In these circumstances, therefore, it can no longer be said with certainty that the issue at the Lambeth Conference is still what it initially seemed to be: the avoidance of schism in the Anglican Communion. A schism there is already; but a real communion there isn't. The issue, rather, is whether to start one; and whether any of the independent churches which call themselves Anglican would want to pay the entry fee. Whatever "modified autonomy" might mean, and whatever "minimum structuring", another Runcie phrase, might be necessary to make it work, a condition of membership of the Anglican Communion would have to be that individual churches could not do some things they would like to do without the consent of the rest.

Clearly, after this first week, that is a novel and difficult notion, so far with few friends.

THE CHURCH AUTONOMOUS

25 July 1988

No-popery is the residual religion of the English, it has been said, though so far the celebrations of the anniversaries of 1588 and 1688 have passed off without any overt anti-Catholic manifestations. These anniversaries are a good test of the present decline of this national trait, as was the Pope's visit in 1982 – some British police forces then, half expecting public disorder, were stuck with a huge over-provision of police manpower and large, unnecessary, overtime bills. Perhaps that particular streak in the English character has died out, carried away by a tidal wave of indifference to religion in general: people who have not the slightest idea what the Reformation was about are hardly going to riot in its defence.

But the no-popery principle went deep into the soul of the English national church, and still exists as a general and vague suspicion of "foreign" interference in domestic religious affairs. It was in due course exported by missionary Anglicanism, and lingers therefore in the subconscious of the various churches of the Anglican Communion worldwide.

As the bishops of those churches struggle at the Lambeth Conference to find some better method of co-ordinating their various tendencies so that none may drift too far or fast from the norm, they are faced with their own intuitive and not completely rational prejudice against the shades of popery, even a purely Anglican popery. So when they talk about the importance of the principle of the autonomy of separate Anglican provinces, they are really reflecting this historical attachment to national religious sovereignty, without knowing why. It is residual no-popery, inter-Anglican style.

Nevertheless, institutions sometimes have a need to turn to parallel models for comparison, particularly when they are not sure how to proceed. Ironically the only helpful comparison that the Lambeth Conference is likely to find is with the Roman Catholic Church. In the days when the international Anglican scene was relatively calm, that is to say relatively English, it was still possible for Anglicans to feel comfortably superior to the Roman Catholic model of international religious authority, and to regard it as unnecessary, oppressive, and a threat to national pride. The Pope, after all, was a foreigner. They would, if pushed, tend to regard the Orthodox model as closer to their ideal, ignorant of the fact that the Ecumenical Patriarch in Constantinople had the power to sack the Archbishop of Great Britain by telex overnight – as he recently did.

Even when the work of the Anglican-Roman Catholic International Commission (ARCIC) on authority in the church was published in 1982, it seemed to many Anglicans that the outline proposal for an international Christian "focus of unity", some sort of universal primacy in a united church, was little more than a theoretical – and not very attractive – solution to a problem that as far as they were concerned did not really exist. But now that the problem definitely does exist and is even a threat to Anglican survival, the *raison d'être* of the Roman Catholic pattern of international church government will begin to look more obvious. When the Lambeth Conference bishops turn to the discussion of this ARCIC document, they will have had first-hand experience of just how difficult it is to hold together an international Christian communion. This is an insight no single province could have gained by itself.

One significantly Anglican blind spot is evident from the

current state of the argument at the Lambeth Conference as it enters its second week. There has been a good deal of theology about the ordination of women, and even more about the principles of authority in the Anglican Communion. All aspects of the matter are being examined theologically, it seems, except the notion of the "national church" and its claim to autonomy. That is taken for granted. It is fenced off from critical theological examination by the ideology of nationalism. American Anglicans are American first, evidently, and they are not alone in such an attitude.

It makes some historical sense that the Church of England should have been declared totally independent of the Church of Rome, in the days when the latter was incapable of distinguishing between religion and power politics. It makes no sense at all that as a result four centuries later the Church of Kenya should be totally independent of the Church of Uganda and vice versa – yet that is what Anglican provincial autonomy means. Most provinces follow political boundaries, and the national church is normative in Anglicanism. Only a few, such as those of Ireland, the Indian Ocean or the West Indies, transcend nationality, usually for administrative or historical reasons.

A theological critique of provincial autonomy would start by asking whether and to what extent it serves the purposes of the Gospel, and whether it leads to the confusion of national identity with Christian identity, a potentially dangerous ideological corruption of Christian faith. The independent nation-state may be the dominant political idea of the latter half of the twentieth century, but nationalism does not deserve to be deified. It can in certain circumstances be a source of great evil. It erects barriers between peoples, and generates dangerous feelings of national and racial superiority, which are often unconscious. Autonomous Anglican churches organized on a basis of national identity are bound to be seen as part of all that, helping to strengthen and perpetuate it, condoning and sanctifying it. And in the church it can turn even a fellow Anglican into a stranger and a foreigner. That was precisely the reaction of the Church of England, when asked to recognize the ordination of Anglican women priests ordained abroad. They were not "us": they were "them". They were easy to reject.

In their campaigning for international social justice, however, these autonomous Anglican churches never fail to preach to governments the virtues of global co-operation, of strengthening the United Nations and of respect for international law, all of which require some sacrifice of national political sovereignty for the sake of a greater good.

They oppose rampant nationalism, and discrimination based on nationality and race. They believe in world citizenship. Yet as Anglican churches, in their relations with each other, they jealously guard their autonomy almost as if it was the fifth mark of the true church: one, holy, catholic, apostolic, and national.

LOOKING BACK ON LAMBETH

8 August 1988

As one of a series of statements on the Christian attitude to violence, the Lambeth Conference of 1988 approved a clause saying it "understood" those who resort to armed struggle when other means for correcting injustice fail. This was in spite of warnings from the bishops of the Church of Ireland, who said that the clause gave comfort to the IRA.

*

Many of the bishops at the Lambeth Conference developed in the course of it something of a phobia towards the media: to be precise, the English secular press. This newspaper, the *Telegraph*, the *Independent* and the *Guardian*, were present more or less throughout; and the English tabloids were mostly absent but ready to pounce from London, as last Friday, over the "armed struggle" resolution, they duly did.

63

It has some bearing on the way the Lambeth Conference went, and so no record of the conference would be complete without mention of it. That in turn would not be truthful without some account of this correspondent's own role in the matter. Of all the papers, *The Times* gave the Lambeth Conference most attention, and we received most attention back.

Half way through the conference the issue came to a head, when thirty-two bishops from Australia published an open letter in the Lambeth Conference daily newspaper (*The Lambeth Daily*) making a cluster of unspecific complaints about the English press, which boiled down to the charge that at least some of the reporting was slanted according to a pre-conceived intention to damage the church. They named no names. Later, organized by the conference staff, they had a formal meeting with a few of the journalists to air their grievances, and this time they did name names: mine. I was not present, though loyally defended in my absence by those journalists from other papers who were.

These grievances were the subject of a discussion among the bishops on television at one point, and the Archbishop of Canterbury, Dr Robert Runcie, mentioned the phenomenon in his final summing up speech on Saturday, saying: "We shall miss *The Lambeth Daily*. Some of you may miss the British press. Whilst some have been critical, others have been envious of the attention which the secular press actually gives us in this country. It is something we have begun to live with, even cheerfully." In a private meeting with some of the journalists he praised the coverage of all the specialist correspondents who had been at Canterbury, but it was not an appreciation he put on the record.

The Times and this correspondent were singled out for criticism by the Australians and some others because of one article in particular: it had asked whether the Anglican Communion really existed, and concluded that at least according to a narrow definition, it apparently did not. None of the points it raised was considered worth taking seriously by the Australians, who instead claimed to believe the article was written on the instructions of Mr Rupert Murdoch: he wanted the Church of England cut down to size because it had dared to criticize Mrs Margaret Thatcher, and *The Times*'s coverage of the Lambeth Conference was therefore part of a right-wing plot.

This fascinating construction was raised by them openly in their official meeting with journalists, and privately repeated many times. Even the non-Australians seemed to be beginning to believe it. Dr Runcie himself was well aware of it, and remarked to me he thought it was close to the heart of the tension between the press and the bishops. At no point did it seem to occur to anyone that there was no evidence for it and plenty against, or that the spreading of malicious calumny is a sin.

In response to the Australians' letter, a long article by me was published in *The Lambeth Daily*, explaining the history and general *raison d'être* of religious coverage in the English secular media. Many of the other bishops seemed to regard it as a more than satisfactory explanation. As if in reaction to the Australian paranoia, *The Times* was almost "flavour of the month" by the end: and it has been promised numerous new international readers among the bishops when they get home.

The effect of this controversy on the conference seemed to be very significant, which is why the issue deserves to be aired. The "Anglican Communion does not exist" article in *The Times*, which appeared at the end of the first week, was said by many bishops to have transformed the mood of the conference decisively, directly affecting the final outcome, either by driving them in the opposite direction to the one they (mistakenly) believed was intended (by Mr Murdoch or whomever), or showing them starkly how close they were to the abyss. So they drew together.

The crucial influence in the growth of this togetherness was their daily Bible study in small groups, prior to their group discussions of the issues allocated to them. This is where, many of them have said, they found the true meaning of the sense of communion that *The Times* had called in question. The article at the centre of the row had said, though in harder language, nothing very different from what the Archbishop of Canterbury had said in his opening address, when he had asked

"Do we want the Anglican Communion or don't we?"

The price of keeping it, he had told them, was the development of what he called inter-dependence in place of independence, of "modified autonomy" for the twenty-seven provinces of the Anglican Communion in place of their previous absolute autonomy. Decoded, that meant some provinces which wanted women bishops agreeing not to have them, in the interests of preserving full communion with other provinces. In fact they voted to keep their absolute autonomy, and the price they will pay is what is called "impaired communion". What they now have as well, though, is a strong sense of corporate identity and mutual support as a body of bishops.

Yet one New Zealand churchman of radical persuasions remarked privately at the end of the conference. "Of course the Anglican Communion does not exist", and the Bishop of London, from the opposite end of the spectrum, felt it was fast becoming no more than a federation of churches. But by the end no bishop was saying that publicly in the conference itself. Such remarks were by then the wrong side of the intellectual picket line.

SEDUCTION OF THE EVANGELICALS?

10 September 1988

If Evangelicals are about to inherit the Church of England – and more than half the present number of ordinands in training are in Evangelical colleges – they do not seem to view the prospect with much enthusiasm. The rise of Evangelicalism in the Church of England has caused little public nervousness, so far, from areas of the church out of sympathy with them, somewhat surprisingly; but it does appear to cause nervousness among Evangelicals themselves. It is as if the opportunity they have always prayed for but never expected to have, had now come upon them and they see it being missed.

Traditionally it was the heir to Puritanism, at least in morality and lifestyle; and the claim it sometimes still makes, that Anglican Evangelicalism was for generations the normative version of the Christian religion in England, is not unfounded. The Church of England has been well described as a Catholic Church of a Protestant nation, and by and large most English people's perception of Christianity, whether they agree with it or not and whether they like the current Church of England or not, is close to traditional Evangelicalism. It is also what is commonly meant by "Victorian Christianity".

But it is a house with many mansions, and Evangelicals can disagree with each other almost as strongly as they disagree with those who are not of their kind. Church Society, for instance, represents a school which has preserved most of the attitudes and convictions of past generations of English Protestants, not least a deep suspicion of Rome. "Modern" Evangelicalism, on the other hand, contains some of the church's greatest enthusiasts for that mode of ecumenism. But it is itself so diverse that there is no single body which can claim to represent it, and any attempt to state what is true of modern Evangelicals as a whole will be immediately challenged by some of them as a wicked caricature. If there is a good deal more in-fighting than among Anglican liberals or Anglo-Catholics, this is not necessarily to its discredit: Evangelicals do care for truth.

A new round of Evangelical self-criticism has been initiated by one of the movement's more famous characters, the Vicar of Ealing, the Rev. Michael Saward, who has recently published *Evangelicals on the Move*. Though his general account of the scene is a fair one, and is from an Evangelical point of view optimistic or even triumphant, it has had mixed reviews largely because the Evangelical vision he describes from personal conviction fails to match the hopes and expectations of at least some of the sub-sections of Evangelicalism.

Dr Gerald Bray, for instance, editor of the Evangelical magazine *Churchman*, dismissed it as "choruses and miracles". His is a serious theological and Biblical Evangelicalism, strongly rooted in the Reformation, whereas many Evangelicals seem more than a little embarrassed by the past. The middle mainstream in the Church of England is mightily seductive, and many a theological student who began his days in the ardour of a university Christian Union has since become a middle Anglican with mildly Evangelical colouring. It is the way to get on. If it is to be such people as that who inherit the Church of England, it would make little real alteration to anything: and that is what worries Dr Bray about Mr Saward's book.

Nevertheless Evangelicalism has managed to maintain, in all its forms, one characteristic difference from other varieties of Anglican belief, namely its emphasis on conversion. Elsewhere in the Church of England it is widely felt to be wrong to erect any sort of barrier or hurdle to church membership. The very concept of "becoming an Anglican" is elusive in a church which regards the entire community as its community, so the distinction between a church member and a non-member is more a matter of practice than of belief. Evangelicals make more of the difference, and tend to refer to themselves as "Christians", suggesting at least that there is another clear category, non-Christians. Evangelicals, as their name implies, want to evangelize the latter to make them into the former. Other Anglicans would not exactly reject the very idea, but tend to regard it as resting on too many questionable assumptions to be useful.

The Lausanne Committee for World Evangelization, an international meeting ground of Evangelicals of various denominations, issued a rousing "call to conversion" earlier this year after a consultation in Hong Kong, which concentrated on this distinction. "We recognize with concern that the Biblical mandate to call all persons everywhere to be converted is eschewed by large segments of Christianity," it said. "Conversion is disputed as a genuine Christian goal; it is decried as mere proselytism stemming from an attitude of spiritual arrogance or religious intolerance." It was being widely abandoned, in favour of other forms of church involvement with the world, such as working for the humanization of political structures, or "give-and-take dialogue" with other religions or ideologies.

Conversion, the statement declared, meant "turning from sin in repentance", a passage from spiritual death to spiritual life. Stated thus, it is impossible to dispute that this is an essential component of Christianity, whatever denominational or party label might be given to it: and that is a truth the Church of England at large tends to dismiss too sniffily. Unfortunately the emphasis on conversion has for so long been seen as an exclusively Evangelical preoccupation that the idea is now unconsciously translated as meaning no more than "becoming an Evangelical" – doing things according to the cultural language of a particular socio-religious sub-group rather than as a profound spiritual journey towards truth and life.

"OUTREACH" OR OUT OF REACH?

8 October 1988

The churches have lived for more than a generation with the hope that things would get better more or less of their own accord. In spite of the gradual long-term decline in church membership in Britain, there has been little sustained effort within the churches to explain or reverse it, or to devise policies accordingly. Yet any commercial organization finding its sales continually reduced would either prepare itself for ultimate disaster or take steps to improve its product and its marketing. The campaign of press and poster advertising launched last week by the new inter-denominational Christian Enquiry Agency is the beginning of a move in that direction.

Even the Evangelical movement, which is more interested than most in recruitment and conversion, has been open to criticism for competing with non-Evangelicals rather than with genuine "outreach", as they term it, in the community at large. For a substantial proportion of the crowds drawn in by their occasional preaching crusades have on closer inspection been found to be on the fringe of church membership already. Nevertheless sociological studies of the factors leading to growth or contraction in church membership have supplied some justification for this tactic. This analysis has shown what appear to be four different degrees of relationship with church activity, which could be regarded as concentric circles. The first two consist of an inner core of "activists" and a larger body of "ordinary worshippers", and the fourth consists of those with no personal or family history of church involvement at all, a present and past of non-relationship.

The group in the third circle, the most significant in these terms, consists of those not currently involved with a church but still with an old or distant connection, either personally or through the family. They might crudely be referred to as "lapsed", or as members of lapsed families. A church with growing membership, either nationally or locally, would usually be one where there was movement from that third level into the second; and the declining church would be one with the opposite flow.

In a generation or two the descendants of those in the third level may drift into the fourth outer one, way beyond contact with any church. And that would almost certainly be one-way traffic, unlike the reversible flow between the second and third. The most serious numerical danger to a church in the long term would come from a generation by generation transfer from the third to the fourth level, from being nearly out of reach to being cut off completely. And that has proved a very difficult drift for the churches to try to influence, even just to slow down.

But the third of these concentric circles, sometimes described as a "penumbra", represents a church's vital reservoir of potential members (in the absence of any strategy to reach people in the fourth level); and so it has been towards them that recruitment efforts have in the past been directed. This presupposes the existence of an emotional and spiritual umbilical cord which has not yet been broken, and on which a church can gently pull when the time is right. Among those in the third group denominational loyalties probably still matter, though their image or memory of the church they tend towards will inevitably be out of date and distorted by misconceptions.

There was a time when the Church of England treated the whole population as being at this "penumbra" third-level stage – in effect "lapsed Anglicans" – and only now is it adjusting to its gradual shrinkage over the years. The Roman Catholic Church has often seemed to be exclusively interested in evangelizing its own third-level group, the so-called "lapsed Catholics", and uninterested in the rest of the community: but according to this analysis it is acting on exactly the same basis as the Church of England, except its third-level group is numerically much smaller.

But of all the churches the Catholic Church has also made some effort towards the fourth level, the totally unchurched, and it is not surprising that the new Christian Enquiry Agency has been greatly assisted by advice from the Catholic Enquiry Centre, which has been fishing in these relatively unpromising waters for a long time. The Centre's advertisements and follow-up material are deliberately not designed to appeal to lapsed Catholics, and such inquirers are gently discouraged.

Even so, any programme for the evangelization of this section of the population will require considerable sensitivity. The approach adopted by the new agency which started last week, for instance, recognizes that it is particularly in times of personal crisis that people feel an absence of, and a need for, a sense of meaning and "someone who cares"; and that loneliness, emptiness and mental distress are not just emotional aches but also spiritual ones. In this respect the marketing analysis is a shrewd one, for it identifies a need and offers a "product" to meet it. The question that will soon arise is whether the product offered is actually in stock.

This kind of appeal to those previously beyond the churches' outer reach is evidently religious at the deepest meaning of the word. But the reception given to that fourth-level group, and the pastoral care provided, would have to be subtly different from that usually available to "new" church members of the more familiar sort, those moving from the third level to the second level. Their kind of entry into church membership

71

and activity often occurs not at a time of spiritual crisis but with the arrival of a sense of stability, and well-being, for instance after a happy marriage and the birth of children. Those are very different needs.

AN UNSTABLE COMMUNION

15 October 1988

The bishops of the Church of England returned from the Lambeth Conference this summer obviously moved by the spirit of brotherhood and unity they had experienced there. But the Church of England at large did not participate in that experience, and has now to contend with the rough bits without the smooth. And so there is an emerging feeling that the church seems to be heading for the worst of all possible worlds, with stalemate on every front. Various parts of the church have various ambitions for its future, not all of them incompatible, but it looks increasingly likely that there will be no joy for any of them and they give the impression they know it.

The General Synod machinery is beginning its long grapple with the ordination of women, and the measures for paying off priests who would not be able to live with it. The three years of bitter argument that this involves can only weaken morale on all sides, though it could still be redeemed if the church then received a tonic from the ordination of the first woman priests. But the smart money says the measure will not receive the two thirds majorities it would require at its final stage, which will depress a large part of the church without any offsetting reinvigoration among the rest.

The key factor will be the 1990 elections for a new General Synod. Previous synods which have debated some aspect or other have divided roughly 60–40, and surveys of opinion in the church suggest that that is a fair reflection of opinion.

Attempts were made to make this a major issue at the 1985 election, and the synod which emerged was if anything more conservative.

Supporters of women priests have a formidable task ahead of them to gain the extra 40 votes they need; and by then the church at large will be very conscious of the possible damage, much less aware of the possible benefits. Furthermore, if the proportion of the synod wanting women priests remained above half but below two thirds, the issue would be likely to return to the agenda repeatedly, without any prospect of a final resolution one way or the other, again the worst of all possible worlds.

Meanwhile the American, and probably the Canadian and New Zealand Anglican churches, are unstoppably heading towards the consecration of woman bishops, which will seriously jeopardize the unity of the Anglican Communion, and move it, as the Bishop of Chichester, Dr Eric Kemp, predicted recently, towards being a mere federation of separate churches.

For the future of Anglicanism the worst combination of these two circumstances, which is also the one most likely, would be a more or less permanent blockage on woman priests in the Church of England, while there were women bishops in three or four Anglican provinces abroad. Even maintaining the internal unity of the Church of England itself would be difficult, particularly if any English bishop is bold enough to take part in the consecration of a woman bishop overseas. It has been mentioned as a possibility, and it would in fact be quite difficult for someone like the Bishop of Bristol, the Right Rev. Barry Rogerson, to refuse such an invitation. In such an event the church will be lucky if the Bishop of London, Dr Graham Leonard, was content merely to declare himself out of communion with Bristol, and carry on as before.

One possible bonus the Church of England could hope for if it decided not to ordain women itself would be an improvement in relations with the Roman Catholic Church, which is desirable for all sorts of practical reasons as the two churches between them account for the greater part of English Christianity. But the Catholic Church conducts its bilateral relations at an international level, and deals not with the Church of England as such but with the Anglican Communion. The damage done to that process by women bishops elsewhere would not be adequately compensated by the Church of England's refusal to ordain women: it is again the worst possible combination.

There has even been some talk of the Church of England establishing a relationship of its own with Rome, cutting out the rest of the Anglican Communion. That would theoretically make it possible for the Roman Catholic Church to recognize the validity of Holy Orders in the Church of England alone, thus avoiding the issue of women priests elsewhere in Anglicanism. But to co-operate with such a step would require Rome to make decisions which could look like interference in internal Anglican affairs, which it has so far carefully avoided.

While many of the bishops who were at Lambeth were persuaded that the Anglican Communion was a Good Thing, it is not hard to detect a contrary opinion at lower levels in the church and all shades of churchmanship. Evangelicals can be particularly cutting about the "sentimental romanticism" of the Anglican Communion as a world-wide body. Most Evangelicals, it is said, judge the Anglican Communion by whether it is practically useful, and regard the finer distinctions between "full communion" and "partial communion" as beyond them. Such distinctions appeal more to Anglo-Catholics, however, for they adopt a quasi-Roman Catholic theology for the Anglican Communion; but they now see it as a source of danger to the Church of England rather than a strength.

Progressive churchmen are more enthusiastic than either of these two more conservative groupings, particularly as worldwide Anglicanism offers them some of the advantages of being an international body without the disadvantages of Roman Catholic discipline and centralization. Some even talk as if the present shape of the Anglican Communion is virtually the definitive picture of an ideal international church.

But to leave the Anglican Communion in its present unstable state, as they seem to want, would itself be the worst of all possibilities: it can damage the Church of England, but it cannot undo the damage.

A Question of Leadership

3 December 1988

Religion in Britain has a leadership problem. Critics of the churches tend to see it as a failure of effective personal leadership, a criticism directed at the style of leadership of such persons as the Archbishop of Canterbury or the Cardinal Archbishop of Westminster. But it is a structural problem. The style is dictated by the structure.

The negotiations to find a suitable body to replace the British Council of Churches have drawn attention to the contrasting styles and concepts of leadership in the various Christian denominations, and the near impossibility of satisfactorily marrying them. One of the proposals taking shape is for something like a national caucus of church leaders, which would act as a corporate centre of Christian leadership spanning all the major denominations. But in trying to reconcile so many different views and interests, there is an obvious danger of producing something so large, unwieldy and out of focus that it will not actually be able to lead at all.

The present president of the British Council of Churches is the Archbishop of Canterbury, Dr Robert Runcie. This is not an *ex officio* appointment, but arises from a consensus among the Anglican and Free Church members of the council that he is an acceptable visible figurehead. Without them being so rude as to say so, he would not be so easily accepted in such a role by the Roman Catholic community, which is why an ad hoc triumvirate, the Archbishop of Canterbury, the Cardinal Archbishop of Westminster, and the Moderator of the Free Church Federal Council, has emerged in practice, to make public statements or sign letters to *The Times*, when occasion demands.

That threesome ought really to be at least a foursome, with the Moderator of the General Assembly of the Church of Scotland; or even a fivesome, with the Archbishop of Thyateira and Great Britain, leader of the substantial Greek Orthodox community. But as soon as it starts to expand to that size, the question is bound to be asked why the President of the Methodist Conference is excluded; and so on. It soon becomes impossible.

A presidential committee consisting of all the leaders of all the churches participating in the post-British Council of Churches process would be enormous. The Cardinal Archbishop of Westminster, for instance, cannot speak for the Roman Catholics of Scotland; and the Archbishop of Canterbury cannot speak for the Anglicans of Scotland and Wales. And there are some thirty smaller churches involved. The various groupings of the Black churches have no agreed leader, and would need two or three to feel properly represented. And in some denominations, lay members would not necessarily accept that a cleric can speak for them, and would want their own representation. What such a hypothetical group begins to look like, in fact, is the British Council of Churches.

In hierarchical churches such as the Anglican, Orthodox or Roman Catholic Church, personal leadership is emphasized; and the classic and ultimate case is the Papacy. The "lower" and more Protestant a church, the less it will like the idea of personal leadership, and the more it will emphasize that the only voice with any authority is the voice of the whole assembly. The belief that an assembly of Christians has an authority of its own, a characteristic belief of Presbyterianism, was carried over intact into the ecumenical movement to give authority to such bodies as the assemblies of the British and World Councils of Churches. It meant that the resolutions of the British Council of Churches were regarded (though in practice with varying degrees of enthusiasm) as having weight, over and above the weight contributed by the member churches themselves. The council was somehow seen, or expecting to be seen, as "speaking for and on behalf of" something important, even though the member churches would rarely have been consulted in advance.

And this is the fundamental reason why the Roman Catholic Church did not feel able to join such bodies. And spurred by such Roman Catholic reservations, the Church of England has gradually realized that it shared them too. They gave a basis to the creeping Anglican suspicion that the British Council of Churches did not really represent anyone. The embrionic structures to replace the British Council of Churches, still prosaically called "ecumenical instruments", are not intended to be invested with such collective authority. Nevertheless the wish for a council of church leaders to head it, a body able to command the headlines, brings the question of authority back on stage again.

The Roman Catholics have been insisting that it could speak only on behalf of the individuals who composed it, and its collective authority would therefore be no more than the sum total of the various degrees of personal authority possessed by the individual church leaders. But if it is to have any influence, the sum will have to be greater than the parts, regardless of such theological reservations. It will have to have a name; it will have to have an identity the public can grasp.

Leadership as popularly understood demands recognizable and familiar figures, such household names as Basil Hume and Robert Runcie. But the Free churches do not like such cults of personality, and change their head man every year, precisely to prevent such "prelacy". The price of such purity, however, is that moderators and presidents are never around long enough to become known and familiar. They lack popular visibility, and therefore lack popular authority. To some extent this is the media's problem rather than the churches'; but journalists and broadcasters are not going to change their ways. If public leadership is to be exercised beyond the confines of a particular denomination, it will necessarily have to be done on terms set by the needs of the mass media. While in practice that is likely to be the last of the churches' concerns, it is on such considerations that the success of the venture will depend.

Healing the Racial Rift

22 April 1989

Archbishop Desmond Tutu is arguably the most famous Anglican churchman of all, perhaps more so even than the Archbishop of Canterbury. His visit to Britain this week was a powerful symbol of the multi-racialism of the contemporary church, which has at last thrown off its all-white image. After a poor start, racial equality is doing rather better under the auspices of Christianity than it is under any equivalent secular ideology. It is not absurd to talk about the next Pope being black, just as, at the Lambeth Conference last year, the present Archbishop of Canterbury was speculating about the possibility that his own successor could be black.

But these are international appointments, where black churchmen qualify for consideration because of their seniority in countries where the whole church and nation is black. The record in countries where the church is mainly white, such as Britain and the United States, is not quite so good, though it is notable that the new woman bishop whose consecration has precipitated the crisis in the Anglican Communion, Bishop Barbara Harris of Massachusetts, also happens to be black.

Nevertheless the relationship between the races in the British church scene has substantially improved over the past decade. Before, the black (or so-called black-led) independent churches were isolated and fragmented, and still very conscious of their painful origins in white rejection. Now, the institutions being fashioned by the "Inter-Church Process" to take over from the British Council of Churches next year will have full Black Church participation, which will mean for the first time the possibility of their real integration into British church life.

A great many of the West Indians who emigrated to Britain came from a culture where church-going was normal, and their affiliations were to the local branches of the major European church traditions. But in England they experienced a frosty welcome from those same churches, not least because their language and style of worship lacked the spontaneity and exuberance of West Indian Christianity.

It was bound to feel cold; and traditional English reserve towards newcomers, no doubt often tinged with racism, completed the impression of racialist rejection. It was from these bitter origins that the Black Churches in Britain mainly sprung. But the consequent division of Christianity in Britain into black and white sectors, understandable though it was, was a lamentable and unchristian development.

The Church of England in particular has been working hard to make amends. It now has a black suffragan bishop, Bishop Wilfred Wood of Croydon, and a black member of the standing committee of the General Synod, Dr John Sentamu, who is priest of a parish in Brixton. Mainly black Anglican congregations are no longer quite the rarity they were; and there are mainly black Methodist congregations too. Apart from Roman Catholics, the black working class population is the only segment of that class which is not yet completely lost to the church.

The latest move in the development of black Christianity in Britain is the foundation of a new theological centre in Wandsworth, south London, to be known as the Simon of Cyrene Theological Institute. Though originally an Anglican initiative – its first principal will be a distinguished black Anglican clergyman from Barbados and financial support for the project is almost wholly Anglican – it will be as ecumenical as possible, and it already has links with the Baptist, Methodist, Roman Catholic and United Reformed Churches as well as some independent Black Churches. Its main work will be with black students prior to their more conventional training for the ministry, or supplementary post-ordination training. Students will still receive most of their pre-ordination training in their own colleges and seminaries, where they can expect, as blacks, to be in a small minority.

The institute will emphasize what is called black theology, a mainly American product of the 1960s and 1970s which sought to illuminate and articulate the black experience of poverty and racism in religious terms. For a while it even seemed to rival liberation theology, and it can now be regarded as a department of that branch of theology though its origins were separate – one may speak of a black theology of liberation. But the West Indian experience in Britain is only superficially similar to the black experience in the United States, and the institute may find itself having to generate a more home-spun black theology to suit British conditions.

The most urgent and most delicate item on this agenda is the need for a black ecumenical theology, capable of spanning the gap between the mainstream British denominations and the new Black Churches. It will require a quite different ecumenical method, for the divisions between them do not originate, as they do in the cases to which conventional ecumenism addresses itself, from European church squabbles of the more distant past.

In conventional terms, the Black Churches do not have much explicit theology behind them at all, and tend to be fundamentalist in belief and pentecostal in style. A black theology of liberation could say a great deal to them, however, and if it became their own, could deepen their sense of identity and self-understanding. That would enable them to treat with the mainstream denominations on a more equal basis, and ecumenism demands such an equality between the partners if it is not to degenerate into condescension. It needs push as well as pull.

It is not yet clear that the Black Churches want to be committed to eventual unity with the mainstream churches, though the principle is implied by their participation in the Inter-Church Process. The fact that their separateness is essentially racial and cultural rather than doctrinal is both an opportunity and an obstacle to the possibility of such a reconciliation. It might well require them to undertake the careful unravelling of all the layers of meaning in the ambivalent term "black", including some theological probing of the secular ideology of "blackness" which may well owe more to militant Marxism than to Christianity.

Some black theology has spoken of this condition of blackness as if it were almost a precondition of salvation, by investing it with the attributes of the blessed that are listed in the Beatitudes. But it could also be that this idea of blackness is the brand-mark of oppression – precisely that from which the Gospel offers liberation. Sooner or later, if there is to be any ecumenical progress between the Black Churches and the rest, this profound issue of black identity will have to be faced. And it is also a question of white identity.

A TOLERANT CHURCH, WORTHY OF A GENEROUS OBITUARY

19 August 1989

The "Anglican Way" in religion – questioning, doubtful, undogmatic and tolerant – is in serious decline, according to the Rev. Nicolas Stacey, one time member of the South Bank *avant garde*. Yet it is the only sort of religion that to him is credible: and so still say thousands of others. In a recent sermon he contrasted it with the buoyancy of virtually all forms of fundamentalism, which know all the answers and condemn "all gays, divorcees, adulterers and condoms as anathema". Those who live in the real world, he added sadly, "know that it is not like that".

Credibility means capable of being believed, and Mr Stacey may be saying no more than that his capacity for believing is limited; therefore he prefers a religion which does not ask him to believe too much. But it is in the nature of Anglicanism not to ask too much; this Anglican Way he refers to is typically Anglican to an extent Anglo-Catholicism and Anglican-Evangelicalism are not. It was the normative form; they are departures from it. Their very existence arises from special stress on a particular source of authority – tradition in the one case, Scripture in the other. But the Church of England from its origins in the Elizabethan Settlement of the late sixteenth century has been an institution marked above all by comprehensiveness, the principle of which is that those of differing theological emphases can nevertheless share one church, provided that no single emphasis is stressed so hard as to unchurch those who differ. And historically those who have taken their particular theological emphasis beyond such limits have either left the Church of England or refused to join it.

The Elizabethan Settlement was as much a political as a theological solution. The sharing of one church by all shades of opinion was a device of government for the peace of the realm, not a profound religious insight. Tolerance of dissent was originally not part of the package, but had to become so once the enforcement of religious uniformity was abandoned as impossible and unjust. It is an attitude manifested not just by doctrinal comprehensiveness but by social "all-embracingness"; the idea, still general in the Church of England, that the Vicar of Bray serves the entire population of Bray, and the population of the parish is the population of the whole neighbourhood which is still notionally deemed to be Anglican.

This is an attractive vision of a unified society, for it means there is no "them", as everyone is part of the "us", and hence there is no "us-and-them". But it means also that there can be no doctrinal or moral test of membership. The relaxed spirit of the Anglican Way which those like Nicolas Stacey found so congenial is not so much the creation of a group of gentle like-minded persons, therefore, as the product of a particular history and ideology, above all the idea of a national church whose membership shall consist of the entire nation.

The decline of the Anglican Way as a home for religious-minded scepticism is likely to be coupled with the decline of Anglicanism (in England) as this ideal national church, under the pressure of secularism and agnosticism. At some critical turning point in that decline, all-embracing comprehensiveness became part of the church's problem and not part of the solution. In the very long term, perhaps, the Elizabethan Settle-

82

ment is slowly unravelling and showing itself to be unstable. And the intellectual tools by which the English nation has slowly turned itself away from religious faith were first learnt from the Anglican Way itself. Agnosticism and Anglicanism share a common frontier, without much frontier control.

There are still a lot of people left in the Church of England who rejoice in this scepticism, or like Mr Stacey himself feel great nostalgia for it. To them the very attractiveness of Anglicanism lies in its lack of certainty and its unwillingness to lay down the law. Part of the evidence for the beleaguered state of the Anglican Way to which he refers is the incessant protest at this condition, and the demand from the theological and political right-wing that the Church of England should "believe something definite". But that can only mean the Anglican Way giving further ground to the Anglo-Catholic or Anglo-Evangelical tendencies, for those are the only two available Anglican sources for finding such a "something definite". But whichever it gives way to, if it does, will tend to unchurch the other.

This "Anglican Way" Anglicanism is not a systematic scheme of theological ideas, like German liberal Protestantism, though in the past it has found some of that thinking to its liking. Nicolas Stacey is of the *Honest to God* generation of South Bank churchmanship, and the publication of that mid-1960s best-seller demonstrated the existence of an appetite for a more rigorous intellectual framework of support. But a whole generation of Anglican liberal theologians in the universities has grown old without a generation of younger men and women of bright minds to follow them. Liberal theology needed a new idea to give it new life; and none appeared; or a new leader: perhaps Mr Stacey should have stayed at his post and written books, instead of taking himself off to do social work. Neither the Bishop of Durham nor Dean Don Cupitt have managed to start a "school" or movement, and Cupitt's rebellion was not only against Christian dogmaticism and fundamentalism, but also a rejection of the Anglican Way as not a rich enough seam to mine. So the weakness of the intellectual content of the Anglican Way in its contemporary manifestation has diluted it down to the point where its enemies can dismiss it as no more than a half-hearted semi-detachment to Christian faith.

It is not clear to an outsider, any longer, what it is trying to say. And those who are sceptical about doctrines and churches but still have warm feelings towards religion feel less need to belong to anything. For them the Anglican Way has succumbed at last to its own sharpest instrument, Occam's Razor: those ideas which are not necessary should be abandoned. But it deserves a generous obituary when the time comes. It was a most decent and civilized way of faith.

DR RUNCIE'S BAD PRESS

14 October 1989

The English churchmen who took part in the Archbishop of Canterbury's official visit to the Vatican two weeks ago are said to be privately surprised and dismayed by the negative tone of the British press coverage. They felt it was a successful visit; but it was reported, by and large, as a papal rebuff. As at the Lambeth Conference last year, the role of the press has emerged as part of the story of the event itself, and once again it has proved an accident-prone relationship. Last year the coverage was held to have influenced the way the conference, which lasted three weeks, actually developed. The effect was different this time, as the event was over a much shorter time-scale and further away.

One of the primary purposes of the archbishop's visit to Rome was undoubtedly to signal to the British public how fruitful and close Anglican-Roman Catholic relations still are. That was not entirely the effect achieved. Either something went amiss with the signalling, or the message was not clear enough to signal. The coverage was not quite all negative, for *The Times*' concluding Leading Article was more optimistic.

Most papers just did not know what to make of it.

There was in the event a different and louder message reaching Britain's newsdesks, in the Archbishop of Canterbury's "Pharisee society" interview in *The Director*, and more especially the accompanying press release from the Institute of Directors which hyped it and about whose sensational tone Lambeth Palace has since protested. Here was a story they thought they understood. The controversy broke right in the middle of the visit, and Lambeth Palace, not realizing how wicked the world can be, had not been expecting it until November.

Some parts of the British press have an obsessive dislike of Dr Runcie, for reasons which will probably never become completely clear, and their aggressive concentration on him makes him "news" for the rest, whether the rest follow that hostile line or not. The coverage of the interview that day effectively sabotaged the press coverage of what was happening in Rome, thereby no doubt giving immense satisfaction to Dr Runcie's press enemies.

As if that was not enough, some journalists suddenly started to pay close attention to the thoughts of Mr Ian Paisley and Dr David Samuel – men whose ideas on Anglican-Roman Catholic church unity are usually ignored in order to whip up the pretence of a constitutional crisis involving Dr Runcie. It was even wildly proposed in one paper that Dr Runcie's proposals for a papal "universal primacy" had caused the Queen to summon her constitutional advisers.

In those circumstances the public could only have received a confused impression of the actual events in Rome. The Vatican was playing its cards close to its chest, and the careful symbolism of the public occasions was carefully ambivalent, capable of supporting almost any interpretation the journalists felt like giving it. The Pope, listening to Dr Runcie explaining the significance of the episcopal ring he was wearing, wore an expression of fascinated inscrutability, and spoke likewise. The ring had been given to Archbishop Michael Ramsey by Pope Paul VI, and was, so to speak, an engagement ring, Dr Runcie told him. It was not a symbol of courtship the Pope was in a mood to respond to.

It was in much the same spirit that the Pope failed to welcome Dr Runcie's suggestion of a universal primacy for himself. He chose to emphasize that the See of Peter is more than an Anglican-type focus of unity, but has a living magisterium, a teaching office (with bite). In other words, if anyone wants to know whether the ordination of women is permissible, he only has to ask the Pope.

The Church of England spokesman invited the journalists present to conclude that this degree of candour was a sign of how close things now were. There was also talk of an exceptional atmosphere of amiability. But the Vatican declined to brief the journalists at all until the very end, when the saintly Cardinal Willebrands insisted that obstacles were, after all, things to be removed. Prior to that no attempt had been made to soften what the Vatican must have known would sound like hard sayings to Anglican ears. The Anglicans were suggesting a much looser style of papal primacy; the Pope replied, in effect, that his office was not negotiable.

In such cases terms like "success" and "failure" are not hard objective facts but judgements made by journalists on the spot; but nor are they purely subjective, because the journalist himself is professionally neutral and will equally happily report a triumph or a disaster. Here the evidence for a rebuff was concrete, the evidence for success was soft.

The Vatican agreed to respond at last to the Anglican-Roman Catholic International Commission's report but it had been due to respond by the end of last year anyway. Dr Runcie met various heads of the Vatican departments but no one was quite sure when he had met them before. The Pope did not call the whole thing off but he wasn't carried away by it either.

Last year's Lambeth Conference had been described as a success because of the warmth of the relationships established, even though the conference represented the start of a formal split between those Anglicans in full communion and those in partial or "impaired" communion. This year's Anglican visit to Rome is now being said to be a success for similar reasons;

and good relationships are indeed essential to ecumenical progress. But they are a little intangible.

The truth of the matter is that things could have been much worse. Influential figures in Rome were beginning to feel they were being led up the Anglican garden path (a sensation not unfamiliar to Methodists and the United Reformed Church in England) and had been tempted to take the whole Anglican-Roman Catholic show off the road. Dr Runcie bravely went to Rome to try to keep it running, and in that he certainly succeeded. The Anglican side could never have admitted this in advance nor can they admit it now and so it could never have been the sort of success of which headlines are made. For that, there had to be a clear picture of what failure would have looked like, for comparison: but no one had been candid enough to offer one.

THE WORLD IS HIS CLOISTER
Dr Robert Runcie

26 March 1990

As he climbed into the pulpit at St Paul's to preach his famous Falklands sermon in 1982, for an instant the light caught the Archbishop of Canterbury's Military Cross, discreetly pinned that day to his cassock. It was a sudden and unexpected reminder that here was a brave man who once saved a fellow soldier on the battlefield at the risk of his own life, who once took a tank into an open field under close, intensive fire from German guns.

It is a sterling characteristic of Robert Alexander Kennedy Runcie, MC, that he does not lack courage when he knows what he has to do. But even to this day he has hardly made up his mind about the wisdom and righteousness of the Falklands campaign. Then and since, he has neither defended it nor attacked it; he is by temperament and principle neither a pacifist nor a nationalist. But he did not shirk from delivering the sermon his conscience felt was right at the national Falklands service, in which he called for prayers for both British and Argentine casualties and their families. Quite calmly, and without regard for the consequences for himself, he told the congregation, which included royalty, politicians and servicemen, that "war springs from the love and loyalty which should be offered to God being applied to some God substitute, one of the most dangerous being nationalism . . . ".

It was he, above all, who had insisted beforehand that the service should be a service of reconciliation and not a jingoistic "thanksgiving for victory", and he also knew, because they had told him so, that neither the Roman Catholics nor the Free churches would agree to take part in the service, and that the Dean and Chapter of St Paul's would revolt, if it were allowed to become a celebration of British military triumph. From that moment on, the more blimpish parts of the Tory party and press had him marked in their sights as an enemy, a softy and a wet; and in the long run some of the mud stuck to him, as mud does. It is, however, merely a myth circulated by her courtiers that the Prime Minister was angry with him. In fact she congratulated him on his sermon that day. Since then Dr Runcie has said that he is puzzled by the common press perception of a state of war between himself and Mrs Thatcher, which has never corresponded to the way she actually treats him personally. Nevertheless they are, temperamentally, poles apart. It has never seemed to him that there was very much wrong with the post-war British welfare state consensus, and the more dramatic moments of its breaking up, such as the miners' strike in 1984, pained him greatly.

There is in his make-up a streak of indecisiveness which has sometimes been mistaken for lack of courage. Successive visitors of opposing views, meeting him in his study in Lambeth Palace for a reassuring word, are likely to come away glowing with the warmth of their welcome, convinced he is on their side. Probably, at the moment he was speaking to them, he was. But while this tendency to run with the hare and hunt with the hounds has made him personally popular in the church and a good pastor of souls – he is a warmly affectionate man – it has been at the expense of clear leadership. Too much sensitivity to all the pros and cons of every argument is an asset in a theology lecturer (which he once was), but does not make for firmness of purpose in a Primate of All England. For that, one has to be prepared not only to win friends, but also to lose them.

He has sometimes been reluctant to seize the initiative, therefore, or once having seized it, he has let it slip again. Dr Runcie tends to want conflicting and irreconcilable things for the Church of England, and for the Anglican Communion whose worldwide leader he also is: women priests and full communion with Rome, for instance; a united church in which everyone of whatever persuasion feels at home; a close relationship with the nation and a distance from the government the nation has elected. Mostly this brings an unfair impression of weakness, but it brings him one great strength – very many ordinary Anglicans share this optimistic or confused vision, and so their leader is just like them. Had he chosen a different career, a country solicitor, perhaps, or breeder of prize pigs, he would have been a mainstay of the local church: churchwarden, school trustee, deanery synod member, one of the nicest men in the diocese whom everyone liked and trusted. There is a Mr Anglican Everyman quality to the present Archbishop of Canterbury, which perhaps explains the unkind comment sometimes heard that too many of his fellow bishops are "Runcie clones".

In truth, they are just typical Anglicans like him. The most notorious of the grievances aired by the late Dr Gareth Bennett in his famous Crockford Preface was that the Archbishop had peopled the bench of bishops with his friends and familiars, almost as a kind of conspiracy. He had failed to notice that the whole preferment process in the Church of England had become a smooth machine for moving nice men like Dr Runcie upwards. All these apparent weaknesses have corresponding strengths, however, and Dr Runcie has never buried his talents in a field. If it is possible to hold the Church of England together by charm, goodwill, affection and tolerance, then he has succeeded.

Even more, the Anglican Communion – no insignificant world body, with 60 million members, and growing – is ideally suited to such a leadership style. It does not want a Pope, and each of the twenty-six separate churches or "provinces" likes to create an Archbishop of Canterbury in its own image. He lent himself to that, deliberately and magnificently. It is a quite undefinable thing, an Anglican Communion; except that, for the moment, it can be defined by its enormous affection for its head man, and that it will miss him. He has become, briefly, himself, its source of unity. That is no small achievement.

CAREY ON THE SCALES

28 July 1990

Dr George Carey's appointment as the next Archbishop of Canterbury was announced on 27 July 1990.

＊

On Wednesday afternoon the BBC wanted to know whether he will be "a good archbishop". "Well," I said, realizing it was both an impossible question and the whole point of the interview, "perhaps."

What is a good Archbishop of Canterbury? Would an atheist think a bad archbishop was one who believed? A Catholic, one who did not accept the papacy? Good for whom? Good for journalists? The appointment of Dr George Carey to succeed Dr Runcie will be good for those who believe in women priests, because he strongly does, but not good for those who do not. There are no answers, only opinions. Not so, as you say later (and if it were so, why should we read on?).

Behind the assumptions in the question lies a heap of other assumptions, all undeclared, chief of which is that there is a clear and agreed role for the Church of England in our society by which a new leader can be measured. Paradoxically, what has most often been said about Dr Carey so far is that he may help it to find such a role, which must mean that the ruler to measure him by has not yet been fashioned. John Wesley was a good Methodist perhaps. Was Christ a good Christian?

A good archbishop presumably means one capable of leading the Church of England in the successful fulfilment of its purposes, which must include the saving of souls. Aside from those who hold a hard doctrine of "assurance" (which everyone else regards as a doctrine of presumption or spiritual conceit), there is no way of knowing for sure whether the Church of England or any other church saves any souls at all, or whether Dr Carey's presence at Lambeth Palace will, by the time he finishes, have increased or reduced the proportion. The means to this invisible purpose is the more visible one of preaching the Gospel, and here it is a little easier – but not much – to judge the Church of England's performance and an Archbishop of Canterbury's contribution. However, the Gospel is no simple package. Its contents have never been beyond dispute.

Those who have been most critical of the Church of England's record in the 1980s accuse it of having laid aside the Gospel in favour of left-of-centre politics or for social and moral fashion. But for many members of the church, identifying with the poor is part of the Gospel, and they have biblical texts to prove it. For many, tolerance towards homosexuals or the cause of female equality with men is of the essence of the justice for which the Gospel calls. For others such attitudes are a great betrayal – who is to say?

Those who call most often for a return to doctrinal certainties cite the Bishop of Durham as the archpriest of doubters, but it is just as likely that he is a man of deep faith who wants to present the Gospel in its most credible form, without what he regards as its miraculous red herrings. He claims to be a better evangelist than those who insist on obscuring the true message with lots of false ones; his critics retort that without miracles there is nothing to preach – again, who is to say?

The commonest assumption among those who have abandoned the faith and practice of Christianity in their own lives is that there is still such a thing as "ordinary" Christianity out there somewhere. The next most common assumption is that it is a good thing, in some generalized sense, so long as they can get on with their own lives and ignore it. So it would be good, the editorials in Thursday's newspapers seemed to be saying, if Dr Carey could reverse the apparent decline in that ordinary Christianity, and persuade more people, though not the writers themselves, to believe in it.

They are fooling themselves, of course; projecting their own memories and expectations of whatever version of Christianity they were most familiar with before they decided it was not for them. This projection, naturally, has scant resemblance to the present Church of England, so Dr Carey's task is to start from here and get back to wherever that was. Well, a bad archbishop is easier to define than a good one, and one who followed this advice would be crazy.

The criteria of competence, intelligence and maturity apply to any leader, and may be applied to an Archbishop of Canterbury too. More relevant is the criterion of holiness, which is not quite so subjective as it may sound; that Francis of Assisi was holy, for instance, is not simply a matter of opinion – but as with the saving of souls, only God really knows.

The only question which makes any sense is whether Dr Carey can be utterly true to his beliefs, whatever they may be. There is a certain authority that comes from complete spiritual integrity, which is more to do with the way a man looks you in the eye than with his opinions, more to do with the quality of his prayers than the quality of his thoughts. If it is meaningful to talk of institutions in such a way, then this quality which is spiritual rather than doctrinal is one the Church of England needs more of, for it is a quality valuable in itself, regardless of its impact on society.

The more Dr Carey can persuade the Church of England

to leave its future to providence and to concentrate on the rebuilding of its inner spiritual life, the better a church it will be, and the better an archbishop he will be. The creed offers four marks of the true church, that it is one, holy, catholic, and apostolic. We have heard much quarrelling about the first, third and fourth, but too little about the pursuit of the second since the days of Michael Ramsey.

Now he was a good archbishop.

Part Three

No Half-way House

The Ordination of Women

THE HAND THAT ROCKS THE CHURCH

20 June 1988

It is hardly disputed that the Church of England would inflict considerable damage on itself by the ordination of women. Supporters of women's ordination acknowledge as much. But they say that not to ordain women would do even more damage. That is still not quite the kernel of their argument; which is that the church has a duty to do what is right, and comparative calculations of consequences are secondary. In short, God wants the church to ordain women: it would be wrong not to do so, and the church must not do what it knows to be wrong.

This summary of the case "for" is woven through the pages of *The Ordination of Women to the Priesthood*, a theological report from the House of Bishops of the Church of England, and is as well argued there as it has ever been anywhere. It does not make the mistake, for instance, of offering the argument that ordination is a "right" of women, for ordination, like salvation, is a right of no one. Indeed, the argument is not primarily that for the sake of women they should be ordained, but for the sake of the church and of everyone, female and male.

In that respect female ordination is unlike any other issue involving the correction of inequalities between women and men. It is different from the campaign to give married women a right to property, to win for women the vote or the right to be in Parliament, and not to be discriminated against in employment. It is only similar to them in that all these inequalities are said to spring from the same mistaken theories of human nature, or from the same male desire to protect male privilege and power. So if in the secular world these theories have been exploded and the roots of sexual inequality exposed as unjust, the church will be seen to be aligning itself with error and injustice if it continues to resist women priests.

The case can only be answered adequately by an equally strong insistence that the church, in refusing to ordain women, would be holding out for some basic and transcendental truth that the secular world has missed, offering itself as a witness to that truth as a "sign of contradiction". There could be such an answer. It involves pointing the arguments of radical feminism in the opposite direction.

For a long time, feminism seemed to hover uncertainly between two contradictory assertions: that male and female were fundamentally identical, and their differences purely the result of social conditioning; or alternatively that male and female were basically different. It is the debate about whether the dominance of the characteristics generally known as masculine was innate in males, and the feminine in females. And it is complicated by a certain moral bias against masculinity, and in favour of femininity, the former being characterized as aggressive, competitive and indeed brutal, the latter as gentle, compassionate and generally more sensitive to feelings.

Feminism seems gradually to be settling in favour of the second alternative: that males are innately imbued with the so-called masculine aspects of human nature, in other words that they are uncurably that way. And the feminist hope of the 1960s that an attack on role conditioning would produce an androgynous New Man, without all those objectionable masculine characteristics, has faded.

If, as feminism would say, masculinity is responsible for most of what is wrong with the world, the redemption of the world must involve as a high priority the redemption of masculinity. Whether desirable or not, it does not now appear possible to eliminate it, nor to neutralize it by diluting it with femininity into androgyny. This is where the maleness of Jesus becomes entirely relevant, and the maleness of the priesthood. They are symbols of masculinity crucified, of masculinity redeeming and redeemed – and not by femininity or androgyny.

Crucifixion of a man by men is a kind of ultimate statement of the collision of good and evil within masculinity: femininity can do nothing with it, except draw back in uncomprehending horror.

A female priest could not therefore be a symbol of crucified and redeemed masculinity. All the other things a priest does, no doubt she could do very well, or even better. But she would be a symbol that the church has turned away in embarrassment and disbelief from admitting that at the very heart of Christian redemption is an apocalyptic crisis of extreme physical violence meeting extreme physical courage, masculinity *in extremis*. It is not possible to read the text while mentally substituting a woman for Jesus, and think it means anything like the same. It becomes a quite different story, with a distinct flavour of sexual violence. Nor therefore can it mean anything like the same for a woman priest to pronounce at the altar the words of Christ's offering – the anticipation of his Crucifixion – "This is my body". It would be emptied of its deepest meaning, and a new and unsavoury sexual suggestion introduced exactly where it was least appropriate.

If the opponents of women's ordination have not yet met the moral case, this, the other side of the coin, is the case the proponents of women's ordination have yet to answer.

DELAY THE DECISION ON WOMEN PRIESTS

---

4 July 1988

The General Synod of the Church of England assembles in London today to address some of the most important decisions in that church's history. It will be asked to debate at length the theological background to the ordination of women, and then to give its first consent to the legislation required to make that a reality.

So the pressure is on to grasp the nettle at last. It is thirteen years since the synod declared that it saw "no fundamental objection" to the ordination of women, and it could be as many as five more before that can be translated into action – time enough, most members of the synod will no doubt reckon. Whether the legislation does finally reach the statute book in 1992 or later, or falls at the last hurdle – the test of two thirds majorities in each of the Houses of Laity, Clergy and Bishops – at least the issue will have been settled for better or for worse.

Yet the most intelligent and courageous option for the synod to take would be to put it off. There are powerful arguments for an adjournment of the debate after the reception of the House of Bishops' theological report, before it turns to consider the legislation. The strongest of these arguments is that the next Lambeth Conference is less than a fortnight away, and the ordination of women priests and bishops will be the dominant question before it.

The Lambeth Conference is the nearest thing to a collective representative expression of the mind of the Anglican Communion. It has no juridical authority over its member churches, but its past resolutions concerning the ordination of women have had their effect nevertheless. The 1978 Lambeth Conference resolution said it was up to member churches whether they ordained women as priests or not, and it should not prevent them staying in communion with each other. It was that resolution which sanctions the proposal the synod is to debate today and tomorrow. But the Lambeth Conference will want to look at it again, and will certainly have new things to say. The General Synod of the Church of England, by going ahead so close to the Lambeth Conference, will in effect be signalling that it is not interested in the results of that review.

The Lambeth Conference will concentrate this time on the ordination of women as bishops, which is imminent in the United States and possibly elsewhere. On this the conference is bound to be deeply divided, and some commentators doubt whether the Anglican Communion could long survive in one piece. But whatever comes out of the conference is bound to make a significant difference to the ecclesiastical landscape. The general synod would be wise to wait, and take a good look at that new landscape, before deciding what is then in the best interests of the Church of England.

It is not easy to say at this stage whether the outcome of the Lambeth Conference would favour the case for or against ordaining women priests in England, which is one reason why a proposal for an adjournment of the synod debate on such grounds as these would probably find few friends among the partisans on either side. From their point of view, it would be a gamble. But it would be difficult for the synod as a whole to claim that it has acted as wisely as it can, on the best information available, if it has turned down the chance to listen to what the Lambeth Conference might have wanted to say to it first.

The imminence of the Lambeth Conference has a bearing in another important respect. It is due to give its final verdict on the agreed reports of the Anglican-Roman Catholic International Commission (ARCIC); and Rome is due to give its own official response later this year. It can be confidently anticipated that the Archbishop of Canterbury, Dr Robert Runcie, will want to visit Rome to meet the Pope after all that is over; and there is speculation that Rome might by then be ready to make some fairly bold move in its relations with Anglicanism.

Again, this would alter the ecclesiastical landscape; and again it is good reason for the general synod to wait and see. Convinced supporters of women's ordination would regard this as a reason for proceeding post-haste, lest the warmth of Rome's response to ARCIC starts to whittle away their voting strength; but the more doubtful supporters, still trying to weigh the pros and cons, might well prefer to make their decision in the light of the facts as they are in six months' time rather than now.

The Church of England already has a credibility problem about its ecumenical seriousness, having in the past first wooed and then turned away both the Methodist Church and the

United Reformed Church. At least the Church of England would be acting consistently if, being on the very brink of a breakthrough with Roman Catholicism, it chose to throw away that opportunity too.

This Lambeth Conference falls in the middle of a long theological debate about authority in Anglicanism, where it lies, how it is exercised, and who is to decide what is Anglican and what is not. The lack of clear answers so far has given rise to the impression that members of the Church of England may believe anything they like about anything, or nothing at all; a church where everybody "does their own thing" and then calls itself unanimous. This is a fundamental difficulty for the present reputation of the Church of England in national life – far removed from the women priests issue, and in its own way far more serious, for it undermines the authority with which the church preaches the Gospel itself. To wait for the Lambeth Conference out of respect for its moral authority would be an important step towards restoring a higher view of authority in the church generally. It would start to put flesh on the elusive concept of communion, *communio*, or *koinonia*, which is what holds the church together.

If one church, and not the least important one, were to signify that it was waiting for a lead from this council of all the world's Anglican bishops, it would challenge them to see themselves as a vital organ of the church, a necessary part of the church's structure of authority, and not just as an episcopal debating society that no one pays much attention to. It might even make a difference to their answers.

IS PARTIAL SCHISM A REALITY?

11 July 1988

Events at Econe* the week before were briefly cited last week during the debate at the General Synod of the Church of England on the ordination of women, but it seemed characteristic of the mood of synod members to draw in on themselves rather than to look elsewhere, as part of the process of bracing themselves for a tough decision.

Probably as a symptom of the same inward-looking mood, the forthcoming Lambeth Conference received even less attention, though like Econe that could soon present another modern example of the rare phenomenon of schism. But it may also have been the very vagueness of the concept of schism in Anglicanism which made it hard for the synod to focus on. It implies a generally agreed systematic theology of the church, the sort of ecclesiology still in its infancy in Anglicanism.

It seems a feature of schism that while both sides acknowledge it as a sin, each side always accuses the other of committing it. In the Roman Catholic schism, Archbishop Marcel Lefebvre claims it is the papal church, the post-Vatican II church, which has left him, not he it. In the Anglican case, the minority against the ordination of women claims that it is the majority in favour, which is proposing to leave them, and not the other way round.

The schismatic anti-women-priests Anglican churches in America actually call themselves "continuing Anglican churches"; and one possibility in England would be the appearance of a "continuing Church of England", without women priests, which would claim to be the "true" Church of England.

* On 30 June 1988 Archbishop Marcel Lefebvre consecrated four bishops into his "Fraternity of Pius X". In the eyes of Rome this action constituted the sin of schism, breaking the unity of the Church; the Vatican excommunicated the Archbishop and his bishops.

But such a possibility lies several years ahead: the more imminent Anglican schism would be an international one, arising from the consecration of women bishops in America and the refusal of other Anglican churches, or parts of them, to recognize those bishops. Some dioceses, and perhaps some whole provinces, would consider a diocese headed by or containing a woman bishop to be "out of communion" with itself: and that would be schism.

Schism comes in more than one form; but it is part of its definition that it involves a breaking of full communion. In the Roman Catholic case, the juridical and sacramental systems are so closely aligned, by design, that it is fairly clear when schism has occurred. So the breaking of full communion also involves the repudiation of jurisdiction. It was Lefebvre's refusal to acknowledge papal jurisdiction concerning the ordination of four new bishops which led automatically to his excommunication.

In the Anglican Communion, however, there is no universal juridical system, only a series of local jurisdictions confined to each province. There is a kind of universality about the Anglican sacramental system, nevertheless, in that all parts of the Anglican Communion have managed to apply compatible criteria for the recognition of Holy Orders. One of the marks of "full communion" between different parts of the Communion is therefore the interchangeability of ordained ministers.

But the compatibility of criteria is already breaking down. A church like the Church of England does not recognize the priestly orders of a woman ordained in the Episcopal Church of the United States, though it does seem that she could be recognized as an ordained deacon. The American Episcopalian view is that no other Anglican church ought to set itself up in judgement over the validity of Episcopalian orders, for to do so is to breach the principle of the autonomy of each independent Anglican province.

That view is not taken in England, and so logically there is already in existence a breach of full communion between English and American Anglicans, some sort of schism. But a new concept has been creeping forwards for attention, the idea of

104

"partial" or "impaired" communion. It suggests there are not just two alternatives, full communion and "out of communion" – in effect, excommunication – but a spectrum of degrees of communion in between. The origin of the concept of partial or impaired communion appears to come from the Second Vatican Council, and has been applied by the authorities of the Roman Catholic Church to Anglicanism. It will require a redefinition of the notion of schism, however: if there is such a thing as partial communion, there would have to be such a thing as partial schism too. And it is significant that the Roman Catholic recognition of a state of partial communion with Anglicans is aside from any claim of jurisdiction, though if or when full communion with Rome becomes an issue, jurisdiction will become one too.

The concept of partial or impaired communion could be immensely useful in handling certain immediate problems in the Anglican Communion. In the first place it sets the direction towards which all parts of the church must aim: to strive to increase and not to reduce the degree of communion. In that respect the Church of England's duty towards the American Episcopal Church is exactly the same as its duty towards the Roman Catholic Church – to increase the degree of communion. They cease to be two different processes, one ecumenical and the other internally Anglican, but become two aspects of the same process.

By the same token not to seek to increase the degree of communion, or to act in such a way as to reduce it, is to act in a way which is schismatic. And the same duty towards the Church of England would apply to the American Episcopalian Church and to the Roman Catholic Church; and the same charge of schism would lie against them if they ignored it.

The Roman Catholic position remains to be answered: is full communion really possible without at least a minimal degree of common jurisdiction? And even leaving on one side its future relations with Rome, it is a pressing internal question for the Anglican Communion. Without at least a few basic rules, which every part subscribes to, it is hard to see how it can survive much longer.

LAMBETH'S RECEIVED WISDOM

1 August 1988

It always seemed possible that the Lambeth Conference would eventually have to settle for a "fudge" on women bishops by agreeing to a deliberately ambiguous and less than totally honest form of words that could mean almost anything. But the official resolution which is being presented to the conference for approval today is not of this kind. It will not make the mess worse than it is; and does not pretend it is less than it is. And though forged in the heat of Anglicanism's biggest crisis for decades, it offers a way forward that is theologically coherent. The conference owes a considerable debt to the small group which devised it.

What the Lambeth Conference has been searching for is what the Anglican Communion has lacked so far, a theory and practice for doctrinal development. This is beginning to emerge. A church without a theology of development was safe so long as its doctrine was anchored firmly and unchangeably in the formularies of the past, and "development" could be dismissed as a dubious theory used by Roman Catholic apologists to justify such new doctrines as the Immaculate Conception.

Conservative biblical Christianity had no time for such developments: the Bible said all that needed to be said. Eastern Orthodoxy had no time for them either: the tradition was set in stone and could not be altered. Anglicanism contains those who think like that, but more who do not. For the latter, the ordination of women to the priesthood or the episcopate must be at least a possibility. But Anglicanism also has no central authority mandated to judge and rule which developments are legitimate and which are not. Any development that is resisted by a substantial section, therefore, is likely to threaten the Anglican Church's unity. That is what has happened, with the added complication that the proposed development in question – the creation of female bishops – would attack Anglican unity at its most vulnerable point.

For the Anglican Communion is defined as a group of local churches whose bishops are in full communion with one another and with the See of Canterbury. If some bishops are out of communion with each other, as is bound to be the result once the first female bishops appear, the knots holding the Anglican Communion together automatically start to become untied. But that does not have to be seen as the ultimate Anglican disaster, if it is a necessary stage in a proper process of development.

Doctrinal developments usually start on the edges of the church, perhaps where local conditions throw up problems that are not felt universally. In Protestant churches they quickly lead to division and to the appearance of new sects. In the Catholic Church doctrinal developments are often at first vigorously opposed by central authority – many of the theologians who were ultimately responsible for the achievements of the Second Vatican Council were at one time under grave suspicion in the Vatican – but as that example shows, they do sometimes ultimately and even spectacularly succeed.

The new Anglican theology of development, as implied in the resolution the Lambeth Conference is about to debate, makes ingenious use of the theological concept of "reception". Its history is surprising in view of the context in which it is now being applied. The First Vatican Council in 1870 was anxious, in defining papal infallibility, to eliminate the view that papal *ex cathedra* definitions were subject to a subsequent test, the approval of the whole church. That concept, called "receptionism" was rejected. It was not entirely discredited or discarded, however, and in recent years the Anglican-Roman Catholic International Commission (ARCIC) revived it when it addressed the question of how such papal definitions ought to be regarded in the Anglican church. The Roman Catholic side found it more illuminating to say that Anglicans had not "received" such definitions than that they did not agree with them; for the concept of reception does not rule out the possibility that they might agree with them one day. It implies a dynamic process, and possible future convergence.

Reception, at the Lambeth Conference, has been lifted straight from these ARCIC sources, with all due acknowledgement. It is still a somewhat raw idea, and until theologians can deepen it there is bound to be a feeling that for a theological novelty it is being made to bear too much weight too soon. There is plenty of scope for such refinement, and some interesting material for the theologians to work on – they could start by plundering the archives of ARCIC. The Lambeth Conference would therefore be wise to see such work was urgently set in hand.

Doctrinal development in Anglicanism, in the theory now emerging, starts with local innovation. It may spread and quickly gain the approval of the whole Anglican Communion, in which case there is no internal Anglican problem (though there might still be an ecumenical one). It may, on the other hand, cause reaction; and on a serious enough issue, that will result in temporary "impairment of communion" – another concept that seems to have come straight from the pages of ARCIC.

The theory requires that that should be tolerated, albeit as second best, while efforts are made to test whether the new development can be received by the whole church, the *sensus fidelium*, which is not limited by this theory just to the Anglican part of the church. Until it is "received", if it is, the development has to be regarded as provisional and possibly mistaken. But churches structured as they are in Anglicanism must in theory have some method of development, and this is probably the only one available to them. But it too must be provisional – for it is itself a development. And it leaves one fundamental question for the future: how is it to be decided when the process of "reception" has given its answer, and what the answer is?

NO HALF-WAY HOUSE

21 October 1989

The great post-war revolution in the consciousness of women is about "women's sense of existing in and for themselves, in the same way that men do", writes Monica Furlong, one of the founders of Christian feminism in Britain and one of its best and most articulate advocates. In an article in *The Tablet* recently she went on to say that women drew from this self-discovery "a new strength, with a subsequent insistence on a different recognition – a demand, for example, of work being valued, of opportunity for education and fulfilling work, being available, of a realistic control of child-bearing potential, of the same sort of freedom from fear of sexual harassment, domestic violence or casual rape that most men enjoy".

Her case, and it is the case, however differently it is sometimes presented, is that this liberation of women from having to define themselves exclusively as "someone's daughter, wife or mother" leads irresistibly to women's ordination. She lamented in passing that even the liberal bishops in the Church of England had failed to grasp that a real revolution was taking place which would leave no sexual stone unturned.

Opponents like Pope John Paul II and the Bishop of London saw more clearly that what is at stake is "a change in the whole Christian landscape; nothing less is involved". And the ordination of women is "a far more significant challenge" to men than women doctors or women lawyers or women engineers. It involves the recasting of the entire traditional pattern of relations between the sexes, including the sexual relationship itself and the entire transformation of the church, including the rejection of the idea of hierarchy.

Being a radical, she has the radical urge to push her case to its limits; not all women who support the ordination of women would wish to emphasize how revolutionary and far-reaching it would be; and some of those who oppose it would claim to "possess themselves" rather than be possessed by men no less than she does. But her case is the more convincing one, not least because it is on the same wavelength as the most profound of her opponents. It also justifies a parallel which is often put forward but usually sounds stretched: that the ordination of women is of a type with the most radical step in the first moments of Christianity, when it was suddenly grasped that Gentiles did not have to become Jews in order to become Christians. From that moment the relationship between Judaism and Christianity was totally transformed. It was the birth moment of separate Christian identity. Although it was not explicit in the teachings of Christ, it was seen to be implied; and the primitive church claimed that competence to make explicit what was implicit with His authority. And that is the claim urged on the Church of England in the case of female ordination.

The Furlong position has one great strength: that it is almost impossible to imagine a respectable argument against it, for it would have to be an argument in favour of returning to the gross repression of women and their subordination to men. There seems to be no half-way house where moderate opponents can lodge. It also has one great weakness, however, of the same sort. She is, quite consistently, more scornful of liberal support for women's ordination than she is of the attitude of her opponents. If there is no half-way house in which to come down against women priests by just a tiny margin, there is no half-way house to come down in favour of them by the same hair's breadth.

It is all or nothing. Revolutions are like that: liberals just get in the way. To vote for the ordination of women is to vote for the completion of women's liberation in its most radical form, the overthrow of what the feminists call patriarchy. And it is a political programme as well as a sexual and theological one, concerning the ending of the dominance of white over black, rich over poor, technology over the earth. Furlong has the courage to say that too. But it is not going to catch votes.

110

Faced with the choice between two radical extremes with political consequences, most people are going to crowd into the "don't know" pen and cover their ears with their hands. Always the best hope of persuading the more or less conservative Church of England in favour of the ordination of women was to present it as one more small but obvious step, raising no particularly new issue apart from the complication it introduces into relations with the Roman Catholic Church. Such a church is not comfortable taking a radical lead in society: it wants things to stay more or less as they are, or get gradually better.

It has been the tactic of the Bishop of London, Dr Graham Leonard, to paint the call for women priests as a radical departure, not only because he believes it but also to frighten the horses. The General Synod will have all this on its plate next month, when it discusses the shape of the legislation which will authorize women's ordination. The more it is a technical debate about legal formulae, the more likely it is that the legislation will go through. But the deeper the water the synod swims in (and with Dr Runcie intending to remind it what the Pope said to him,* it will be hard to stay at the shallow end) the more the synod will take thought and take fright. Whether that would be a victory or a defeat for radical feminists, only they can say.

* In September 1988 Dr Robert Runcie, then Archbishop of Canterbury, had visited Pope John Paul II in Rome. The Pope had virtually ignored Dr Runcie's suggestion that the papacy could evolve into something Anglicans could accept as a "universal primacy" and had instead restated traditional Roman Catholic teaching. The Anglican delegation attempted to present the issue of the ordination of women to the priesthood as a surmountable difficulty, but the Pope showed no flexibility, saying "we cannot but acknowledge that events in recent years have seriously aggravated the difference between us".

OUTSIDERS ON TWO COUNTS

2 June 1990

Had there never been a woman's liberation movement, the Church of England would hardly have dreamt one up for itself. So all arguments for the ordination of women which rest on purely religious considerations, claiming for instance that women priests were always part of God's plan but that He left it 2,000 years before letting anyone know, can be taken with a pinch of salt.

The equivalence of men and women is an insight to which the church came late, and learnt only from watching what was happening outside. If women had a right equal to that of men to be judges, doctors or even prime ministers, the church eventually had to ask itself whether they did not also have a right to be priests and bishops. But before such arguments were fit to be tossed around in synod and cloister, they had to be translated into church-speak. The word "rights", in particular, had to be heavily qualified, for anyone who knows anything about ordination knows it can never be demanded as a right. It emerged from the shuffle as a women's "right to have her vocation tested", which essentially means the right to be judged as to suitability and seriousness, for no one can verify the validity of a mystical calling.

Inevitably, before long, this ecclesiastical edition of the secular argument took on a theological life of its own, and at the present stage of the debate it is commonly put forward as if it had no connection with anything which has happened outside. One such proposition states, for instance, that the all-male priesthood is (and hence must always have been) defective, because it is representative of only the male half of humanity. But, as Mrs Thatcher might have said, there is really no such thing as the priesthood, there are only individual priests, each of whom can only be male or female.

To declare 2,000 years of the church's history defective is not a very secure basis on which to commend the truth of the church's message today. That is what happens when secular values are dressed in ecclesiastical vestments. Secular values can be valid today, but not yesterday; if a religious truth is true today, it must always have been so. And it has to be admitted that some of the arguments against female ordination cobbled together by conservative theologians also tend to prove too much.

What has happened to women's rights outside the church will no doubt ultimately prove decisive inside it, irrespective of who scores most points in the theological tennis match. This is particularly so for a church which cannot drift too far from what the majority of the population regard as right and decent without calling into question its special relationship with the nation. The public certainly thinks the issue of women's ordination is about the rights of women, which is why people with no stake or interest in Christianity nevertheless tend to have strong opinions about it.

Those who celebrate Holy Communion also happen to enjoy power and status, for they are the professionals among the amateurs, and this, rather than the question of access to the sacramental mysteries, dictates how the issue is seen, inside the church as much as outside. The church is a hierarchy, with the laity at the bottom, the clergy in the middle and the bishops at the top. And the laity are regarded by the rest as those who are not quite serious about being Christian – the amateurs, half-baked, ignorant, second-class folk with mere baptism to their name. So a layman in the Church of England who feels the urge to deepen his spiritual life must sooner or later think of ordination: the approved way to signify and fulfil his greater commitment. Some people are hounded by the thought for years before doing anything about it, but the whole ecclesiastical system is shaped to convey to them the nagging subliminal message: half-hearted Christians are laymen, wholehearted Christians are clergy.

There is a significant difference here from the Roman Catholic Church, where a layman who gets married knows that the possibility of ordination can be crossed off the list for ever. He can proceed at peace with the life he has, and be as devoted to his faith as he feels called to be. But because the Church of England abolished statutory celibacy for priests in the sixteenth century, it has no way to distinguish the call to the devout life from the call to orders. If the first applies to everyone, which no one who reads the Gospels can doubt, then so must the second; or so it must seem.

If all lay males, married or not, are always subject to this call, it is absurd to argue that no lay female can ever be. Some of them do indeed hear a clear call to do Christ's work to the utmost, but for centuries all the ecclesiastical signposts have been pointed to ordination as the only proper response; and, incomprehensibly, the signposts read "Men Only".

Women are now demanding the right to be admitted to the ranks of first-class Christians. It is indeed an argument about equal rights and opportunities, and the secular perception is entirely correct. But below the surface, it is also an argument about the clerical monopoly of religious seriousness. The very word "layman", originally just meaning a non-cleric, now means "outsider", one who is excluded. And that, for the Church of England, is a still deeper problem. Ordaining women will only make it worse.

But Men Just Don't Wear it

1 December 1990

At the very moment Mrs Thatcher's career was wobbling on the brink, a memorial service was held at Westminster Abbey for Lady Home, a more conventional former female occupant of 10 Downing Street. In the congregation of past and present government luminaries, the women mostly wore hats, the men were all bare-headed, for that is the custom. Its origins are well enough known; and from its origins, its meaning. Women should cover their heads in church, said St Paul, out of respect for male authority and to show that it is wrong for women to have authority over men.

It hardly needs saying that this is not why most women wore hats in the abbey that day. The convention is enough. What does need saying is that for women to have authority over men is not yet as fully accepted as the other way round. There has been little comment so far on the possibility that the mixed feelings about Mrs Thatcher, even her downfall, may stem partly from the fact that she is a woman.

People's minds may tell them women are the equal of men, but the amen from their hearts is often muffled. As Jung discovered, religion is an excellent short cut to the depths of the human psyche. How people behave in church is an indication of what goes on in those depths. While 99 per cent of the population appear to accept that women may exercise authority in the political sphere, the proportion hesitant about or downright opposed to women having authority in the religious sphere is substantially larger. Among active members of the Church of England they constitute about a third. Whether a typical member of that third has an unconscious distaste for the idea of a woman prime minister, only his (or indeed her) psychiatrist could say. Those who criticize Mrs Thatcher's style sometimes mention her voice or even her hair and the famous handbag. Listening to the debate on female ordination in the Church of England, the similarity of the prejudices unveiled there is striking – "handbags on the altar" is a favourite sneer (in private).

Straight misogyny they will deny, as emphatically as do Mrs Thatcher's detractors. Even chapter 11 of St Paul's first letter to the Corinthians makes them vastly uneasy, because it is so far the wrong side of the contemporary liberal picket line. "For a man it is not right to have his head covered, since he is the image of God and reflects God's glory; but woman is the reflection of man's glory. For man did not come from woman; no, woman came from man; nor was man created for the sake of woman, but woman for the sake of man; and that is why it is right for a woman to wear on her head a sign of the authority over her . . . "

The Archbishop-elect of Canterbury, Dr George Carey, wrote a memorandum on this subject in 1987 for a church commission which was discussing women bishops. It has only now been published, having been rejected as a draft for a chapter in the report, after, we are told, "heated exchanges". In his draft, Dr Carey argues that women have been admitted to roles of authority in society and have shown their ability as leaders, and that this may be pointing the church towards the need for a break with its own tradition, overriding St Paul.

At the beginning of the debate twenty years ago, supporters of female ordination did not base their argument on woman's equal status in society. Rather, they said that in the name of justice, the church should lead secular opinion to accept women clergy, just as a church in a racist society should ordain black priests to confront white prejudice with the justice demanded by the Gospel. What is now argued is the exact reverse, that women feel alienated in church, and will stop going or not start to go unless the ordained ministry is as fully opened to both sexes as are leadership roles in secular society. So is this a circular argument, or can they have it both ways? They can, but only if the *a priori* assumption of the justice of female equality is based on some other ground than social acceptability. "We are agreed", wrote Dr Carey, in the tone of a drafter of a consensus document, "that the ordination of women . . . has to be justified on theological grounds" and not "simply" by reference to what has happened in society. He might have added that the church must also decide if what has happened in secular society can be justified on theological grounds.

But his problem is that the normative Scriptural text on male authority over women is 1 Corinthians 11, the memory of which is so entrenched that it continues to dictate customs in headware among the rulers (and church-goers) of secular Britain and their wives and husbands. It is not enough to say, as Dr Carey does, that "the entire passage bristles with exegetical problems", as if that raises a theological doubt, because the only problems it bristles with are those arising from its rejection by society. Virtually the entire content of Christianity has that problem.

The Church of England cannot answer the question of whether or not St Paul had a good point just by referring to contemporary secular practice, particularly if it reads that practice only one way, by excluding all the evidence that female equality, particularly equality in authority, is still a tender plant. Attitudes as deep as these change only very slowly, generation by generation. They may yet change completely; but it is much too soon to be certain. The Church of England will have to be patient.

Part Four

THAMES AND TIBER

REMOVING THE DIVISIONS

22 August 1988

The Anglican-Roman Catholic International Commission (ARCIC) meets in Edinburgh this week to resume its dismantling of the walls which still divide the two churches. It will find that another course of bricks has been added since it last met, by the Lambeth Conference's refusal earlier this month to restrain those Anglican provinces which want to ordain women as bishops.

The talks are international. Anglican provinces which have women priests are represented as well as the contrary opinion. What the Catholic negotiators face, therefore, is not a unified Anglican position in favour of women priests and bishops, but a double one, and no party line.

Female ordination is by no means yet official policy in the Anglican Communion, and both the 1978 and 1988 Lambeth Conferences deliberately avoided a decision on the principle. In so far as any doctrinal judgement has been made, it is that the division is enough to impair full communion between Anglican provinces with women priests and bishops, and provinces without them. It is admitted to be a "serious obstacle" to internal Anglican unity. There does not seem to be much disagreement here.

Providence has smiled on the work of ARCIC so far, and the Edinburgh meeting will be able to digest the Lambeth Conference's very favourable response to the four joint doctrinal statements which past labours had produced. The statements on ministry and on the eucharist received the full endorsement that the conference was asked to give; the more tentative statement on authority got a rather better reception than expected; and the conference warmly approved the most recent statement, on justification by faith.

The conference's general approval of the authority statement means that international Anglicanism is now looking for some kind of reconciliation with the Roman Catholic Church which would incorporate a "universal primacy" – ecumenical shorthand for the Pope. The condition being asked in return is reform of the papacy, and the modification of its stronger claims such as "universal jurisdiction" in all parts of the church.

In practice there is more common ground than there seems to be. For the only sanction which nowadays backs up the Pope's universal jurisdiction in the Catholic Church is the threat of breaking full communion. Though the Lambeth Conference did not call it a sanction, it told Anglican provinces that those that proceeded with the consecration of women bishops would be breaking or "impairing" full communion with the rest. "Excommunication" is an ugly word that ought to be dropped, but apart from the phraseology the warning the Lambeth Conference gave to the Anglican bishops in America, Canada and New Zealand is not so different from the warnings Pope John Paul II gave to Archbishop Marcel Lefebvre.

The bilateral relationship between Catholicism and Anglicanism will, as a result of the Lambeth Conference and any subsequent consecrations of women bishops, become in a sense trilateral: between Catholicism and two forms of Anglicanism. That could prove entirely creative, for the theological issues being discussed, such as relations between parts of the church which ordain women and parts which do not, will not be purely abstract, but actually represented round the table.

Although the ARCIC statements were addressed at the Lambeth Conference as a specific and separate issue, many ideas from them surfaced elsewhere. The statement on authority was drawn on in the debates on internal Anglican authority and unity, and it could even be said that ARCIC's vision of a united church of the future has been adopted as an official model for evolution of the Anglican Communion itself.

Meanwhile, Rome's own answer to the first three ARCIC statements is due by the end of the year. There is apparently an internal debate still to happen in the Vatican to decide its shape. The Congregation for the Doctrine of the Faith issued a number of criticisms when the statements first appeared; but most of the responses from individual episcopal conferences round the world seem to have been favourable, and the Vatican's Secretariat for Christian Unity is directly represented on ARCIC itself.

Before the issue of women bishops appeared, there had been hints from Rome that it might regard joint acceptance of the ARCIC statements on ministry and eucharist as grounds for reopening the question of Anglican orders. It is already on ARCIC's agenda and may be discussed again in Edinburgh this week. But until the official Vatican response to those statements has been promulgated such explorations will have to remain hypothetical.

Rome is unlikely simply to state that the judgement of the 1896 Bull *Apostolicae Curae*, which declared Anglican orders null and void, was wrong. But it could well say that acceptance of the ARCIC statements by the Lambeth Conference means that Anglican ordinations could no longer be regarded by Catholics as defective in intention. A greater difficulty is presented by the alleged break in the apostolic succession of Anglican bishops, because of supposed defective intention in the past. One solution would be to acknowledge that the participation of Old Catholic bishops in Anglican episcopal consecrations had restored the apostolic succession; but it would not be very flattering to Anglican pride. If they could bear it, however, it would bring a quicker result than the other possibility, a complete theological examination of what apostolic succession really means. And wiser than backing either of those horses would be to back them both at once.

WAITING FOR THE TIDE OF UNITY

14 January 1989

The Vatican remains a somewhat inscrutable organization, in spite of the efforts of such shrewd and penetrative journalists as Peter Nichols, former correspondent of *The Times* in Rome, who died so sadly last week. He came as near to understanding it as anybody – and it seemed to enjoy being understood by him. But it would probably take a Nichols at his best to work out which way Anglican-Roman Catholic relations are moving at the moment.

He was a man who did not automatically reject the obvious answer, which in this case would seem to be that the Vatican itself does not know where it is going. For there is a major piece of work stuck inexplicably somewhere in the system, the official Roman Catholic response to the final report of the first Anglican-Roman Catholic International Commission (ARCIC I).

The soundings throughout the world were completed long ago; the Lambeth Conference gave its positive verdict last summer; and Rome's official judgement was promised by the end of last year at the latest. Instead, and quite unexpectedly, the Vatican issued its "authoritative" response to a much later ecumenical document, the second international commission's agreed statement on the theology of salvation. The explanation that someone mixed them up is probably too obvious by half. But the Anglican Communion is only just beginning to digest the salvation document – there is to be a preliminary debate on it at the General Synod of the Church of England later this month – and this lack of co-ordination in timing is liable to throw the whole exercise out of gear. The synod, however, is much too courteous to grumble.

It is said that those outside the Vatican and its mysteries usually make the mistake of regarding it as a monolithic body with a single mind, whereas it is in fact an organic community being pulled in all directions at once. The Vatican's recent observations on the Anglican-Roman Catholic salvation statement, for instance, bear some evidence of its preoccupation with an exclusively internal Catholic problem, the decline in the practice of private confession, which has really nothing to do with the ecumenical landscape in which it has surfaced. The observations, issued by the Congregation for the Doctrine of the Faith headed by Cardinal Joseph Ratzinger, were actually rather negative as these things go, despite some ambiguity. So leaders of the Anglican-Roman Catholic dialogue on both sides were quick to welcome and stress the better bits, thereby drawing attention away from the rest.

The attitude of Cardinal Johannes Willebrands, the Vatican's church unity supremo, seemed to be that a setback is only a setback if you admit it, for he simply told the international commission to carry on with the good work. The only section of church opinion which seemed genuinely to enjoy Cardinal Ratzinger's contribution was the Protestant anti-papal fringe of the Evangelical movement, which ironically was particularly gratified by its attack on ambiguity.

It is clear that the Vatican's real difficulty with Anglicanism is the ordination of women, particularly women bishops. It is even possible that it is waiting to see what happens in Massachusetts, where the Rev. Barbara Harris seems to be heading for victory in the nationwide poll of dioceses that Episcopalian rules require, which would make her the first Anglican woman bishop anywhere in the world probably by mid-spring.

To let the shape of its response to the ARCIC I package wait upon such events might seem an unusually political way for the Vatican to reach theological decisions, but it would not be unprecedented. The ARCIC I package is political enough anyway, for the parts referring to authority in the church are by implication highly critical of the way the Vatican currently likes to run things. Opinions of a not dissimilar kind have been coming from the powerful United States Episcopal Conference of late, and a delegation is due to meet top Vatican officials in March to try to reach a better mutual understanding. The endorsement of ARCIC I as officially in line with Roman Catholic Church doctrine, just when the Americans are preparing for a showdown, is the sort of tactical mistake the Vatican might want to avoid.

All this suggests that Anglican-Roman Catholic relations are in fact hostage to a lot of other Catholic concerns, but that is not new either. In its long-term ecumenical strategy the Vatican is more interested in looking East than West, particularly under a Slav Pope. There are interesting ecclesiastical possibilities under *glasnost*, which would be even more promising if Catholic relations with the Russian Orthodox Church could be improved. A papal visit to Moscow, and the emergence from the shadows of the Ukrainian Catholic Church, are the prizes which seem almost within grasp.

But Orthodoxy has no time for the ordination of women at all. Those Anglicans who hope the Roman Catholic Church might change – or at least open its mind – on that issue to help ecumenical relations, are forgetting that the relationship is only symmetrical in England, where the two churches are approximately equal in size and similar in interests. They do not look symmetrical in Rome, where nothing will be allowed to happen in the direction of Anglicanism that could harm the prospects with Orthodoxy.

The Pope has described England as "privileged ecumenical terrain", a nice compliment which gives the English Roman Catholic Church a certain room for manoeuvre and the Church of England a special place in the Vatican's affections. But the ARCIC I final report, approved by Rome or not, is already water under the Thames and Tiber bridges; and if Rome's approval has reservations attached, the appropriately reassuring response was rehearsed last autumn. The good work will continue.

But that, at least until the end of the century, is probably all there is on offer, while the Vatican watches and waits. Compared with a century ago, that is itself a miracle. Compared with what might have been hoped 20 years ago, though, it is a disappointment. Church unity, wrote Peter Nichols, is still "not yet afloat on that limitless ocean which is tantalizingly near".

126

BREAKING THE STALEMATE

29 July 1989

Father Hans Kung referred in *The Times* yesterday to the "suppression" by the Vatican of the joint theological statements of the Anglican-Roman Catholic International Commission (ARCIC I). It appears the Vatican is sitting on them, so it would be more accurate to say they are in limbo. It will be one of the chief hopes of the Archbishop of Canterbury, Dr Robert Runcie, when he visits Rome in September, that he can rescue them from that state. They are becoming a source of inter-church but very unecumenical embarrassment.

The two statements in question record agreement between panels of international experts from the two churches, on the doctrines of the Eucharist and of the priestly ministry. Last summer the Lambeth Conference fulsomely endorsed them, which on the Anglican side was the final step. It was understood – indeed it was part of the deal – that Rome would take its own final step by the end of last year. Cardinal Johannes Willebrands, head of the Vatican secretariat for Christian unity, had already given a half-promise that the acceptance of these two statements would prepare the way for a reopening of the painful question of Anglican orders. It was immediately put on the agenda of the new international commission (ARCIC II), but Anglican expectations were higher than that.

Recognition that Anglican priests were, in Roman Catholic eyes, properly and validly ordained would be a breakthrough in the relations between the two churches. In Anglican self-understanding, the Church of England is part of the ancient and universal Catholic church, one in principle but divided in practice, and Rome is accepted as the senior partner.

Rome's refusal to reciprocate that understanding, and worse in 1896 to have repudiated the Church of England's right to be called a church at all – for a church must have valid priests – throws that Anglican identity off-balance, in addition to the obvious difficulty it creates in relations between Anglican and Roman Catholic clergy. The papal bull, *Apostolicae Curae*, of that year was the lowest point in relations between the two churches since the seventeenth century, and it still exerts its negative influence. Most Anglican clergy claim not to care whether Rome recognizes them or not, in terms of their own ministry, and hence recognition now would make no difference. Methodist clergy say much the same about their lack of recognition by the Church of England; unmarried couples living together say the same about the lack of recognition of their union by the state.

But these things do matter; they make a substantial psychological difference to how people see themselves, which only becomes clear after the event. In 1896 Rome went much further than it ought to have done, largely it seems at the prompting of the English triumphalist Archbishop of Westminster, Cardinal Vaughan, who held the Church of England in profound contempt and reckoned to wipe it out in one generation with *Apostolicae Curae* as his weapon. To answer the question posed, Pope Leo XIII need only have said that Anglican orders were uncertain. Instead he was urged to go to the limit by Vaughan and Vaughan's friends in Rome, Cardinals Gasquet and Merry del Val. He did: he declared Anglican ordinations "absolutely null and utterly void", and announced his decision to be binding for all time. He seemed unaware, however, of the manifest danger of basing an irreversible judgement that claims to be objective on the available historical evidence, for more evidence might subsequently come to light contradicting it. So it did, promptly enough, when the two archbishops of the Church of England issued their dignified reply, in the document *Saepius Officio*, the following year. But it was too late, however good their arguments and historical sources.

Any honest inquiry by the Roman Catholic Church now into this vexed question would have to start from the fact that Anglican belief today, as defined in ARCIC I's statement endorsed by the 1988 Lambeth Conference, would pass all the tests applied by Leo XIII in *Apostolicae Curae*. But that does not quite prove the point, as the papal judgement was based on an alleged defect in Anglican doctrine and practice in the sixteenth and seventeenth century, not the twentieth. Even so, it does identify the key issue. If official Anglican doctrine is now entirely in line with Roman Catholic doctrine on the two essential issues of the Eucharist and the priesthood, the burden of proof has shifted. To justify the judgement of *Apostolicae Curae* today, it has to be shown that the Church of England believes something different from what it believed in the sixteenth century; and it has to be explained how it has recovered doctrines that were mislaid somewhere in the past.

In fact the document *Saepius Officio* shows the opposite: that there is a continuity of Anglican belief stretching from the sixteenth to the nineteenth century (and as *Saepius Officio* was formally endorsed by the Lambeth Conference in 1930, into the twentieth century too). Anglicanism is a very conservative faith, lacking the Roman concept of a living magisterium which can regulate and confirm new doctrinal developments. In many contexts that lack of flexibility is a weakness, but not in this one. It is strong evidence of consistency.

The experts in ARCIC have always tended to say that whatever they might privately think of *Apostolicae Curae*, it was better politics to go round it rather than to try to shift it. Rome also has its rigidities. But ecumenism really is a waste of time if there is no Christian generosity, no willingness to look again at previous decisions in the light of new evidence and arguments. If Leo XIII was mistaken, Pope John Paul II should be prepared to say so. It is possible, but unfortunately not likely, that it is such considerations as these which have held up the Vatican's reply to ARCIC I. When Dr Runcie visits Rome in September, we will find out.

VATICAN TEST OF HOLY ORDERS

30 September 1989

The immediate future of the Anglican-Roman Catholic relationship is more likely to be decided by the General Synod of the Church of England early in the 1990s than by the Pope and the Archbishop of Canterbury at their meetings in Rome this weekend. Some of the moves made in Rome in the next few days will undoubtedly reflect that fact, and may in turn prove influential, even decisive, when the initiative is eventually back in the General Synod's hands.

Somewhere around 1992, the synod will have to decide whether to give its final approval to the Ordination of Women Measure. The Vatican has been sending out signals that what the Church of England does about the ordination of women will be regarded as far more significant than actions already taken elsewhere in the Anglican Communion, even the consecration of the first woman bishop in America last year. The message is that it would alter the whole character of the relationship. This will not be easy for the Anglican Communion to come to terms with, for it likes to think of the Anglican-Roman Catholic dialogue as taking place purely at the international level, and in some parts of the Anglican Communion women have been ordained for more than a decade.

The rest of the Anglican Communion may not much like the idea that what the mother church does is still regarded as normative by Rome, but there is a certain realism in this approach nevertheless. Once the Church of England has women priests, female ordination will begin to feel like the normal and accepted thing in Anglicanism, and those churches which still refrain from it will seem slightly deviant. This would be the reverse of the present situation.

This primacy of one particular church, the founding church of the Anglican Communion, stems partly from the dual pos-

ition of the Archbishop of Canterbury as the leader both of
that one church and of the Communion as a whole. To be
an Anglican is to be in communion with the Archbishop of
Canterbury. The day the Archbishop of Canterbury – this one
or his successor – ordains his first woman priest, the Anglican
Communion will have taken a decisive step. Perhaps it will be
rightly seen as a decisive step towards justice for women. But
it will certainly be seen as a decisive step away from the ecumenical goal of full visible communion between Anglicanism
and Catholicism. The only way that will again become a realistic
prospect would be for the Catholic Church itself to make the
same decision.

The choice the synod will face in the early 1990s will, as
things stand now, be an unequal one. The alternatives presented will be out of balance, even different in kind. It will
have before it a practical proposal with immediate beneficial
consequences, the ordination of women priests. It will also have
before it the vague and general hope that relations with Rome
might continue their steady but tedious course into the next
century, with a very uncertain outcome. As compensation for
not ordaining women immediately, that is a thin deal. The
more the Pope stresses that Anglican-Roman Catholic relations
have already been seriously damaged by recent developments,
and therefore that a successful conclusion to the ecumenical
negotiations has already been made less likely, the thinner it
will look. If that is the scenario when the synod faces up to the
choice, it wil hardly be surprising if it takes the bird in the hand.
Otherwise the Church of England might find itself neither with
women priests nor with a better and closer relationship with
the Roman Catholic Church.

What Rome cannot say, but might like to say, is that
restraint by the Church of England over women priests would
open the prospect of mutual recognition of Holy Orders, if not
covering the whole Anglican Communion then applying to
those parts of it which have not ordained women, the Church
of England in particular. Dr Runcie has even hinted that if
Rome had made that offer earlier, it would have been easier
for him to persuade the American church to hold back from

consecrating a woman bishop, or the Lambeth Conference to distance itself from any such consecrations. He could not condone anything which required him to consent to special treatment for the Church of England, as that would be to imply that the Anglican Communion was no longer a single entity. But as the Roman refusal to recognize Anglican Orders was a unilateral decision, it could in principle be reversed unilaterally, and Anglican consent would not be required.

After the ordination of women, the status of Anglican orders in Roman Catholic eyes is the single biggest difficulty between the two churches. Many solutions have been suggested in the past, but there is one that has not so far been tried, using an individual test-case.

English Roman Catholic bishops are not infrequently faced with a convert ex-Anglican clergyman who wishes to exercise a priestly ministry in the Roman Catholic Church. At present he has to be ordained afresh, because he is technically deemed to be a layman. But instead of re-ordaining him, his bishop could apply to Rome for a formal determination of the status of the orders he received as an Anglican, and ask for Vatican permission simply to reinstate him as a priest.

For such an individual case to succeed it would be necessary to show that the theological and historical conditions behind the 1896 papal bull *Apostolicae Curae* no longer applied. That might not be so difficult. The Anglican doctrine of the priesthood is now substantially the same as Roman Catholic doctrine, and if there was any breach in the apostolic succession in the sixteenth century, it has long been repaired by the participation of Old Catholic bishops recognized by Rome in Anglican consecrations.

It would not be surprising to find that some Catholic bishops are already wondering whether they are doing the right thing when they ordain former Anglican clergy, knowing as they do that a valid ordination is in principle unrepeatable. An application to Rome for a determination, therefore, would be a matter of conscience. A favourable decision in favour of one case, provided it was truly representative, would have to apply to all subsequent cases of the same sort. An unfavourable decision could be treated as applying only to that case, leaving the general question for further study and things no worse than they were before. Without some such breakthrough as that, however, the Church of England will be drawn to the conclusion that there is no end in sight for the long and gradual process of inter-church dialogue, and therefore the result is not worth waiting for.

A BASIC LESSON FROM THE POPE

7 October 1989

While he was in Rome courting the Pope, the Archbishop of Canterbury had the extraordinary experience of seeing himself upstaged by himself, by the publication of a controversial interview he gave to *Director* magazine. So "Runcie attacks Thatcher" headlines knocked "Runcie woos Pope" headlines off the front pages just when he least wanted them to. They look like two different issues. But there is an important connection between them. If among the papers Dr Robert Runcie brought back from the Vatican there was a social encyclical or two, then perhaps he has seen the link himself.

A social encyclical is a papal document setting out what Catholics call "social teaching", which refers to authoritative theological commentary on political and economic affairs. "Social teaching" is what Dr Runcie was up to himself in his *Director* interview, though the theology was more Anglican than rigorous.

While in Rome he repeated his call, this time in the presence of the Pope himself, for the Bishop of Rome to become the father-figure of world Christianity under the heading of "universal primacy". He insisted it had nothing to do with supplanting the Queen's role in the Church of England, but was a plea for moral leadership crossing denominational bound-

133

aries. The Pope sometimes made declarations on issues touching the Christian faith, he explained, which were not only of interest to Roman Catholics. It was not clear what Dr Runcie thinks is stopping people paying attention to the Pope already, but if he wants to help the process along, all he has to do is set an example.

He could do worse than start with the social encyclicals. They represent a continuous tradition of analysis going back centuries, each one building on the last, and setting out how societies could best organize themselves economically and politically for the greater good, under the insights of faith. They are the firm theoretical bedrock, for instance, beneath the Solidarity movement in Poland – solidarity is itself a key word in Catholic social teaching. The Christian Democrats in the European Parliament, who have been holding the British Tory MEPs at arm's length for reasons which should interest Dr Runcie, have the social encyclicals as a key element in their basic philosophy. And if anyone doubts that Catholic social teaching can influence continents they have only to look to South America, where the church is busy acting as midwife to fundamental political change.

There is no equivalent in Anglicanism. Such theology as there was in the famous report "Faith in the City" was, by general consent, bland and vague. Dr Runcie's *Director* interview was a good deal tougher, but it lacked the armour-piercing power of rigorous analysis from clear first principles. And because its theological basis was understated, the archbishop inevitably left himself open to the counter-attack. His grim view of the present state of British society may be more Christian than the Government's optimistic one. The Government, the most theologically minded administration Britain has had since the war, does not agree. The conflict may be fascinating, but who is to say who is right, or how even to decide? There is no genuine theological debate, because there is no agreed and available theological method for conducting it. When two theologically minded enterprises cannot find a common language to talk to each other, something has gone wrong.

This might be just the point to introduce a touch of the

"universal primacy" whose teachings, Dr Runcie declared in Rome, should be accessible to all. In fact the lead he has called for has already been given, page after page of it, by Pope after Pope. And some of it is brilliant stuff. The present Pope is in his element in this sphere; he is a world-class philosopher, which is one of the main reasons he was elected Pope. His encyclical *Laborem Exercens*, for instance, had a great deal to say concerning the creation and distribution of wealth, about which church and government get so touchy. It is even possible that Dr Runcie and Mrs Thatcher could at last find common ground under such a papal umbrella, and their public dialogue would lose that frustrating sense of cross-purposes which has been its tone so far.

Two principles run through Catholic social teaching, solidarity and subsidiarity. The meaning of the former is clearer than the latter, though it is not quite the meaning with which the British will have come across before, in the jargon of old-fashioned trades unionism. Solidarity describes the duties members of the community – any community – owe to each other. The idea that individuals have natural duties towards each other is one that both sides can accept: whether one calls that collection of individuals bounded by solidarity "society" or not is a matter of mere sociological semantics. Solidarity may be expressed by having a Government, to represent the totality of those with duties towards one another, and to discharge those duties more efficiently and conveniently. But it keeps Government in its proper place, as a means rather than an end. And the other principle, subsidiarity, is a powerful warning not to go too far. It is firmly against "big Government".

The subsidiarity principle is subtle. It says the decisions affecting people's lives should be made as far down the chain of command as possible, as close to the people concerned as possible – by the people concerned if possible. Could any Anglican disagree? But is that not one of the tenets of basic Thatcherism?

As ideas, solidarity and subsidiarity are powerful tools of analysis. In practice, they are powerful allies for social reform. But they are not logical opposites, as are individualism and collectivism, for they can and should be complementary. A community where they are not in equilibrium will be a troubled one. But design it so they balance, and the good is maximized, the bad minimized. Subsidiarity speaks for personal freedom, solidarity for mutual caring. The theory says you can have both, if you get the combination right.

It would be even more interesting if the vast British experience of social and political life, once it had learnt how to express itself in these philosophical terms, could begin to feed back its own wisdom into the formation of new social teaching, for the benefit of others. If there is nothing exclusively Roman Catholic about its appeal, as Dr Runcie seemed to be suggesting in Rome, there need be nothing exclusively Roman Catholic about its sources either. Anyone can join in, once they grasp the principles.

Part Five

THE VATICAN
AND
THE FAITHFUL

A SPIRIT OF DISOBEDIENCE

2 July 1988

In the sultry heat of the Swiss Alps in summer, the familiar plainsong melodies of the *Missa de Angelis* wafted over the crowd on the hillside like musical incense. There was a beer-and-sandwiches tent further up the hill, beyond the little queues of people waiting for open-air confession or groups just watching in the humid sunshine. While at the far end of the giant marquee Archbishop Lefebvre was busy breaking with the Pope, his followers seemed to be enjoying a day in the country. This is the Econe paradox; and the better the church understands it, the better it will be able to handle it.

Monsignor Lefebvre has always held one trump card: his adherence to the Tridentine rite (named after the Council of Trent). His quarrel with the Second Vatican Council on various points of theological principle does not have the same appeal, and it was not what his ordinary followers were talking about on Thursday. The Tridentine mass was a card he was handed by the church itself, by the inept and insensitive way it was suddenly swept away in the late 1960s. What was compulsory one day was forbidden the next, with hardly a word of explanation. All those disturbed by the change, and dismayed by the flat modern-language services which came in overnight, were potential recruits to any protest movement around at the time.

One lady from Strasbourg, on her sixth visit to Econe, volunteered the comment that neither she nor two thirds of the others would have been there if they could have heard the Tridentine mass in their local parish church. Her rebellion is

139

therefore precisely like the campaign in the Church of England to preserve the 1662 Book of Common Prayer. She, and her Anglican counterparts, of whom she was certainly unaware, are victims of that modern scourge, the intolerance of liberal reformers.

Lefebvrism, as we will now have to learn to call this new Christian denomination, is a much more complex phenomenon than that, however. Probably too much has been made of its links with Le Pen's National Front in France; for the passions that drive Lefebvre have attracted thousands outside France who know nothing of such matters. The difference may be that in France he has popular appeal, whereas elsewhere Lefebvrism is a private choice made by individuals. They are not unlike the seventeenth century Jansenists who sought a scrupulous ideal of perfection and purity in their religious affairs. They were, said a contemporary, "as pure as angels and proud as devils".

A young Econe seminarian was cheerfully dismissive of the imminent excommunication of Lefebvre and the four bishops he was ordaining that morning: "You cannot be excommunicated for being a Catholic." This relaxed spirit of disobedience, in the name of truth or conscience, is a further part of the Econe paradox. For Lefebvrism is at first sight the very incarnation of ultra-conservative Catholicism, an attempt to perpetuate the strict faith of the 1890s or the 1930s, and a refusal to recognize that the modern world has anything to teach it. But what marked the "Brideshead Revisited" kind of Catholic was a profound, sometimes almost pathological, sense of obedience. To be excommunicated by the Pope was just about the very worst fate such a person could envisage. Yet at Econe on Thursday they were almost revelling in it.

It will take the church authorities some days to work out all the implications of Thursday's schism, in particular how widely the excommunications apply. Because it is an automatic penalty, laid down in advance in canon law but still needing expert interpretation, the exact status of a Catholic who attends a Lefebvrist mass tomorrow is not yet clear. Cardinal Basil Hume of Westminster has already issued a statement that to support Lefebvre and worship with his Fraternity of Pius X would be "to leave the Catholic Church", but that was couched as an exhortation, not a canonical sentence. He is disposed to play it very carefully, and to wait for Vatican guidance.

All heresies contain a truth, it has been said, and maybe the same applies to schism. The cardinal told *The Times* yesterday he believed the church must look to the quality of its worship, and ensure that all the spiritual riches of the Tridentine rite were properly preserved in the rite that has replaced it. Cardinal Hume accepts that there is a case for going even further, and instituting a regular Tridentine mass in Westminster Cathedral every Sunday, as he has the authority to do. It could be a powerful beacon to Lefebvrist waverers, as they try to decide where they go from here.

England has led the way in rolling back the original prohibition of the Tridentine rite. In the early 1970s the late Cardinal John Heenan, Cardinal Hume's predecessor, was granted by Pope Paul VI a unique "indult", or canonical exemption; and this was more recently made universal. So on special occasions organized by the non-Lefebvrist Latin Mass society, Tridentine masses still take place in England from time to time with official approval; and the fact that Lefebvre's followers in Britain number no more than a few thousand may be the result. The Tridentine rite was not, after all, dropped because there was something wrong with it. And there was a hint of thoughtless vandalism in the sudden repudiation of a text which has done so much to enrich Western culture: it is the mass which inspired Vivaldi, Bach, Haydn, Mozart, Beethoven, Schubert and many others to produce some of their greatest work.

Such a move would also help to identify the real heart of the matter, which is not about the liturgy at all. Here too Lefebvre is playing back the cards the church itself has dealt him, for there is a certain weight to his claim to be "more Catholic than the Pope". The Roman Catholic Church never likes to admit that it has changed its mind, for it is feared in the corridors of the Vatican that it might weaken its command of the faithful's allegiance. But the Second Vatican Council did represent a U-turn on several fundamental questions, not least over religious liberty and freedom of conscience. Error has no rights, they used to say: it was almost the motto of the Inquisition. But in the new climate yesterday's heretics have become today's "sister churches", partners in ecumenical dialogue.

"Ecumenism" is a word Lefebvre pronounces with particular scorn. It is hard to dispute his claim that he is the more faithful to the old tradition, unlovely though the tradition was. This is also where he is most vulnerable to counter-attack. If Rome is sensible, it will force him into the corner he is already backing towards, identifying him not as an ultra-Catholic but as a neo-Protestant, one who sets up private judgement against the church's living authority. The charges of heresy and apostasy he makes against Rome, to explain how Rome has lost the right to rule him, are just those made by Martin Luther at the Reformation.

It is the extreme irony of the Lefebvrist crisis that once it is passed, and the new denomination establishes its place in the Christian firmament, Rome will be bound to extend to it all the ecumenical courtesy and goodwill it shows all the other non-Roman Catholic churches. Error, in other words, has some rights; and Lefebvrism can eventually look forward to being hailed as a sister church, invited to sit round the ecumenical table to discuss its differences. When that happens, the 82-year-old archbishop will no doubt be dead, and will no doubt turn in his grave.

MAKING PEACE WITH THE DISSENTERS

31 December 1988

Twenty years after the publication of Pope Paul VI's encyclical on birth control, *Humanae Vitae*, dissent to its teaching continues to be a fertile source of controversy and anguish in the Roman Catholic Church internationally. The year just passed saw both celebrations of the anniversary of the encyclical's publication and further demonstrations of opposition and dismay; but also just the first glimpse of an approach that could ultimately begin to resolve the division.

At an international gathering in Rome in November, attended exclusively by bishops and theologians who support the encyclical, there was much praise for Pope Paul's "prophetic vision" in publishing it. The general view was that contraception, and the pill in particular, had proved in the intervening years to be a malign influence, leading to marriage breakdown and promiscuity and even contributing to the spread of AIDS. The encyclical's condemnation of the separation of procreation from sexual intercourse was seen as having been fulfilled by the later development of *in vitro* fertilization, which in such circles is viewed with even more alarm than contraception itself.

Some speakers at the conference admitted that the encyclical's arguments still lacked the sort of detailed support from moral theology that the Pope at the time had asked for. The question was beginning to be asked why this was so. And one of the explanations offered, which was evidently becoming widely accepted, was that conventional moral theology still relies heavily on what are termed pre-conciliar methods and procedures, meaning those pre-dating the Second Vatican Council, whereas *Humanae Vitae* itself was a new departure.

Thus the rejection of *Humanae Vitae* on theological grounds is actually, in this view, the more conservative position. What is needed, therefore, is a new moral theology which gives better answers.

Opponents of *Humanae Vitae* will greet this as a damaging admission of the weakness of the encyclical's case, and as an attempt to change the rules of the game having been beaten under the rules as they are. It certainly raises new difficulties. The strongest argument for *Humanae Vitae* has always been that it was in line with Catholic tradition, a restatement of the church's consistent teaching down the ages, and the only answer the Pope could give, therefore, that preserved the authority of that tradition. But pre-conciliar moral theology is very much part of that tradition too.

It is also true that much of what has been said in the past about the interpretation and implications of *Humanae Vitae*, by those Catholic bishops and theologians who accepted it, has been based on this same conventional or pre-conciliar moral theology. But read without these preconceptions, it becomes a rather different document. It has always been assumed to mean that any and every married Catholic who used a contraceptive device for whatever motive was guilty, unless his degree of responsibility was reduced, of mortal sin. For that is what comes from applying conventional moral theology to the basic judgement the Pope made in *Humanae Vitae*. It is also the heart of the dissent: for many Catholic couples who use contraception are as sure as they can be that they are not guilty of sin; and if the encyclical says so, then it must be wrong.

What proportion of the whole they are is largely unknown, but in a country like England it is revealing that very few clergy care to preach on contraception, and very few bishops care to make an issue of it, suggesting that the level of dissent is either very tiny or very large. Such surveys of opinion as have been conducted point to the latter. The decline in the numbers going to Confession, and the decline in the Catholic birth rate, suggest the same. The long term effect of *Humanae Vitae* has been to reduce the authority of the church in the eyes of such dissenters, for if it is regarded as fallible on one such matter it could be so on other matters too.

As happened at the time of the encyclical's twentieth anniversary, such views erupt from time to time in the correspondence pages of the Catholic press in Britain, where they are usually accompanied by sincere expressions of distress that Catholics who think themselves loyal, or want to be loyal, have been driven into disobedience. Some even claim to have left the church over it. The more exaggerated claims in support of *Humanae Vitae*, including some uttered by the present Pope (such as his famous remark that those who used contraceptives were in reality "atheists") have only added to the depression. Ecumenically, full union between the Church of England and the Roman Catholic Church remains quite incredible if the rejection of contraception, resting on papal authority and little else, is regarded by the Catholic side as an acid test of Christian orthodoxy.

The theology to extract the church from this impasse does not seem to have been written yet, though it may have started to emerge in the treatment of the related issue of *in vitro* fertilization. This has broken free of the legacy of the old penitential manuals of moral theology, which existed primarily to guide priests on the gravity of the various sins they heard in the confession box. It was a characteristic of pre-conciliar Catholicism to be excessively pedantic about what was or was not a mortal sin, thereby reducing moral behaviour to mere rule-keeping.

Perhaps *Humanae Vitae* was assumed too readily to be an instantly applicable supplement to such manuals, rather than a statement of principle whose implications remained painfully to be worked out, and whose bearing on confessional practice was neither obvious nor the primary question. In other fields, such as social theology, the Catholic Church does not move in one step from general statements of moral principle to the simple attribution of personal sin; nor has it done so in its recent official statements on embryo experimentation. If the same change of perception were to occur with birth control, the church could at last make peace with the dissenters in its ranks, and they with it.

THE POPE'S DIVISIONS

I   CHALLENGING THE RULE OF ROME
24 July 1989

Twenty-one years ago the Roman Catholic Church was plunged into turmoil and division by the publication of Pope Paul VI's famous encyclical on birth control, *Humanae Vitae* which condemned artificial contraception as intrinsically wrong. Gradually the opposing sides learnt to live together, and the quarrel subsided. There followed two decades of uneasy peace. Now the bitter war of words has flared up again and the Vatican is facing the most serious challenge for a generation to the way it runs the Roman Catholic Church. All over Europe, theologians and other churchmen have added their voices to a chorus of complaint, alleging that Vatican departments have been attempting to stamp out dissent by persecuting those who step out of line. "Ten years of the pontificate of Karol Wojtyla", says Father Hans Küng, a prominent Swiss theologian who has been disciplined by the Vatican for his views, "have brought the church to a precarious position. At all levels we have to deal with a loss of credibility on the part of the church with regard to the modern world."

Küng is one of more than 500 theologians, including many with world reputations, who have joined the growing international protest at the way the official line was being imposed from the top, and the way priests who object to it have been disciplined. Theologians play a central role in the affairs of the Roman Catholic Church, and the Vatican body which tries to keep them in line, the Congregation for the Doctrine of the Faith, is the senior department in the church's administration, which is known as the Roman Curia. The Congregation was once called the Holy Office of the Inquisition, and it still has the right to investigate secret denunciations against the clergy, and to impose penalties. It is being accused of pursuing a

146

strenuous policy of clamping down on freedom of speech among theologians, particularly in the area of sexual morality.

There are literally thousands of theologians who hold academic positions in university departments under church control all over the world and many of them do not endorse the official Roman Catholic teaching on various issues such as contraception, homosexuality, divorce or even abortion. Increasingly, those who say so in books, articles or lectures are being called to account, asked to retract, and if they do not, dismissed from their jobs. One theologian has accused the Vatican of engaging in "spiritual terrorism" against its critics.

Meanwhile the Vatican has announced a new oath of loyalty, by which all priests, including theologians and parish clergy, would be required to swear that they agree with official teaching, drawing an expression of "serious concern" from the Catholic Theological Association of America, with a more outspoken condemnation in preparation. And the Vatican has used its power over the selection of bishops to appoint men strictly loyal to the official line to certain key dioceses, often in the teeth of local church protest.

It was one such appointment to the archdiocese of Cologne in West Germany that triggered the latest wave of dissent. Theologians from Germany and elsewhere were already smarting at the Vatican's refusal to allow the publication of a book recording the proceedings of a conference on moral theology last year, because questions had been raised about official Catholic teaching on contraception. Then German Catholicism was convulsed by a major public quarrel concerning the appointment of the new archbishop by the Vatican over the heads of the cathedral chapter, which had the ancient right to nominate a successor to the late Cardinal Joseph Hoffner. The Vatican eventually broke the deadlock over the appointment by changing the rules of episcopal election.

The first public declaration (the "Cologne Declaration"), signed by 163 theologians from Germany, Austria, Switzerland and the Netherlands, was issued in January. They have since been joined by more than 200 from France, Spain and Belgium as well as 63 from Italy – this last group causing particular annoyance in the Vatican as some of the signatories held teaching positions in Rome itself.

Vatican sources have described this unprecedented wave of dissent as a "crisis in European Catholicism". But while the first reaction from the church's leadership was indignant – Pope John Paul II was said to have lost his temper when he first read the Italian theologians' declaration – some observers claim to have detected recent signs of a more conciliatory approach. This mood was not apparent, however, when the Pope addressed the Italian bishops shortly after the theologians published their protest. He declared: "The bishops are the authoritative teachers of the faith. How can one legitimately claim space for a parallel and alternative magisterium, whether it be in open or covert form?" Speaking of dissenting theologians, he added: "From them, one must demand a particularly close, loyal and respectful collaboration with the bishops. The truth of Christian ethics is too often distorted and contested, not only in practice but also through teaching."

In the United States more than a thousand theologians are said to be considering similar action, as well as condemning the new oath of loyalty. But their anger was somewhat abated by the recent publication of a report by the United States bishops, which calls for a more live-and-let-live relationship between theologians and the authorities. The Association of Catholic Theologians of Great Britain and Ireland has the issue on its agenda. Groups of theologians elsewhere are also believed to be considering adding their voices to these protests.

The *National Catholic Reporter*, a liberal American Catholic weekly, remarked recently: "It is not the numbers involved that are important here. Several hundred European theologians have spoken their minds. What is critical is who these theologians are among the elite of Europe." It urged American theologians to join their European colleagues in speaking out, and listed their grievances: "Roman centralization of authority, the imposition of bishops, the bans on theologians out of favour with Rome, the over-extension of papal authority, and an unacceptable disregard for a traditional Catholic hierarchy of truths, as if *Humanae Vitae* and the Trinity were of equal standing for the faith."

Most of the subsequent statements by national groups of theologians have been implicit or explicit supportive commentaries on the original Cologne outburst. The German-speaking theologians, who claimed the support of many others who did not sign it, identified particular areas touched by events in the Church as "depressing": first, that "the granting of artificial permission to teach is being abused by being made a means of discipline". The declaration called on the Vatican to respect the rights of local churches, which were sometimes now being "disciplined" by the appointment of tough conservative bishops. They also attacked the operation of the Vatican diplomatic service through local nuncios (ambassadors from the Holy See accredited to national Governments and Catholic hierarchies), saying that their role was "becoming continually more questionable".

Bishops, the Cologne theologians alleged, were being required to submit to the Pope in "blind obedience", whereas obedience in the Gospel, they claimed, includes the possibility of constructive opposition. In their protest at the disciplining of theologians, they declared that "bishops are not executive organs of the Pope", but had the right to exercise discretion in granting or withdrawing official permission to teach.

"The contemporary practice of violating the principle of subsidiarity within the church in cases where the local bishop is clearly competent in matters of faith or morals is intolerable." Arbitrary action, unsupported by arguments and not "justified according to recognized academic norms", jeopardized the very existence of Catholic faculties of theology in state universities. And the appointment and removal of professors of theology by such means threatened the reputation of theology in the academic world. Not all doctrines were of equal weight, the theologians went on, and matters of detail "cannot arbitrarily be blown up to become questions concerning the very identity of faith".

Then they come to what is probably at the heart of the matter: the 21-year-old controversy in the Roman Catholic

Church over contraception, which is no nearer being settled than when *Humanae Vitae* was first published: "Recently . . . the Pope, without consideration for the degrees of certainty and the different weight of church statements, has linked the teaching of birth control with fundamental truths of faith like the divinity of God and salvation through Jesus Christ. As a result, critics of the papal teaching on birth control are now charged with 'attacking fundamental pillars of Christian doctrine' and indeed of falling into error by appealing to the dignity of conscience." They went on: "The concepts of 'fundamental truth' and 'divine revelation' are enlisted by the Pope in order to advocate a very particular teaching which cannot be justified on the basis either of Holy Scripture or of the church's tradition." And they assert that the ban on birth control in the encyclical *Humanae Vitae* "does not replace the responsibility in conscience of the faithful", which is Catholic theological code for saying that married people should be allowed to make their own minds up: "The dignity of conscience does not consist only in obedience but also precisely in responsibility."

II   IS THE INQUISITION ALIVE?
25 July 1989

It is possible to defy the Vatican and survive. One of Roman Catholicism's most eminent moral theologians, the 76-year-old German Redemptorist Father Bernard Haring, is proof of that. But he has likened his experience to that of being brought before Nazi courts, which he also survived.

He was called by the Vatican to account for his views on contraception, and was accused of "showing fidelity" to the official teaching without really believing it. At the end of the investigation of his case by the Congregation for the Doctrine of the Faith in Rome, he was told he had to promise not to express further dissent, and to stop criticizing the Vatican and the Congregation. When he refused, saying "that which goes against conscience is a sin", Pope John Paul II intervened to halt the proceedings. But Haring is still bitter, and has called publicly for the Congregation to be temporarily suspended and its function drastically reformed, saying it would "let the church live for a few years without this nightmare".

Just how bitter the dispute between the Vatican and progressive theologians has become in 1989 is demonstrated by Haring's comparison of the methods of the Congregation with those of Nazi Germany. During the Second World War Haring served as a medical orderly on the Russian front, and was brought before Nazi courts four times for advocating non-violence. "The processes of Hitler were more dangerous," he said, "but they were not an offence to my honour, while those of the Holy Office were a grave offence." (The Holy Office of the Inquisition was renamed the Congregation for the Doctrine of the Faith after the Second Vatican Council. Some of its critics use the old title, arguing that nothing has really changed.)

Haring escaped being disciplined, but his treatment and the high regard in which he is held apparently by the Pope as well as his colleagues was undoubtedly one of the factors which provoked the Cologne Declaration protesting against the Vatican's "persecution" of dissenters. Another leading moral theologian, Father Charles Curran, was not so lucky. He held a professorship in moral theology at the Catholic University, Washington, DC, and was for a time chairman of the Catholic Theological Association of America. The Congregation began a long process against him which reached the end of the road this year, when his appeal against being sacked from his professorship was dismissed in the American courts. Concluding a case which had become a *cause célèbre* in American Catholicism, the judge held that it was for the Roman Catholic Church to decide who was entitled to function as a Catholic theologian, not for the academic authorities or the court itself. "I have fought for academic freedom at the Catholic University for 20 years. I have lost," Curran said after the verdict. "In future we are going to have to live with greater differences, and we have to do it with respect for one another. I think I have shown how that can be done."

There is no Roman Catholic university, nor a Catholic theology department in a secular university, in the United Kingdom, much to the relief of Catholic theologians here. Their appointment to an academic post does not, therefore, depend on their having a "dog-licence", as some disillusioned priests call it – an endorsement from Rome authorizing them to teach as an officially recognized Catholic theologian. A good deal of Catholic theology is, in fact, taught in departments of theology in Britain, and the bishops have been happy to link their seminaries with such departments. They do not have jurisdiction; and it seems they are content that they do not. This explains why the current "crisis in European Catholicism" has largely bypassed Britain.

But Curran did require official recognition if he was to teach. His offence was that he had put forward the view that official Roman Catholic teaching on sexuality was unsound, because it gave insufficient weight to the human and "personalist" element in sexual relations, in other words to the moral value of sexual love, while over-emphasizing the procreative element in sex as the primary arbiter of sexual morality. At the back of it, however, was a sharp disagreement about the nature of authority in the church. He was never told he was not entitled to his opinions: he was told he was not entitled to teach them as Catholic theology. But his is a common approach to sexual ethics among Catholic moral theologians. It came near to becoming the official line prior to the publication of *Humanae Vitae* in 1968, as it was the view taken by the majority of a special commission set up by Pope Paul VI to advise him on these matters. He rejected their majority report, and the documentary evidence shows that one of the main reasons, apart from the need to uphold papal authority, was that this line of argument could ultimately be used to legitimize homosexual relations. Father Curran took precisely that step. But homosexuality was not the main issue: it was his challenge to the authority of *Humanae Vitae* and of the magisterium of the Catholic Church.

There are two sharply contrasting views in the Roman Catholic Church on these matters. One, now dominant in Rome, is that even if *Humanae Vitae* was not technically infallible, it has to be regarded as the only position in accordance with Catholic tradition. The magisterium is the church's official teaching voice, which is treated as comprising all the routine utterances of the Pope and of the Vatican congregations, particularly the Congregation for the Doctrine of the Faith. The duty of the faithful is to hear and obey this magisterium; and of theologians, to expound and explain it.

The other view is held by Haring and Curran and all those who have signed theological declarations in the past six months. It is that Catholic teaching exists at various layers of importance, from the most fundamental – that God exists, for instance – to the most marginal, such as the doctrine of indulgences. This is known as a "hierarchy of truths". Deviation on a fundamental point, these theologians readily concede, is a fundamental matter; but on a marginal point, it is a marginal matter. And they maintain *Humanae Vitae* is a marginal matter.

Some moderate theologians in Rome, aghast at the intransigence of both sides, see the present crisis as part of a continual struggle between the theologians and bishops. Since the Second Vatican Council the theologians have been in the ascendancy. Under the present strong Pope, however, and with a strong German disciplinarian in Cardinal Joseph Ratzinger, head of the Congregation for the Doctrine of the Faith, the emphasis is being pushed back the other way. It is ultimately, therefore, a struggle for power, and who wins it may well shape the future of the Roman Catholic Church, by far the world's largest and most powerful religious organization.

III   CONCEPTION AND CONSPIRACY
26 July 1989

It is no secret that a great many Roman Catholics in Britain use birth control methods which were firmly ruled out by *Humanae Vitae* as sinful. They still regard themselves and are treated by the church as good Catholics. Many priests quietly support them; many agree with them. So a major part of the two million practising Catholic population in Britain regularly and repeatedly defies the official teaching of the church. Otherwise they are remarkably loyal. It is, nevertheless, a serious problem for the integrity of British Catholicism.

Some have left, adding to the two million lapsed Catholics on the very fringe of the church, but most have remained. Although the Catholic church-going population has declined in the last twenty years, contraception has not been a major factor except as part of a more general sense of disillusionment and the trend to secularism.

Father Brian O'Sullivan, chairman of the National Conference of Priests of England and Wales, said the "frank and open atmosphere" between priests and bishops in this country had prevented any confrontation over birth control. "Most of the priests take a pastoral view, while still holding to official teaching as the ideal. In pastoral practice we have to accept people where they are."

The publication of *Humanae Vitae* in 1968 sparked a brief and furious row among British Catholics, which was quickly extinguished by the calming influence of senior church leaders. The influence of the *modus vivendi* they reached then is still very much alive. It has been called a conspiracy of silence; but it has kept the peace for two decades. Cardinal Basil Hume's predecessor, the late Cardinal John Heenan, cooled the controversy in 1968 when he was asked in a television interview what he would say to a practising Catholic who admitted in confession that he used a forbidden birth control method; but who then added that he did not, after careful thought and prayer, believe it was wrong. Cardinal Heenan replied that he would simply say: "God bless you." And at about the same time Archbishop Derek Worlock, then Roman Catholic Bishop of Portsmouth, uttered a remark which was subsequently much quoted by Catholics, that "birth control was not the acid test of Christianity". These two observations ultimately carried more weight than the conservative bishop who called the use of contraception "the morality of the farmyard". Behind the observations there seemed to be an impression Heenan and Worlock had gained the year before, that the Vatican had come very close to changing the official line, before pulling back.

Heenan had been closely involved in the work of a confidential international commission set up by Pope Paul VI to review the issue. The publication of some of the documents of

that commission showed that there was, at one time, a considerable majority for change. Soon after *Humanae Vitae* appeared,
a leading English Catholic doctor who had served on the papal
commission announced that he had changed his mind in the
course of it, as he no longer regarded the reasoning behind the
traditional teaching as convincing. And in one public statement
before the publication of *Humanae Vitae*, Heenan had seemed
to be preparing opinion in the church for a change.

Thus were the foundations laid for the present climate of
live-and-let-live. So when the senior Catholic layman, the
Duke of Norfolk, unguardedly remarked some years later that
the trouble with the approved "natural" methods was that "they
don't bloody well work", a few ultra-conservative Catholics
were quietly ignored when they tried to have him denounced.
He is still president of the Catholic Union of Great Britain,
for instance, which of all Catholic lay organizations has most
prestige; still leader of the Catholic peers in the House of
Lords, in which capacity he is consulted and trusted by the
bishops; still chairman of the trustees of the leading Catholic
journal *The Tablet*.

The Roman Catholic Church in England and Wales is
governed by a standing conference of all the 42 Catholic bishops, both diocesan and auxiliaries, whose president is Cardinal
Hume and vice-president Archbishop Worlock. They meet
twice a year, and their general secretary briefs the Press on the
agenda both before and after each meeting. It is clear from
these briefings that the issue of contraception among English
Catholics is rarely discussed by the bishops, and even then only
tangentially.

In 1980 Hume and Worlock represented the English and
Welsh bishops at a Vatican synod on family life. They were
delegated to urge a new approach, and in particular to report
a widespread feeling among British Catholics that church
teaching on this point needed to "develop". But in the Apostolic Exhortation from Pope John Paul II called *Familiaris Con-
sortio* and published the following year in the light of that synod,
the previous papal teaching was reiterated as firmly as ever.

The word "develop", in theological language, is more deli-

cately nuanced than "change", though on the essential point
the serious immorality of every use of contraception it is in
practice the same thing. The significance of the word is that
the possibility of "development" is uncontroversial in Catholic
theology, and does not necessarily imply that the previous position was totally erroneous. To call for "change", on the other
hand, is to suggest the church has made a serious mistake in
a major point of its moral doctrine.

It is impossible, however, to reconcile this low-key approach
in England and Wales with some of the more outspoken utterances of Pope John Paul II, particularly those quoted with
alarm by the 163 theologians in the Cologne Declaration. They
recalled that the Pope has on various occasions likened the use
of contraception to making "Christ's cross in vain", as tending
to "shatter the mystery of God" and to denying the "dignity
of man". The bishops of England and Wales have certainly not
behaved as if they agreed with him, though it is unacceptable
for them to contradict him publicly. Nor have they been subjected to the process of "stiffening" by the appointment of
conservative bishops to certain dioceses, as has happened in
Holland and elsewhere. For a long time this was attributed to
the decisive influence over English appointments exercised by
the former pro-nuncio to Great Britain, Archbishop Bruno
Heim, who was a friend and admirer of Pope John XXIII. But
the first recommendation of his successor, Archbishop Luigi
Barbarito, of Bishop Crispian Hollis as the new Roman Catholic Bishop of Portsmouth was very much in the same mould.

Several factors appear to explain this apparent immunity of
English Catholicism to the chill winds which have produced
recent Continental storms. In the first place, the Vatican takes
very seriously the delicately growing relationship between English Catholicism and the Church of England. The Pope himself
has called England "privileged ecumenical terrain". A heavy-
handed crackdown on English Catholics because of their dissent on contraception would abruptly end all Anglican interest
in unity, defeating the historic progress made in the last half
century.

Second, in Hume English Catholicism has a head man with

unusually high international standing, who is by all accounts respected and admired by the Pope. He was for a time president of the European Council of Bishops' Conferences, which demonstrates his reputation. So the Vatican would think twice before challenging the judgement of such a man. Hume has been entirely loyal to papal teaching on birth control, but by his actions he has signalled exactly the same point made by Worlock in 1968, that it is not "the acid test".

Third, Britain has a certain international prestige in Roman Catholic circles. The Pope went to enormous trouble not to offend British public opinion during his visit at the height of the Falklands crisis in 1982. He was more guarded in his references to contraception than on any other papal visit.

And finally, the Catholic Church in Britain has learnt to conduct itself with extreme care, to avoid drawing on its head the bludgeon of Vatican discipline. The native tradition of understatement, together with profound loyalty to the Holy See that comes from having been a persecuted minority, has discouraged militancy and extremism.

Only one English moral theologian, Father Jack Mahoney SJ, who is a professor at King's College, London, has had a slight brush with authority, as far as it is known (if others have, they have kept quiet about it). His book *Bioethics and Belief*, published in 1984, had the imprimatur taken off its second edition, at the request of Cardinal Hume, after it was somewhat belatedly spotted that parts of Mahoney's argument were out of step with Vatican thinking on the moral status of human embryos. No other action was taken against him, and Mahoney continues to be held in high respect in the church. His theological professorship is not, however, deemed an official position in the church, and he is not officially appointed to teach "Catholic theology". And London University is not a Catholic university, although it does have a Catholic constituent college.

Otherwise the calm has rarely been disturbed. When the head of the Vatican's Council for the Family, Cardinal Edouard Gagnon, tried to order a Scottish priest, Father Andrew Monaghan, to stop his regular series of radio "agony aunt" advice programmes, alleging he had been soft on abortion, Archbishop

Keith O'Brien of Edinburgh, his superior, told him to carry on, with the full backing of Archbishop Barbarito.

CATHOLICS IN CONFUSION

7 April 1990

No-popery, it has been said, is the residual religion of the English, suggesting that the worst fate that can befall a residually religious Englishman is to want to marry a Roman Catholic. For his children, it is well known, would have to be brought up Catholics too. And Catholicism is an earnest sort of religion which has the temerity, in secular English eyes, to believe itself to be true.

In Northern Ireland, many well-meant English solutions to the communal rivalries – non-sectarian schooling, say, or more inter-marriage (which mixed schools would undoubtedly lead to) – founder on this sharp rock. It is true that one of the ways in which different communities have commonly learnt in the past to get on with one another has been the practice of exogamy, which, as differences dissolve in the intimacy of kitchen and bedroom, gradually becomes indistinguishable from endogamy. But not when religion is the dividing line and one of the religions is Roman Catholicism, for rather than coalescing, it tends to absorb other tribes into itself. Many a non-Catholic married to a Catholic will know what this feels like, at least once they have children. Even in "Protestant" England there must be at least a million such families.

The Roman Catholic Church seeks to control the religion of the children of such mixed marriages by requiring from the Catholic partner, as a condition of the marriage being allowed, that a formal promise be made. The other partner is no longer required to agree to it, nor, in England at least, does it have to be in writing. Nevertheless it is a formal and formidable

158

commitment, and the other partner has to know about it. From the end of this month, for Catholics in England and Wales, the key passage in the promise will have a slightly different form: "I sincerely undertake that I will do all I can within the unity of our partnership to have all the children of our marriage baptized and brought up in the Catholic Church." The words "within the unity of our partnership" are new, and represent a response to the complaint that without such a qualification, the promise could wreck the marriage itself. The security of the marriage, clearly, is even more important than passing on the Catholic faith to the children, which is therefore no longer insisted upon as the absolute priority.

All official Catholic documents, particularly those based on Canon Law, require considerable deciphering, and this new Directory on mixed marriages is a classic of the type. As well as the regulations, it contains a long commentary which makes decoding it only slightly less of an adventure. This states, for instance, that the obligation on a Catholic to have his children raised in the same faith is *A Divinis* – a matter of Divine Law, not a man-made rule of the church which could be altered: "individual Catholics must recognize a God-given obligation to do all that is possible to preserve their own faith and to pass on that faith to their children."

Nevertheless it is said that non-Catholic partners "will certainly recognize for themselves an obligation to do all that they can to pass on to their children their own deeply held religious convictions". What this seems to be trying to say is important, for it is probably the first time an official Catholic document has been so generally sympathetic towards the rights of the other party. On the other hand, it does not say that the Catholic Church or the Catholic partner ought to "recognize" that obligation. "Recognize for themselves" is an odd and empty phrase.

In this context, recognition of the obligation by the Catholic Church is the only recognition that means anything. But for the Catholic Church to say it recognized the obligations of the other partner would be for it to accept a symmetry of moral obligations of equal and opposite force, which, by cancelling each other out, would leave the couple free to do whatever they agreed. Nor would it help (even if it made sense) to recognize the other obligation yet think of it as somehow less binding. When a card is going to be beaten by an ace, it makes no difference whether it is a king or a two. A lesser obligation is, in this context, no obligation at all.

For all its quiet reasonableness, the Directory is unconvincing in its argument at this point: the faith is a "precious gift"; a good parent would therefore want to pass it on; the Catholic Church believes it is not just one church among many, and others cannot expect Catholics to deny their deepest beliefs. All this is unexceptionable, and indeed will impress many non-Catholics as evidence of a church confident of itself, but non-Catholics could just as well say the same about their own faith, or even lack of one.

Now that the promise has been made subject to the overriding qualification "within the unity of our partnership", the door has been opened for the introduction of another overriding qualification, for which there is already good authority in Catholic doctrine: the duty of everyone, Catholic or not, to obey his own conscience. The curious phrase "recognize for themselves" seems to imply that non-Catholics should not expect the Catholic Church or their Catholic partners to recognize that they have such an obligation. That is contrary to Catholic doctrine on the rights of conscience. And that too is held to be *A Divinis*.

GOOD ENDS BY NO ILL MEANS

28 April 1990

The Archbishop of York, Dr John Habgood, put forward a Church of England view on embryo experimentation in *The Times* on Monday which was startlingly different from that presented on the opposite page by five Catholic archbishops.

There is evidently potential for an interesting ecumenical conversation between Dr Habgood and his Catholic opposite numbers.

Abortion and embryology are in some respects different issues, although the Catholic approach tends to mix them. Destroying an early embryo is considered as wrong as killing a well-established foetus, for the same reason. But this begs the very question Dr Habgood had raised: whether an embryo in its early stages can be recognized as human life. As he knows, because he reads it regularly, *The Tablet* has recently hosted a Roman Catholic debate between distinguished theologians on this point, and the score was about even.

If a pre-14 day embryo is not strictly speaking "human life", then its destruction is not equivalent to abortion. Its destruction is not what the Catholic archbishops and later Cardinal Hume himself had condemned, the doing of a wrongful act on the utilitarian ground in aid of research that good may come of it. So the Catholic riposte overlooks the possibility that non-utilitarians like Dr Habgood might reach different conclusions because of a different view of the status of the early embryo, rather than different moral principles.

The Catholic Church's implacable opposition to abortion stems from the application of one basic principle: that it is never permissible to choose a wrong means to a good end, never permissible to justify such a choice as the lesser of two evils. That a well-established foetus is "human life" is not disputed by either side in the argument, as it is in the case of embryo research; what is disputed is whether there can ever be circumstances in which ending its life is, in the moral sense, the least-worst course available. In the case of abortion, the principle has not been much discussed by Catholic moral theologians (the church does not like clerical dissent on abortion), but they have intensely debated the parallel question of nuclear weapons. The principle says it is never permissible to achieve a good end (deterrence of war) by a wrong means (preparing to kill millions of innocent people). In the US, many Catholic bishops have been persuaded by this argument virtually to espouse unilateral nuclear disarmament, and some say they were pointed in this direction by thinking about abortion.

It is not clear, however, that this absolute moral principle that the end can never justify the means ought strictly speaking to be called Christian at all. It is neither explicit nor implied in the Bible. It is essentially a philosophical rather than a theological judgement. So why is the Catholic Church so attached to an absolutist morality, and so opposed to a utilitarian one? There is no infallible papal dogma on the point. As it is essentially a matter of philosophical method rather than revealed doctrine, there could not be, for dogma applies only to revelation.

The Catholic moral tradition has been substantially shaped by the practice of private confession. Moral theology as an area of specialized study arose from the ancient penitential codes, which set out a precise tariff of penance according to the severity of the sin. This has long ceased, but what to say in the confessional remains a preoccupation among priests, for they understand themselves to be exercising a divine power. Necessarily the emphasis in such a context is on individual acts of sin. Each has to be described sufficiently by the penitent so that it can be quantified by the priest, and so that sorrow for each sin can be declared and duly acknowledged, leading to absolution on condition of a firm intent to mend one's ways. It is a process which fascinates psychiatrists, who recognize in it a certain psychological truth.

At its best, the regular practice of private confession can help to cultivate a kind of translucent personal integrity and simplicity which is very attractive; at its worst it leads to an almost amoral obsession with avoiding certain thoughts and actions, and an unpleasant attitude of dry righteousness. This form of spiritual discipline places great emphasis on the avoidance of specific sinful acts and on what happened in a particular moment. It is very individualistic. Inevitably it enlarges the importance of those sins on a time-scale that it is well suited to deal with, such as individual sexual acts, to the detriment of others it cannot so easily cope with, such as relational, social or collective behaviour. Thus racism, which may easily be the more serious sin, is hard to pin down in the confessional, while masturbation or fornication (or abortion) are easy. Such a concentration on specific actions, and the avoidance at all costs of those actions which used to be called "mortal sins", is likely to lean towards moral absolutism. If sinful acts must be avoided at all costs, there can be no choosing between different sins, to select the lesser, no choosing of a sinful act because of some greater good. The confessional is not the place for a utilitarian seminar. It is the place where sin is healed by holiness, for the avoidance of damnation.

Rome's Rigid Patriarchy

18 August 1990

The largest organization in the world, the Roman Catholic Church, claims to have 890 million members, 18 per cent of the world population. It has a full-time manpower (and womanpower) of 1.7 million. It has one pope, 4,126 bishops, 402,000 priests, 893,000 nuns and 400,000 others. That is a lot of each kind (except popes). It is also a lot of power for good or evil.

The priests are the backbone of this extraordinary body. How they fare will determine the future of the whole. Much has been said and written in the last ten years about a crisis of identity and numbers in the Catholic priesthood, but the latest official statistics do not altogether confirm this impression. The number of priests dropped by 4 per cent during the decade, but ordinations increased every year. In Europe the vocation rate – the number of candidates for priestly training per million Catholics – rose from 85 to 105, equalling the rate in North America (where it dropped from 165). But North America still has the highest proportion of priests per head of Catholic population.

Despite these apparently healthy figures, a priestly identity crisis is officially admitted, and the Vatican has called a special conference of world Catholic leaders this autumn to address it. The concern is primarily with quality and function. In every country, it seems, there is some uncertainty about what a priest is for, and how he ought to go about doing what he is for. In Western Europe, this questioning has become acute. If the church is not careful, Catholicism in Europe will follow the pattern of Anglicanism in England, with 20 per cent church attendance dropping to 5 or 3 or 2 per cent. French Catholicism is already well on the way.

In an increasingly literate and educated world, a priest is likely to spend much of his time among his intellectual equals, many of whom will be fellow professionals. There is a characteristic movement in virtually all societies to recognize authority and grant respect only where it is earned by performance rather than status, which presents a particular difficulty for a priest. His identity still largely comes from what he is rather than what he does. What he is will mean nothing much in increasingly urban and secular societies. As the world becomes more democratic, the idea of a divinely ordained hierarchy, of which a priest is a member, may seem inimical to the democratic ideal of equal rights and universal participation in the exercise of government. Even in the church itself responsibility is moving towards the laity, who are having to learn that they possess a certain kind of priesthood of their own – much to the puzzlement of those who thought they had a monopoly of it.

These accelerating trends are mystifying and demoralizing to the older clergy, while the younger ones may embrace them too uncritically. Both reactions are likely to be distorting, and 400,000 misdirected personalities occupying leadership positions among 890 million people is bad news for almost everybody.

If the preparatory papers are any guide, this autumn's synod of bishops will set out to find the narrow middle way between these two destructive tendencies, neither embracing change unconditionally nor rejecting it out of hand, so achieving an idealized "identity" for the modern priesthood which avoids all the traps. But because the institution is so vast and disparate,

Roman Catholicism tends to be suffocated by meaningless generalizations. Not much can usefully be said that applies equally to 400,000 people of some 150 nationalities aged between 25 and 90. Even less that can be said now will still be true in ten years.

Despite all the complaints about overcentralization in this enormous church, the Vatican is fighting a rearguard action to retain control. There is no databank in the Vatican with 400,000 names on it, let alone the 1.7 million total. The staff of the Roman curia, the church civil service, can just about keep half an eye on the 4,000 bishops. So order is kept in the church not by the Vatican but by canon law, the universal regulations, locally enforced, that apply to every priest. These are the rules which make the priestly body a disciplined body; they impose on the priesthood its shape and pattern. They create stability and cohesion. They also inhibit adaptation as conditions change, and this leads inevitably to an identity crisis when the failure to adapt passes a critical point.

This crisis will be greatest in those societies that have changed most, for it is there that the model of the priesthood enshrined by these rules is most out of place. Canon law is static, and even the latest version describes the priesthood as it was ideally imagined to be thirty years ago. It is based on the picturebook rural dream of the priest as father of his flock, but such a patriarchal ideal is no longer appropriate.

The church needs more flexibility, to allow experimental patterns of ministry to emerge: worker priests, part-time priests, married priests, even female priests if the theologians can agree. What canon law imposes, above all, is the rigid idea of the priesthood, a caste or class embodied in the notion of a clergyman. This is at the root of the identity crisis of the Catholic priesthood. Yet it need not be so: nowhere in the Bible is it laid down that priests have to be full-time, celibate, professional men.

Part Six

Jewish-Christian Relations

THE NAZI LEGACY

19 July 1988

There is no more distinguished chronicler of the Nazi geno-cide of the Jews than Elie Wiesel, the Nobel Prize-winning author and campaigner who was in Britain last week for the international Holocaust conference in Oxford and London. As it happens the subject of his concern is one of the items on the agenda of the Lambeth Conference of Anglican bishops, now meeting in Canterbury: the state of Jewish-Christian relations in the light of (or perhaps one should say the darkness of) the Nazis' atrocious crime against the Jews and against humanity. The conference will be asked to agree in particular that Jews should no longer be encouraged to convert to Christianity.

In the course of Dr Wiesel's remarks to the London confer-ence on Friday, there was one heated exchange which brought to the surface very raw and deep feelings. Though the hurt and anger which suddenly erupted should not be viewed too negatively, it indicated that the usual courteous exchanges of Jewish-Christian dialogue, and the efforts of scholars in search of some healing for these relations, are in reality conducted on the edge of a precipice. Both sides need to take stock not just of the arguments, but also of the emotions; otherwise well-meant attempts to make things better could make them much worse.

Jews have good enough reason to be angry with Christians. Jewish survivors of the concentration camps know very well that what happened to them under the Nazis was only worse than, but not really different in kind from, what happened to them before under Christianity.

Hitler exploited the long European Christian tradition of antisemitism: he did not invent it. When it came to the point, the great majority of members of both the Protestant and Catholic Churches in occupied Europe turned their backs on the Jews. The British like to think it would have been different here, but there is enough wartime evidence of antisemitism in high places even in Britain to make that an uncertain hope. Dr Wiesel is clearly convinced it is still present in Christianity.

Speaking at a public meeting in London on Friday, he declared himself concerned, puzzled and angry at the behaviour of Pope John Paul II in particular. He had visited Auschwitz in 1979, and had not prayed for the Jews; he had said Mass there, which to Dr Wiesel was a further grievance: it looked like an attempt at "posthumous conversion" of the Jews who died in Auschwitz. Dr Wiesel did not say so, but the innuendo was that the Pope is an antisemite. Members of the audience got to their feet to protest, shouting that the Pope had in fact prayed for the Jews: and Dr Wiesel conceded that he had prayed for the children of Abraham; but that meant everyone, not just Jews. There were strong feelings in Central Hall, Westminster, at this moment, and the chairman had to intervene to calm things down.

Of all the current problems in Jewish-Christian relations, the issue of conversion is both the most painful and the most difficult. As was apparent from Dr Wiesel's remarks and the enthusiastic response to him from what was presumably the Jewish sector of the audience, any and every attempt to convert Jews to Christianity is deeply resented.

The Pope could not possibly have been trying to bring about "posthumous conversions" by saying Mass for the victims of Auschwitz, for the dead are obviously quite beyond such things. But somewhere in Dr Wiesel's reproach is the idea that Christians do not think Jews are quite good enough to get to heaven on their own, as Jews. It must be very doubtful whether the Pope thinks any such thing, as it would contradict the plain teaching of the Second Vatican Council.

Not very many Jews – and Dr Wiesel is apparently no different – have been prepared to appreciate how extremely difficult these matters are for Christians. Jews do not believe in conversion, as a policy: they are happy for Christians to get to heaven as Christians. And there are some liberal Christian scholars who encourage them in their protest, rejecting as Christians any Christian claim to exclusiveness or uniqueness. It is easy for Jews to believe that if some Christians say that, the rest of them could do so too, if they were not so blinded by anti-Jewish prejudice.

In the main, however, the Christian churches do believe they have a duty to preach their Gospel, to Christians, Jews, Muslims and everyone because they believe it is true, and because they believe no one is excluded from the right to hear that truth. Forced conversions are abhorrent, of course; so are manipulative and deceitful missionary tactics. But to ask the churches to agree that Christian teaching is not in any circumstances to be offered to Jews, is equivalent to asking them to agree that the teaching is not true at all or that Jews are uniquely not allowed to hear it, which would be a doctrine with very objectionable implications that Jews themselves would hardly welcome.

The most that Jews can expect from Christians is that conversions from Judaism should be handled with the ecumenical courtesy the mainstream churches now show towards each other. There are conversions between all the Christian denominations, in all directions, and there are activities by the separate churches designed to facilitate or even encourage them. No church likes losing a member to another; but they can all agree on four things: every religion and every church has a right to state its case, provided it does so honestly; every individual has a right and duty to follow his conscience where it leads him; no one is barred from salvation because his faith has the wrong brand label; and conversion is more about seeking a deeper relationship with God than about changing labels.

THE RIFT BETWEEN JEW AND CHRISTIAN

7 January 1989

Jews were disappointed that the Lambeth Conference last summer did not rule out attempts by Anglicans to convert Jews to Christianity. It remains the main bone of contention between the two faiths, and has given rise to fresh complaints by Jews, against aggressive Christian missionary activity. Nevertheless the Jewish community welcomed the general tone of the Conference's long statement on Jewish-Christian relations (also incorporating a statement on Muslim-Christian relations), which was a formal and emphatic repudiation of the antisemitic tradition in Christian thought.

The Lambeth Conference was initially going to be asked to agree to a statement which excluded conversion. In the event the approved text merely described the various attitudes to the Jews within the Christian churches without stating a preference between them. It was no secret that Evangelical Anglicans in particular were not prepared to support a document which appeared to contradict the teaching of Jesus that "No one comes to the Father except through Me."

"At one pole", the Lambeth Conference stated, "there are those Christians whose prayer is that Jews, without giving up their Jewishness, will find their fulfilment in Jesus the Messiah. Indeed some regard it as their particular vocation and responsibility to share their faith with Jews, whilst at the same time urging them to discover the spiritual riches which God has given them through the Jewish faith . . . ". It is this group, including such bodies as "Jews for Jesus" and the Anglican "Church's Ministry among the Jews" which has given most offence, even though they are generally seen as a slightly batty fringe by the other much larger bodies of opinion. It seems to be becoming the common response among Christian ministers who are approached by Jews inquiring about conversion, to refer them first to their local rabbi; and that is the advice given by the Bishop of Oxford, the Right Rev. Richard Harries, who is the Church of England's specialist in these matters.

The style of Christian proselytism among Jews is generally eirenic and by no means overtly antisemitic, though their passion for proving that it is possible to be both a Christian and a Jew makes them seem a special threat to the Jewish community. They insist that Jewish identity can survive a change of religious conviction. But strong attachment to Jewish identity is one of the chief ways in which Jews have traditionally resisted attempts to convert them, which this approach seems to undermine. The repudiation of antisemitism by all the major churches, and the growing willingness of Christians to rediscover their roots in Judaism, can ironically add to the sense of alarm Jews feel. Once their Christian antagonist hated them: the newer kind assures them it loves them, treasures their heritage, and wants to enhance rather than to destroy their feeling of "being Jewish".

There is no interest in proselytism in the Jewish community, and indeed they exceed all but the most most liberal Christian theologians in believing that all religions can be pathways to salvation. Many Jewish leaders interpret the unique Jewish covenant with God not as an easier road but as a harder one: if the Jews have special divine privileges, they also have special obligations to match.

The issue of conversion to Christianity raises a double-sided challenge to inter-faith goodwill. On the Jewish side, the common complaint is that Christian leaders mouth words of respect and admiration for the Jewish faith, emphasizing the deep bonds between them, while at the same time quietly lending their support to conversionist campaigns, or at least not repudiating them. But there is a puzzle in the other direction too, which is more rarely referred to. Jewish leaders are usually very happy nowadays to express their respect and admiration for Christian leaders, again stressing their commitment to shared basic values: it is not clear why they nevertheless think it is such a disaster if a Jew decides to adopt for himself the very faith which is so admirably led, and which so impressively supports such values.

In both directions, therefore, there is an unstated ambivalence. And the long and notorious record of Christian antisemitism has made it seem insensitive to mention that there is within Judaism an old tradition of hostility to Christianity too. There have been Jews who would not allow the symbol of the cross in their households. It was even wrong for a Jew to touch a Christian.

No one remarked on it at the time, but the discreet visit of the Chief Rabbi to the lying in state of Cardinal John Heenan at Westminster Cathedral in 1975 was in this context a most remarkable gesture by Britain's leading Orthodox Jew to the memory of one of the "righteous Gentiles". The very phrase suggests how uncommon Jews accept righteousness to be outside their own ranks. After 2,000 years of persecution they have good reason. But until recently Christianity tended to be regarded as more than unclean: it was felt to be tainted with evil, and not just because of its hostility to the Jews. And this may explain why Jewish parents are much less distressed if their children drop the practice of their religion and profess themselves agnostic or atheist, than if they adopt Christianity.

The historic rapprochement between Jews and Christians, particularly as the latter draw back in horror from the ultimate consequences of Christian antisemitism under Hitler, has made possible an enormous growth of understanding and respect among Christians for Judaism. This is well described in the Lambeth Conference document. But there has been no equivalent warm response from within Judaism towards Christianity, and most Jews will know far less about Christianity than most Christians about Judaism. All that most Jews really ask from Christians is to be left alone; they have no incentive to inquire what Christians actually believe. It may not be as bad as they think it is.

THE VATICAN'S DISTANT VIEW OF JERUSALEM

18 March 1989

The refusal of the Holy See to recognize the State of Israel is one of three or four major grievances that Jews have towards Christians. To some of them it is the most serious of all. It symbolizes a continued unwillingness on the part of the largest Christian church and, by association, other churches too to take seriously the right of the Jews to a land of their own.

Meanwhile Muslim leaders in Britain appealed last year to Christian and Jewish leaders to do something about the plight of the Palestinians. It was an initiative which led to a useful exchange of views and the improvement of friendly contacts: but the condition of the Palestinians, it must be admitted, remained the same.

There is a direct link between these two issues. In reply to the approach to the Roman Catholic Church last year, part of the more general appeal to Christian leaders, it was explained to the Muslim community that the church's influence in Israel was limited. But it would not be so limited if diplomatic recognition and an exchange of ambassadors had taken place. That probably was not explained to the Muslims, as they might well be presumed not to favour the establishment of such relations anyway. But the case for the recognition of Israel by the Holy See has been put in a different context since, by the change of policy of the Palestinian Liberation Organization towards Israel. There is now room for some creative diplomacy by the Vatican, which would be entirely consistent with what it always insists is the reason for maintaining its diplomatic service.

Non-Jews are usually taken aback by the vehemence with which Jews press their demand for the Holy See to recognize

Israel, being not quite able to see why it matters so much to them. The Vatican is not an economic or military world power, and it represents religious beliefs to which Jews do not subscribe. But whatever the reason for it, the fact of it hands the church a unique opportunity for influence. It would be naive to try to break the PLO-Israeli deadlock by offering recognition only on certain conditions, such as the acceptance of direct talks between the parties. It would be wiser if the Holy See could announce its willingness to recognize Israel, while stating its view that direct talks were desirable, and declaring its intention to put its weight behind that objective. Israel could hardly find that too much to swallow; all sorts of states with which it already has diplomatic relations have already said as much.

The Holy See could go even further, expressing a special concern for the Palestinian people and offering them its help and friendship. This would placate the Muslim world, which has in any case found relations with the Vatican too useful to want to jeopardize them, while distancing the Vatican from Israeli government policy; for it is states which are recognized by other states, not governments.

Officially, recognition has been withheld so far on the grounds that Israel is not technically at peace with all her neighbours, and because she therefore does not have defined borders guaranteed by treaty under international law. The logic of this position has always been questionable, for it effectively gives hostile Arab states, such as Syria, a permanent veto over the recognition issue. The Vatican appears to have failed to ask itself the obvious question: whether the supposed irregularity of Israel's status in international law was justified; whether, in short, those states which had not made peace with her were right not to have done so. Behind the legal issue is a moral one, and moral issues are supposed to be the Vatican's speciality.

Jewish commentators usually see additional and more cynical explanations in the Vatican's reluctance, either the risk of estranging Muslim states, or of arousing the hostility of Arab Christians. Some also see in it the residue of centuries of Christian antisemitism. In fact under the present Pope there has been steady progress in breaking the spell of Christianity's antisemitic tradition in the Roman Catholic Church. It still exists, and no doubt still exists in the Vatican itself, but not as a serious influence on the formation of policy concerning the Jews or Israel.

The PLO's announced change of position, and its recognition of Israel's "right to exist", provide the basis for a review of that policy in the light of both the explicit and implicit reasons for it.

Religion greatly complicates the difficulties of Israel's relations with her Muslim neighbours, just as it complicates its relations with the Palestinians; from some perspectives the religious issues are the most fundamental of all. This is an ideal situation for the intervention of a third faith, which is committed to peace, human justice and reconciliation, which has no political stake in the region, and which, in the case of the Holy See, has vast diplomatic experience and a worldwide network of friendly contacts. Not to intervene as fully as possible in the attempt to find solutions to such religio-political conflicts, while being prepared to take a presence on the stage only after they are resolved, would make nonsense of the Holy See's reasons for having a diplomatic service in the first place.

Any progress towards a lasting and just solution of the Palestinian problem would sooner or later raise the question of Jerusalem, in which the Vatican can hardly fail to want a direct voice. But it will not carry much weight if it is the last to arrive at the conference table, and only comes at all in order to protect its own special interests. On the other hand, it could carry a lot of weight if it had been part of the peace process before, and had already earned the goodwill of both sides.

SHADOW OVER AUSCHWITZ

20 May 1989

A small group of Carmelite nuns in Poland have somehow managed to put at risk all the precarious goodwill built up since the war between the Jewish community and Christianity. The problem is not what they are doing – they are praying – but where they are doing it. They have opened a convent in the grounds of Auschwitz concentration camp.

The nuns are defying an instruction from the church authorities to close their convent and move out. They have signalled their defiance by erecting a prominent cross above the old theatre building they occupy in the concentration camp compound. They were supposed to be gone by February 23, a date agreed after top-level Jewish-Christian negotiations. The church has now promised they will leave in July, but there are not many Jews who believe it.

Auschwitz, where millions of Jews were murdered by the Nazis, is uniquely special to the Jewish community: to call it emotive would be a crass under-statement. But Polish Catholics were murdered there too, and the nuns wish to pray for their souls. Despite their pious intentions their presence has generated endless misunderstanding, which is now rapidly turning to ill-will.

The World Jewish Congress recently considered calling a world Jewish boycott of Pope John Paul II wherever he went, and the withdrawal of Jewish participation in joint-faith enterprises all over the world. In the event more moderate counsels prevailed, not least because of impassioned pleas from British Jews. But there was a strong sense of a crisis merely postponed rather than avoided.

The alternative tactic the Congress adopted was to utilize all the points of contact that have been built up painstakingly over the years between Jews and Christians, to apply as much pressure as possible before the new July deadline expires. In this way, however, it has become even more a global issue, even more a make-or-break test for Christian-Jewish relations, for it challenges the sincerity of a far wider group than those directly concerned with the Auschwitz Carmelites. From the Jewish point of view, Christian-Jewish relations are only worth fostering if, over a critical issue like this, they can deliver satisfaction.

Last week Cardinal Basil Hume of Westminster was approached by Jewish leaders, and he has promised to contact Cardinal Jean-Marie Lustiger of Paris, who was part of the church team which negotiated the earlier deadline. A Jewish deputation has been to see the papal pro-nuncio to Britain, Archbishop Luigi Barbarito, without gaining much comfort. And while Jewish leaders in Britain know the difference between Catholics, Anglicans and Protestants, such distinctions are lost on many ordinary Jews. They seem to see the Auschwitz convent as a blatant piece of aggression, which demonstrates the truth of the old suspicion that no Christian expression of goodwill towards Jews, whatever denomination it comes from, can ever really be trusted. There is no evidence, however, that the nuns' motives are consciously antisemitic: they have offered to pray for the Jewish victims of Auschwitz as well. That in itself is a perfect example of the fundamental misunderstanding at the root of this crisis, for many Jews greeted the offer as compounding the offence.

It seems to be the case that even those in the church who have been most sympathetic to the Jewish grievance have scarcely grasped exactly why the issue is, to the Jews, so important. The nuns probably do not begin to understand: no doubt that is why a move this July seemed a fair substitute for a move in February.

Auschwitz stands for the uniqueness of the Holocaust. To regard it as the scene of one more dreadful massacre, only in degree worse than countless other inhumanities of man to man, is to ignore that it was the focus of an attempt to wipe out the whole Jewish race. Even to mention that hundreds of thousands of Christians were murdered by the Nazis there, coupling

Jewish and non-Jewish suffering and death as somehow a shared experience, seems to Jews to threaten the symbolic meaning of Auschwitz as a place of specifically Jewish desolation without parallel on earth.

But the anger seems to go deeper even than that. European Jewry has spent its whole existence in the shadow of Christianity, under perpetual pressure to disappear, to convert, to give up. Jews became aware of every church, chapel, convent or cross as an ominous symbolic reproach to them for remaining as they were. To the Jews of Europe Christianity was not a religion of the love of God but a religion of hostility towards Jews. A Christian chapel in Auschwitz, now topped by a cross, feels to them like an attempt to hound the dead even beyond the grave – or even to celebrate Jewish extermination as a kind of Christian triumph.

The church, or course, would be quite properly outraged by the very suggestion. But very few Jews will have even an inkling of the reason why the presence of a community of nuns in Auschwitz, praying for peace and for the dead, makes perfect Christian sense. The Jewish instinct in a place like that is to leave it as desolate as possible, physically, morally and philosophically. Auschwitz is not sacred to the Jews; it is the very opposite of sacred. To extract solace or meaning from such things, let alone find holiness there, is to try to mitigate the evil, to pretend it was somehow not as bad as it really was, and thus to belittle the millions who died there. The Christian instinct is the exact reverse; it is to sanctify such a place. Christians consecrate their cemeteries, build shrines where accidents or executions happen, celebrate their martyrs and call the place of martyrdom holy. There is also a convent of nuns on the site of the gallows at Tyburn, praying for peace and for the dead.

The total contradiction between these two approaches to Auschwitz has hidden the fact that each side, in its own way, is trying to express its utmost sorrow and grief. But Auschwitz is the last place on earth at which Jews can be expected to look on Christian symbolism with sympathy. And it is the Christians who must give way – for they were not only among the victims; they were among the murderers.

Part Seven

NEW
THEOLOGIES

NEW MEANINGS FOR OLD CHURCH WORDS

21 July 1988

The average income of a bishop in the Anglican Communion is not a statistic the Lambeth Conference staff has at its fingertips: nor, incidentally, is the exact number of bishops present at Canterbury. However many they are and whatever they are paid, they are having to work hard for it. For three days they have been struggling with mind-bending theology coming at them from all directions, some of it breaking what to most of them will be entirely fresh ground.

There are two new "in" words for them to digest this week: ecclesiology and reception. Neither means what the bishops probably thought before they arrived at the University of Kent. The first has nothing to do with church architecture, though that is still the dictionary definition, and the second nothing to do with checking in at Canterbury's excellent hotels.

Ecclesiology is the theology of the structure and nature of the church as an organism, not a building, an idea unfamiliar to most Anglicans, for whom "the church" still means dear old St Mark's in the High Street (or in the US, Main Street). Reception means the process by which a new doctrinal development, such as the ordination of women, gradually soaks in until people can no longer remember not believing it; or doesn't soak in. Reception implies the possibility of non-reception, in the event of which women priests presumably have to pack their bags and go home to mother.

Having had two full days of ecclesiology, including heavy doses of the World Council of Churches, Greek Orthodox, and Roman Catholic versions of it, the bishops no doubt looked forward with relief to a lecture yesterday on the theology of liberation: social justice, the church and politics, and the "option for the poor". But liberation theology turned out to be pure ecclesiology too. It is about the nature and structure of the church as an agent of political change. Everything is ecclesiology these days.

The Anglican Communion was once a rather English pragmatic thing bound by the episcopal equivalent of a gentleman's agreement. The agreement being about to break down, largely because some gentlemen want to let ladies in on the act, there is little alternative but to construct an edifice of theory – an ecclesiology which describes an ideal church in which the relationship between the parts and the whole is governed by rules and principles, based on Christian doctrine. The sources for this ecclesiology are the Acts of the Apostles and the Epistles.

Reception, an idea many bishops are clutching at as a solution to their predicament over women priests and bishops, means that the final proof of the truth of a fresh idea in the church is the general consent of all the faithful, which is not likely to be given overnight. And vice versa. It is, in ecclesiological terms, a way of explaining a patchy pattern of belief over something important. A church still in the process of receiving something need not think of itself as disunited, and therefore need not split up into rival factions. And the Lambeth Conference is desperately searching for a theologically respectable idea which does this particular trick, otherwise it senses its doom.

Whether "reception" can be sold to the General Synod of the Church of England, to resolve its crisis over women priests, is another matter.

THE POWER OF COMMUNION

---

12 November 1988

One powerful idea suddenly seems to be at the top of the agenda in the Church of England and the Anglican Communion, in the Roman Catholic Church in this country and worldwide, in the relations between these two, and in their relations with other churches. Perhaps only a journalist hopping between them all would be struck by the convergence so forcefully.

On Monday morning last, for instance, the secretary of the Roman Catholic Bishops' Conference of England and Wales, Monsignor Vincent Nichols, briefed the press on the agenda for the next bishops' meeting in London. A significant item will be the relationship between bishops' conferences and Rome.

On Monday afternoon the Archbishop of Canterbury, Dr Robert Runcie, addressed the General Synod on the issue of women bishops elsewhere in the Anglican Communion and the Church of England's official attitude to them, in the light of the Lambeth Conference.

On Tuesday an African bishop described movingly to the synod what the Lambeth Conference had meant to him. On Tuesday also, Cardinal Basil Hume introduced his excellent new book by talking further about the relationship of national Catholic hierarchies to Rome, and the need for certain changes in the type and frequency of international meetings to which they send delegates.

The one word all were using was *communio* or *koinonia*, sometimes translated into English as communion (which is not a direct reference to the Sacrament called Holy Communion, though not unrelated). Cardinal Hume's *Towards a Civilisation of Love* has a chapter devoted to it, though in fact it is the theme of the whole volume.

Meanwhile, with the same word in mind, ecumenical representatives have been meeting in England and Scotland to fashion the "new ecumenical instruments" to replace the British Council of Churches which the Lambeth Conference in the summer was really all about. It will also be the guiding idea of Archbishop Eames's Commission, due to meet in London shortly to try to find a way out of the Anglican impasse over women bishops.

Yet it is not an easy concept to grasp. As the cardinal remarked, when he sat down to write his chapter on it he found himself rather short of source material: no one has so far managed an exhaustive definition. Its currency in all these spheres owes a great deal to the work of the Anglican-Roman Catholic International Commission (ARCIC), though it is also an ancient and biblical idea, and one fully understood in the Orthodox churches too. It is gradually becoming apparent that it was also at the heart of the Second Vatican Council, and it is beginning to replace the new images and expressions for the church – "People of God", "Pilgrim People" – which were fashionable immediately afterwards.

The definition of the word is becoming more precise as it is used, and as ecclesial institutions reflect on what it tells them about themselves. It refers to the quality of their inner relationships, the bonds and commitments that hold them freely together, and the criteria by which those relationships are to be conducted. And all the churches, facing similar problems, search for similar solutions.

The Lambeth Conference was preoccupied with the relationships between provinces, using the idea of *communio* which members felt they had tangibly experienced to express what fundamentally united them. Meanwhile the Roman Catholic Church is engaged in its own deep examination of almost the same question, and the English and Welsh bishops are about to prepare their reply to a Vatican document, circulated throughout the world, on the status of episcopal conferences. This too is all about the meaning of *communio*.

The tensions in this exercise seem clear enough. While the Vatican, according to its working document, is prepared only to regard these national or regional bishops' meetings as a convenience, conceding them little real power, some of the conferences themselves are insisting they are rather more important than that. The American bishops have gone so far as to demand the withdrawal of the Vatican document, saying it falls so far short of what is required as to be beyond amendment. The English and Welsh bishops are in no mood, it appears, to be less bold. They are planning to expose the exercise to a thorough dose of ARCIC theology – in the name of *communio*.

One repeated note struck at Lambeth was that the Anglican Communion did not want to evolve towards "centralism", by which they meant the Roman Catholic example of a church dominated by its central institutions. They would have been taken aback had they seen the American Catholic bishops' document. It does not waste words. It accuses the Vatican drafters of engaging in "assertion rather than argument", of "lacking historical consciousness", of "ecumenical insensitivity", and of "failure to attend to legitimate theological diversity". It even accuses them of what journalists call a "cuttings job", meaning a disguised compilation of unattributed material from already published sources.

Their argument is that conferences of bishops participate, of their nature, in the *communio* of the church and the collegiality of bishops. They therefore have, of their nature, an authority to declare and teach (and by implication to interpret) Christian doctrine. This is not to claim, they insist, that they can invent new dogma. And there is not a shadow of a hint that the American Catholic bishops think they are entitled, irrespective of the wishes of the whole church, to proceed unilaterally with, say, the ordination of women. To that extent they are definitely not saying what the American Anglican bishops said to the Lambeth Conference. But they are saying they have a right to a good deal more freedom of thought and action (provincial autonomy) than the Vatican wants to allow them – freedom they claim in the name of *communio*. The Vatican, in other words, has got its doctrine wrong.

Communio has begun to take on a pretty sharp cutting edge if it leads Catholic bishops to say such unexpectedly blunt things to the Roman Catholic Church's central authority. It is a concept that is beginning to be used with confidence. And that is what is now happening in the Anglican Church too. It is obviously a new word with quite a future.

DISCOVER THE GOSPEL AMONGST THE POOR

28 January 1989

D
r John Vincent, director of the Urban Theology Unit at Sheffield, has a reputation as the *enfant terrible* of Methodism, a worthy successor of Lord Soper (who is no longer an infant). As the next President of the Methodist Conference Dr Vincent will wear both Soper's and Wesley's mantle for a year, and command the chief forum in the church for the promotion of his radical ideas.

Methodism is possibly the most fertile ground in Britain for a native growth of the theology of liberation, and Dr Vincent is one of the very few who might even be said to have anticipated some of its thinking. Wesley's original mission was very much to the poorer sections of eighteenth-century Britain, so liberation theology's message of an "option for the poor' rang a lot of bells and was like pushing at a half open door. In Latin American Catholicism, by contrast, liberation theology was a radical reversal of the church's traditional alignment with wealth and power, and the shock waves have by no means yet died down.

Dr Vincent has already foreshadowed what will be one of his major concerns as Methodist President after this summer's annual Conference, in an article in this week's *Methodist Recorder*. As he puts it: "How on earth do you communicate across divided Britain?" The essence of the problem he is

188

referring to, which is by no means confined to Methodism, arises from the church's largely middle-class base in British society, combined with its presence in some of the areas of greatest deprivation, particularly in the inner city and on run-down housing estates.

In the nature of things, Christianity then becomes a middle-class message, one from the better-off to the poor. But, as Dr Vincent roundly declares with only a touch of preacher's overstatement: "In an affluent society Good News comes from the poor." In other words only the poor can reach the poor in a way which does not distort the Gospel, the very message of St Francis of Assisi. This certainly helps to explain the success of the independent Black Churches, who for all their lack of sophistication do not start with the disadvantage of riches.

His dramatic advice to the church, faced with old and costly buildings and small and hard-up congregations, is to sell its buildings and invest in something closer to the scale of what is really needed. Financial self-sufficiency for the urban church is his ideal, if possible turning its real estate into a modest source of income. In its activity, his advice to such churches is to "trust the neighbourhood", meaning that it should respect the existing community spirit and work within it. "Bring in people like the folk already there, and let the worship and the lifestyle of the church be truly based on them . . . Let the churches make an ecclesiastical and cultural journey down-wards."

Dr Vincent favours the concept of "basic communities" as practised in Brazil and elsewhere, which he calls "walking-distance communities". There being few areas of solid Metho-dism left on the urban landscape, such groups would almost certainly have to be ecumenical if they were to work. They could, he envisages, be reinforced in numbers by the sponsor-ship of wealthier congregations, who might be persuaded to support someone prepared to live and work with the poor.

Such basic communities could not exist with exclusively "religious" agendas of their own, in isolation from the problems of life: indeed the whole point of them is that they do not try. Inevitably they must participate in the community's own struggles, for law centres, better buses, housing repairs, street lighting . . . but if they are not to be absorbed and indistinguishable after a time, they must also have a "something else" which is at the heart of what they are about.

Dr Vincent predicts they will discover "the essential Gospel of Jesus, not only for the poor but for all the churches". This is an optimistic view. There are many instances of small groups who have set themselves up with a simple sense of mission, but have quite quickly taken on extraneous or ideological characteristics, or have been riven by controversies of their own making. The communes of the 1960s eschewed authoritarian leadership, or indeed any rules at all; but none of them found the secret of harmonious stability.

In the case of an expressly Christian community there is the added problem of finding a spirituality that controls the wilder flights of fancy that the unbound religious imagination is capable of. Roman Catholic basic communities in Latin America receive their explicitly Christian character from the regular community Eucharist, and their doctrinal stability from being part of the much larger church enterprise. The traditional solution to these far from new problems has been through the foundation of religious orders, and it is often said that Methodism could well have developed as such an order, had it not begun in a religious climate dominated by Protestant suspicion of such things.

But times have changed. The Methodist "option for the poor", which is obviously going to dominate that church at least for the year of Dr Vincent's leadership and if he is successful far beyond, may well be looking – whether it knows it or not – for something like a Methodist Order of St Francis.

TRUTH, THOUGH NOT EXCLUSIVE

14 April 1990

Modern science is familiar with the phenomenon of discontinuity in nature. These breaks are abrupt changes, when one set of laws seems to stop and another to take over. On first discovery, they are intensely disconcerting, for scientific explanation seems to have broken down; but later work can reveal a transcending theory which explains both sets of laws. The understanding of nature, having surmounted its own discontinuity, is thereby advanced.

This is a powerful metaphor for the first Good Friday and Easter, a historical moment of discontinuity par excellence. The scriptural record shows how utterly disconcerted the followers of Jesus Christ were when they realized that all their expectations and predictions were made meaningless by his death on the Cross. They were, after all, orthodox Jews. They had expected a messiah, and thought they had found him. But that his life should end in public execution, charged with blasphemous sedition by the Jewish authorities, was completely contrary to their expectation. This was no triumph; this was disaster.

Although the Gospel record tells the story as comprehensible even to the participants, it was written some time after the event, in the light of the dawning of a new understanding. Inevitably it is read by Christians today with the full benefit of doctrinal hindsight, in the knowledge especially of the credal definition, which took centuries to emerge, that Christ was both true God and true Man. The creed explains the death of Christ as necessary for his resurrection, and his resurrection as necessary for his divinity; and that is how the events of Good Friday are understood by Christians today. Those present at the foot of the Cross had no such insights. Their first Good Friday is beyond recapture. Nevertheless, Christianity has

191

always insisted on the importance of that day. One of the great evolutionary movements of religious thought in the twentieth century has taken as its task the re-examination of that discontinuity, driven by an anxious fear that some of the lessons had for all these years been misunderstood.

The transcendental theory which was the basis for making sense of Good Friday presupposed that all that had gone before was mere preparation for that event, and had no other meaning. Thus Christianity took Good Friday as a sign of God's repudiation of his previous covenant with the Jews, who were thought to have served their full purpose in his plan. That Jesus himself was Jewish, as were all his disciples, was no longer deemed of any significance. In time, the continued right of the Jewish religion to exist came to be challenged; and eventually, in the course of history, so did the right to exist of the Jewish race.

There is a growing recognition that too much of the old was discarded to make way for the new. Despite St Paul's clear statement that God had not repudiated his covenant with the Jews, other Christian leaders, as late as the middle of this century, insisted on treating Jewish survival as no more than a curious anomaly, not part of the hard evidence to be accommodated into their own comprehensive scheme of salvation.

The refashioning of Christian doctrine to make proper room for Jewish existence is far from complete, although the journey has begun and cannot now be diverted. The extent of the required alteration in Christian self-understanding is considerable. It is now hardly regarded as heterodox to believe that Jews are not a proper target for Christian proselytism. So the belief in the unique truth of Christianity will have to be approached by Christians in a new way. No doubt some will not find a way that satisfies them, and will abandon the belief altogether.

Once room has been made for Judaism, it is a small further step to make room for other faiths. The Christian tradition was once proud to insist on its exclusiveness, represented in the phrase "no salvation outside the church", but life is no longer so simple. Few apart from Protestant fundamentalists now regard explicit acceptance of faith in Christ as the only way to heaven, and all the rest as signposts to hell. Yet the radical discontinuity of Easter is still preached universally in all the churches, not only the evangelical ones. They still use the old formulas of faith. The official theology of the churches still stresses the uniqueness of Christ and the unique significance for the whole of mankind of the events of his life, death and resurrection. What they say is the same, but what they now mean is subtly different. Their implicit belief (to which their explicit belief has not yet adjusted) is that the uniqueness of Christ's life remains significant, even though knowledge of it is no longer considered a condition of an individual's salvation. This makes the Christian claim more modest and less likely to offend non-Christians.

The great theologian Karl Rahner invented the phrase "the anonymous Christian" to describe those who are, so to speak, covered by the events of the Christian salvation but do not recognize them as true. This is the beginning of the adjustment of the theory to explain the new discontinuity. It is by no means an official doctrine, but the behaviour of the churches towards other faiths today really makes sense only in Rahner's terms. It is a hypothesis at the very beginning of its useful life: its implications, great as they are, have yet to be fully explored.

THE RELENTLESS DURHAM INQUISITION

24 February 1990

There is an important principle in the criminal courts called *autrefois acquit*, which means no one may be tried more than once for the same offence. Had the Bishop of Durham, the Right Rev. David Jenkins, spoken in his own defence at his trial-by-synod on Thursday, he could have pleaded thus, on the basis that the synod had been over this ground before. He was found not guilty the first time, and the second. But there is an increasingly illiberal faction in the Church of England which refuses to take his acquittal for an answer. He is, to them, a remorseless heretic; and they are, to him, a relentless Inquisition.

Previous synod debates on the doctrines of the Virgin Birth and Resurrection had been theological, but the most recent one was largely tactical. The Bishop of Durham was not named, though he and everyone else knew he was the target. The object of the "prosecution" was to shame the general synod into approving a resolution which would by inference repudiate his views; with the additional offer of an amendment to reject him from the church and anyone else who agrees with him. The tactic of the "defence" was to persuade the synod that adherence to the ancient credal formulae was enough for orthodoxy, knowing that the Bishop of Durham was prepared to declare his adherence to the creeds and thus would escape the theological gallows. That in the event is how it worked. The synod declined to commit itself to a literal interpretation of the virginal conception as the only possible one, or to commit itself likewise to a physical and bodily interpretation of the resurrection, though it seemed had members actually been polled on these points they would have given them a majority.

In Anglican terms, therefore, it is still legitimate to take the liberal view that these doctrines need not refer to historical events according to a literal reading of scripture, but may be true in some other sense. It was also apparent, however, that a majority did not seem to understand what "being true in some other sense" might mean: they merely gave the concept the benefit of the doubt, at least partly because they did not like the intolerant tone of those who were urging them to go much further.

The synod was in fact being intensely traditional in its reticence. There is a principle going back almost to the foundation of Christianity of defining what must be believed as narrowly as possible, and therefore leaving as much as possible outside the scope of formal definitions. Anglicanism has not had much occasion to practise it, for before the creation of the General Synod in 1970 there was no real mechanism for handling doctrinal disputes outside the courts and Parliament.

The principle, still observed in the Roman Catholic Church on those rare occasions when it defines a doctrine, is to make a declaration of what is deemed to be orthodox, and then attach an anathema to anyone who declares the opposite. This is subtly different from making a declaration of what is orthodox, and then demanding that everyone must believe it, which is what the synod was being asked to do. It takes care, above all, of those who do not understand the doctrine in question, and therefore cannot say whether they believe it or not. They may not understand it because they are too simple or ignorant; or they may not understand it because they are intelligent enough to know that all religious doctrines refer to mysteries beyond human comprehension.

It is significant that the Bishop of Durham, who as a theologian will be well aware of this traditional negative way of approaching doctrinal definition, has been careful never to deny an actual physical resurrection or a literal virginal conception. In accordance with the tradition, therefore, he should avoid the anathema, for it only falls on those who contradict, not on those who merely ask questions.

The use of this negative anathema method of defining doctrine has the virtue that it does not stifle further exploration. It has always been accepted as legitimate to ask what a doctrine meant, and to suggest it did not mean what everyone thought it meant. Doctrines – once defined, properly called dogmas – contain religious truths; but the meaning is not always obvious on the surface and has to be extracted before it can be comprehended. This is one of the meanings of the notion of theological reception.

It is a very good question whether a doctrine may also contain a related historical or scientific truth as an adjunct to the religious truth and carrying the same weight, or whether such non-religious truths, even if apparently implied by the doctrine, have to stand on their own feet on the historical or scientific evidence. The doctrine that God created the world, for instance, says nothing about how or when; religion can throw no light on such scientific matters. The area of greatest difficulty concerns the doctrines which surround Jesus Christ, who existed in history. There is at least one doctrine, therefore – the doctrine that Christ existed – which is simultaneously historical and religious, and cannot escape being both. Are there others?

This is precisely where the real issue lies between the Bishop of Durham and his critics. The statement that Christ was raised from the dead on the third day is necessarily a historical statement, in principle at least capable of historical proof or disproof. If a religious doctrine may not say anything outside its own area of competence, and may therefore not make any historical statements about what was or was not the case, then the doctrine of the Resurrection may not mean what it at first appears to mean. It can say nothing about what actually happened; the only part of it that matters to faith is the part that says something religiously, not something historically. The same goes for the doctrine of the virginal conception: the part that matters cannot be the gynaecological part, for religion can say nothing useful about a remote gynaecological event. This approach justifies the Bishop of Durham in saying that he believes in the doctrines of the Incarnation and Resurrection, while reserving his position on "what actually happened". It implies that religion is capable of being an independent realm of meaning and truth, with no need for any grounding on scientific or historical facts (reliance on which could in fact weaken rather than strengthen it).

The eye of strong faith may regard the independent religious realm as the paramount one, and see the detachment of religious truth from scientific or historical "fact" as the separation of what is primary and sure from what is secondary and unproved. That is the Bishop of Durham's (highly dogmatic) position – and if he has erred at all, it has been by imposing an anathema on those who say to the contrary. They too have a case, and in any event they are more numerous and by no means less faithful.

THE PRIESTLY WORK OF THE LAITY

28 October 1989

There is a revealing phrase still commonly used of a young man accepted for ordination in the Church of England. He is said to be "going into the church". Behind that expression lies a whole landscape of attitudes and prejudices, the exploration of which would throw a great deal of light not only on the present condition of the Church of England but of British religion generally.

The exploration has already been started by the publication last week of *Call to Order*, an excellent report of a small committee set up by the Advisory Council for the Church's Ministry. Its most arresting suggestion is that the time has come to dispense with the notion of an almost mystical "inner voice" which calls some to the ordained priesthood. Instead it suggests that call ought to come, quite deliberately and unmysteriously, from the church itself. But the theological context in which it makes that proposal leads to far wider conclusions. It starts with the axiom that the vocation of which Christians speak is universal: a call to everyone to answer the challenge of the Gospel. By no means all who answer will be suitable or needed for ordained ministry, but that does not mean they do not have a perfectly valid vocation to live a Christian life as a lay person. And this is the point at which the theology of *Call to Order* becomes of much more general application. It makes nonsense of the notion behind the term "going into the church".

The traditional attitude, of which the Church of England is by no means the only one guilty, is that only the clergy may really be considered serious about their religious vocation. They are the first-class Christians. The laity are second-class Christians, amateurs, part-timers, the rank and file. And this is confirmed by the special training the clergy receive, the special status they are granted, the exemplary moral life they are supposed to lead, the power in administering the church they share, and the fact that only they are special enough to perform certain special sacred actions. They even look different. The laity, meanwhile, get on with the hunting, shooting and fishing. It is not good for them to be too "religious".

Given this disparity, it is no wonder that many women are clamouring to go "into the church", to get out of the second-class category into the first-class one where the real business is done. And if the distinction between first and second class was valid, so would be their demand for promotion from the lower status to the higher. At the end of the road down which *Call to Order* sets off, however, is a very different world. If "in Christ there is neither Jew nor Greek, male nor female", then neither is there clergy nor laity.

The Church of England has a particular problem here, arising from its origins as an uneasy alliance of high and low, Anglo-Catholic and Evangelical. The Evangelical stresses the "priesthood of all believers" while the Anglo-Catholic stresses the cultic status of the ordained. And each deliberately under-states the other's emphasis. A complete theology would have to contain both. No such complete theology really exists, unfor-tunately, which means that the importance of the insight con-tained in the phrase "priesthood of all believers" has been lost, because the importance of the idea of priesthood has been lost. For an Evangelical it is an empty statement, because of the emptiness of the word priesthood itself. On the Catholic side, not excluding Roman Catholics, the importance of priesthood has been stressed almost exclusively in connection with the status bestowed by ordination. What in theory the priesthood of all believers means to a Catholic is far from clear: but in practice it means "not a priest at all".

The theology is plain enough, however. Baptism is admis-sion to a priestly caste, just as ordination is. Those who are baptized, mere laity though they may be called, have a priestly role. And just as baptism is not only operative in church on Sundays, neither is this baptismal priestliness confined to that special roped-off area behind which the British like to shelter their religion.

A priest's role is to "make the sacred", the Latin for which gives the English word sacrifice. When something is made sacred it is not only dedicated to God but simultaneously offered to Him, which is how the idea of sacrifice has become associated with ritual propitiation. Such ideas need to be dragged out of the sanctuary and into the real world, however. The primary priestly vocation of the church, and therefore of every member of it of whatever designation, is to make the entire world fit as a holy offering to God, as a sacrifice in its literal meaning. That is priestly work; but by and large it is the vocation of the so-called laymen, and some parts of it should definitely be roped off from the intervention of the ordained ministry, whose home territory it is not. Making the world fit as an offering includes all the work which tends towards order and justice, a great deal of which will be political and economic. It is priestly work for lay people, even though the idea just does not exist in the conceptual vocabulary of the vast majority of British Christians.

The repossession by the laity of their priestliness would correct the present severe imbalance between clergy and laity, and would tend to show that the most important priestly work of the church, making the whole world holy, is more proper to lay than to ordained hands, which should be "set apart" for other things. That actual "priests" tend to invade the layman's space from time to time is clear enough from recent controversies, but it is a distorted symbol caused by the unpriesting of the laity. Unless the demarcation is maintained, however, the ordained priest's special priesthood will seem to be just a superior case of the unordained's general priesthood, depriving either of them of any special significance. The relationship between the two remains to be worked out; all that is clear so far is that both are necessary.

This was well illustrated when an assembly of European Roman Catholic clergy spent a week in Britain earlier this year discussing whether and on what terms they might involve the laity in greater collaboration with the priestly work of the clergy, a question becoming fashionable in all the churches. Even to ask such a question was a step forward; but it still deserved a short answer from the laity. Who exactly ought to be knocking at whose door? The real question is whether and on what terms to involve the clergy in the priestly work of the laity.

GARDENING FOR GOD

15 September 1990

The cliché about the enmity between the church and Mrs Thatcher appeared again last week almost as part of the standard rubric of every Church of England report. In 1985, when *Faith in the City* appeared, its critics had a point; it had more than a hint of anti-government rhetoric. But its 1990 sequel, *Faith in the Countryside*, shows the lesson has been learnt.

Whether or not its political observations were well founded, the 1985 report was just not Christian enough. Although the report had a theological chapter, it lacked a clear theological basis. *Faith in the Countryside*, which was published on Tuesday, does have a theological basis. The reflections with which it begins are a succinct, lucid Anglican response to the environmental revolution. But they have much wider ramifications than the present state of rural English society, to which the rest of the report is devoted. They offer a new start to the church's sometimes hostile relationship with the environment, this time a nature-friendly one. The chapter quotes two representatives of the Green movement, Max Nicholson and Jonathon Porritt, who regard Christianity as the arch-enemy of the new Green enlightenment because of its insistence that mankind has an "unqualified right of dominance over nature" (Nicholson), and because of the "central Christian axiom that nature has no reason but to serve man" (Porritt).

The report fully admits the charge, examines the Christian tradition for flaws, and offers an alternative version of the doctrine. Christians are not obliged to run the world for their own exclusive benefit; furthermore, they are not allowed to. This much has been said before, however. What the theology of the environment has lacked so far apart from real theology is any convincing synthesis of the soft bits (the intuitive sense of wonder people feel in the presence of natural beauty) and the hard bits (the doctrine of God as creator and Christ as redeemer).

What has the church to do with protecting the environment, beyond saying that church members should be good citizens and not drop litter? What is missing is the religious eye, seeing the world in the light of faith, how the natural is shot through by the supernatural. It is an intuition which comes to true converts to the Green cause and which explains their almost Buddhist reverence for life and the natural order. Many Christians have lost it or never had it, and some brands of Christianity tell them they do not need it. But the Green reverence for nature can be as ominously anti-human as traditional Christianity has been anti-nature. The theological reflections in *Faith in the Countryside* offer a bridge between the two.

The report argues that God did not give mankind the created world to ruin and plunder, but to tend, as a gardener tends his plot. Love of nature is the instinct implanted by God, urging us towards that care. So, says the report, that instinct is part of a religious (even mystical) bond between mankind and the natural world. Love of nature and love of God are very close. George Herbert's "Providence" is quoted:

> Man is the world's High Priest:
> He doth present
> The sacrifice for all: while they below
> Unto the service mutter an assent,
> Such are springs use that fall, and winds that blow.

The words of a recent world conference on Christianity and the environment say it more prosaically: "The true vocation of the human person is to be the priest of creation, to stand before the creator on behalf of all creation, and in turn to interpret the good intention of the creator to and for all." The term "priest" is at first puzzling, until it is taken back to its original and simple meaning. Then it opens a door.

A priest is one who "makes things sacred" – the literal meaning of sacrifice – and offers them to God, an intercession. Sir Laurens van der Post, in a contribution to this chapter, observes that the feeling of wholeness and healing many people feel from contact with nature in the countryside is frequently expressed in religious language. And studies of the nature of intense religious experiences, incoherent but profound sensations of awe and worship, show how often they are linked to this contact with nature. These experiences are sometimes described as a sense of being close to some great spiritual power, and of being suspended between that presence and the beauty of nature. It is as if some innate sense of the holiness of nature and an innate potential to sacred intercession, priesthood, were struggling to the surface.

This is not the priesthood usually attributed to clergymen, in the narrow tradition, but the universal priesthood of humanity of which Christianity has always had a sense, as in Herbert's poem. It is not cheating to put Herbert's insight alongside van der Post's, though Herbert's deliberate resonance is with the Epistles of St Paul. There, Christ himself is called the High Priest: mankind's participation in priesthood is only possible "by Whom and through Whom all things were made".

Here is a theological key which fits a lock. Adam had a garden, but he spoilt it. Christ, the "second Adam", is the gardener who redeems it. The garden, restored, is the world made well once more, ready to be offered back to its creator, who saw that it was good. We are under-gardeners; we are also the hooligans. It all sounds very simple, very English, green and Christian, as it should.

Part Eight

Whose Fault is it Anyway?

Values in Society

JUST WAR, UNJUST REVOLUTION

15 August 1988

The concept of a "just war" in Christian theology seems to lead logically to the possibility of a "just revolution", but this is not a new idea: St Thomas Aquinas appeared to think as much. Whether Christians may *in extremis* engage in violent subversive activity was a dilemma which exercised the consciences of some who took part in the 1944 bomb plot against Hitler. There is a considerable history, therefore, to the theological issues addressed by the Lambeth Conference in its famous "armed struggle" resolution, which was widely thought to be mainly about South Africa but instead caused a brief storm in Ireland.* It was defended as a valid development of just war theology.

The conference's "understanding" of those who engage in "armed struggle" was conditional upon peaceful means to correct injustice having first been exhausted. It was expressed, as in the theory of just war, as a last resort. There are three other traditional conditions for a war to be deemed just (*jus ad bellum*): a grave and persistent injustice; due proportionality between the damage the war will do and the scale of the injustice; and a reasonable hope of success. There are also conditions attached to the way such a war must be conducted (*jus in bello*), which have found their way from medieval theology into

---

* On 4 August the Conference approved a clause saying it "understood" those who resort to armed struggle when other means for correcting injustice failed.

modern international law in the form of Conventions protecting the rights of prisoners and civilians.

But these conditions for a just war by no means meet the case of violent subversion or revolution. War is between states, and states have a prima facie legitimacy and status, whereas revolutionaries by definition do not. Thus a state may engage in a just war, but who is to say who may engage in a just revolution? Unless it is truly a mass uprising (on behalf of society as a whole), the moral status of a revolutionary movement is bound to be very questionable. The only standing it has is the standing it awards itself. From outside it is indistinguishable from a violent criminal conspiracy, albeit with a political rather than financial objective.

Conventional warfare is fundamentally about armed conflict for the possession and control of space, military contest aimed at replacing one sort of political and social order by another. Revolutionary struggles rarely have such geographical simplicity, and are not about substituting order but destroying it, at least as a means if not an end.

The common analogy with the self-evident morality of the French Resistance in the Second World War therefore breaks down, for though the Resistance had many of the appearances of a revolutionary struggle, its fundamental purpose was to aid conventional armies in their more orthodox measures to wrest control of space from the enemy. The regime against which it was directed was ultimately to be toppled not by subversion or terrorism, but by pitched battle and conquest. This gave it the moral legitimacy of conventional just war, and also established clearly the moral status of the combatants, as agents and representatives of states at war. Revolutionaries have no such positive purpose or status.

The nature of "armed struggle" is also morally problematical, even leaving aside the inevitable contravention of "Thou shalt not kill." When nations make war they aim to prevail by military force, using soldiers, tanks, aircraft and warships against the other side's similar men and equipment. Civilians simply get in the way. But revolutions are nowadays conducted according to sophisticated theories of which the intimidation by terrorism of the civilian population always forms an essential part.

The fundamental flaw in the Lambeth Conference proviso, that peaceful and democratic means have first to be exhausted, is that revolutionary movements deliberately make it their first aim to render such normal political life impossible, so that "armed struggle" is the only way left. They seek the breakdown of social order, for instance, by engaging systematically in terrorist activities in order to provoke the security forces of the state to violations of human rights, thereby alienating the civilian population from the government. They privately welcome the suspension of democratic freedoms and the principles of the rule of law in the name of security for the same reason.

The alienation and polarization of the community is therefore an essential part of any campaign of "armed struggle" if it is to succeed. It is done by propaganda, intimidation and coercion, by the undermining of public confidence and by planned terrorism. But by attacking order in society "armed struggle" creates anarchy and breaks down civilization itself, which must gradually revert to barbarism. In the name of opposition to injustice, it ultimately makes all justice impossible (except "revolutionary justice"), for justice requires a social order. It cannot hope, therefore, to pass the just war test of proportionality. Any state faced with such "armed struggle" will take appropriate measures, which include collecting information and intelligence. For those engaged in such "armed struggle", the existence of informers in the civilian population has to be met by intimidation and ultimately by assassination.

So in all these ways it is in the nature of "armed struggle" that it is widened to include those very non-combatants that in just war theory must be left at peace. They become in fact the battlefield, the "territory" to be fought over and controlled. But by this stage, "armed struggle" will have lost all touch with the concept of a just war.

Thus the theory of a just revolution remains only a theory. For the paradox is that the only kind of "armed struggle" likely to succeed, thereby meeting the last of the four conditions for a just war – reasonable chance of success – is one conducted ruthlessly according to these principles. Anyone playing by the rules will fail; but anyone not playing by the rules does not deserve to win.

PRACTICES MADE IMPERFECT:
Professional ethics

15 April 1989

In their resistance to the Lord Chancellor's proposals for reforming the legal profession, judges and barristers have been confronting the same issues that have been preoccupying the churches in their dealings with the Government over the last ten years. It is at root a philosophical and a moral conflict. The Government's commitment to the principle of the free market necessarily commits it to the progressive elimination of what it sees as restrictive practices, which are obstacles to the operation of market forces. If market forces are good, then restrictive practices are bad.

In this respect the dockers, the doctors and the barristers are in the same boat; the clergy would be too, except there is not the slightest chance that the Government would be so daft or bold as to refer the Church of England to the Monopolies Commission. But the dockers, the doctors and the barristers (and the clergy) see these same restrictive practices not as damaging to the public interest but as protecting important values which serve the public interest.

Restrictive practices serve to define the boundaries of a community of workers, professional or otherwise, by specifying what the conditions are for joining it, or for being made to leave it after a transgression. Inside such a community these practices exist to sustain an ethos peculiar to that community, a localized sense of right and wrong usually described as a professional ethic. It does not necessarily always correspond to common morality based on the Judaeo-Christian tradition: for instance, there is no sin committed against that tradition by a solicitor who advertises his services, as was held to be contrary to the ethic of the legal profession until recently. There is no sin committed when a barrister appears in court without a wig. But these ethical codes, which are often more implicit than explicit, do also incorporate most of the main points of the Judaeo-Christian tradition. A doctor is not supposed to commit adultery with a patient; a solicitor is not supposed to steal money from a client.

These professional values are maintained and passed on by being embedded in the culture of the community in question. The ultimate sanction is professional disgrace, a secular version of excommunication. The rituals and customs of the community are directed towards the continual reinforcement of the collective ethos, which eventually begins to shape the very personality of its members. They are morally formed by it.

Such an ethos can gradually become corrupt, however, its restrictive practices used to rig the market for the benefit of a privileged elite, and a profession then begins to take on the character of a conspiracy against the public. It is a key question whether such an ethos, to stay healthy, needs a common basis in religious morality; and whether, therefore, the secular drift away from religion since the war has pulled away the carpet.

In any event, the Government does not appear to have much confidence in the concept of a professional ethos, and probably most of the public do not either. An ethos requires a particular community which shares and upholds it; and the Government has a bias towards individualism, regarding the idea of "community" as not much more than a sentimental evasion.

The alternative conception, which has caused such ructions at the English Bar, is that the barriers and defences round such communities should be torn down in the name of competition, which has the additional advantage that it is likely to be more efficient in delivering the goods. In this view, the task of maintaining minimum professional standards has to be undertaken not by peer-group pressure and unwritten codes, but by regulatory bodies backed by law and supervised by government, applying detailed published rules. Each individual is alone with his rule book; and the question "How far can I go?" is answered not by the fear of shame among professional companions but by the risk of being caught and published. The sanction of the old way is a turned back; but of the new, a heavy fine.

The supreme example of the old way is not the Bar but the Church. Churches of all denominations nourish their ethos as a precious treasure, and pay lip service at least (much more than that in most cases) to the principle that the collective beliefs of the church as a community even have the guarantee of divine sanction. Their sacraments and rituals are essential to the sustenance of those beliefs. There is virtually no free market inside a church, unless it be the competition between cathedral appeals for royal patronage. They are hierarchical, even those which pretend they are not; they are rife with what in secular terms are restrictive practices.

Churches are particularly quick to detect those values which are held collectively in secular communities; and they are usually themselves a primary source of those values. They are particularly unlikely, therefore, to sympathize with or even understand what the present Government is about. And they do not face the question whether a decline in religious faith can undermine a collective ethos, for theirs is proof against it. But if a collective ethos has turned against the public interest, and is no longer supporting good behaviour but elitist privilege, then the public interest is not served by defending restrictive practices but by supplanting them by a system of discipline which works, answerable to an authority located outside that community. And the reproach will inevitably be heard that those doing the supplanting do not trust the community to uphold its own standards, and are, in effect, treating that community as having no real value. That will be painful news for those who still "believe" in that community, for whom it is their mother and father.

The general drift of moral fashion in British society is largely in this direction, with the national community as a whole relying more and more on the law to tell it what it may or may not do, less and less on an explicit and implicit national ethos founded on the Judaeo-Christian tradition. Ultimately the final arbiters of the difference between legal and illegal, hence between right and wrong, will be Members of Parliament who make the law, and the judges who interpret it. That makes the prospect of a clash between the two all the more poignant and ironic.

FAITH, HOPE AND HONESTY

5 November 1988

Churchgoers are much more likely to behave honestly than non-churchgoers, according to the fifth report on British social attitudes published by Social and Community Planning Research last week.

The survey devised various hypothetical cases to put to the sample, rather as in a game of Scruples, such as whether they would keep £5.00 given them in change by mistake. If it was given in a corner shop, 13 per cent of men and eight per cent of women would keep it rather than hand it back. If it was given in a large store, 28 per cent of men and 20 per cent of women would keep it. But among weekly churchgoers, only one per cent would keep it in a corner shop, six per cent in a large store.

The same distinction was found when the case was posed of £100.00 found lying in the street. Only 11 per cent of weekly churchgoers said they would pocket the money, compared with twice that number in the general population. Those with no religion were, by every measure, the least honest. All those who have argued that religion is good for society, that secularization is undermining the moral fabric of the nation, and that the churches have a unique ability to correct some of the more worrying tendencies towards dishonesty, will therefore claim to be vindicated.

But this would be too easy: a statistical correlation does not prove cause and effect. Both churchgoing and honesty could be effects of some other separate cause; or honesty could be the cause of churchgoing and not the other way round, though that at first sight seems implausible. But someone who knows himself to be the sort of person who would hang on to the money may not want to compound his guilt by pretending to a finer moral character than he deserves.

One of the most persistent attitudes towards churchgoing, among those who do not go, is that one has to be good to go to church – even that to go to church is to stake a public claim to goodness. Churchgoing is associated with respectability; and despite the well-advertised fact that Christianity is for sinners rather than for saints, there is a widespread perception that churchgoers are especially moral or at least pretend to be. There is even a streak of integrity in such attitudes among non-churchgoers, a refusal to appear hypocritical in their own eyes, although their feelings are based on a false premise about whom and what the church is for. Few clergy will have failed to come across individuals who half-apologize for not attending church, on the grounds that they do not think they are good enough.

If churchgoers' answers to the questions are at all to be believed, the survey refutes the suspicion of hypocrisy against churchgoers: they really do behave better. Even those who go to church less than once a week but more than once a month behave better, though less better.

It is very difficult, nevertheless, to separate cause and effect. The most common misconception of Christianity in Britain today is that it is about "salvation by good works", the doctrine named Pelagianism after a characteristically British heretic of the time of St Augustine. Those who believe that that is what the church stands for will certainly equate it with respectability: and, as in some recent hints dropped by Government ministers, will regard the spreading of civic virtue as the church's primary duty. The opposing and orthodox doctrine, salvation by grace, dismisses any possibility that a person may earn a ticket to heaven by good behaviour. But though these two ideas look very different, they have got terribly tangled and confused, not just in the public mind but in the churches too.

The churches which ought from their Protestant background to be closest to pure salvation by grace, such as Low Church Anglicanism and the Free Churches, have in fact become the ones with the strongest image of straitlaced respectability. There is a substantial tinge of Pelagianism in the Protestant Ethic. On the other hand the Roman Catholic Church, traditionally accused by Protestants of believing in salvation by good works, is a good deal less "respectable" and judging from the proportion in the prison population, it has a higher ratio of sinners. But Pelagianism creeps in there too, particularly through the persistence of Jansenism, the Catholic form of Puritanism, which planted the idea that only the super-pious had any hope of salvation.

The influences of the churches on their members is by no means confined to the doctrines they teach officially. As social communities, they are also rife with peer group pressures and homespun traditions which may be at odds with the official view, or relics of the issues of the past. Those oral traditions of the common folk always seem to tend in the direction of Pelagianism and respectability. Free Church members continue to disapprove, by and large, of disrespectable things like alcohol and gambling, though they have long since lost touch with that bottom section of the population for which these were the besetting sins. Catholic culture still has its idea of the "good Catholic", and the tenacious but fallacious belief that Holy Communion must always be preceded by Confession otherwise one is not good enough to receive the Sacrament.

It is as if the doctrine of totally gratuitous salvation is hard to grasp or too good to be true, while salvation by good works seems simple and logical, and like everything else worthwhile in life, has to be earned. But it is the heresy that is closest to common sense orthodoxy that confounds it. So while the churches ought not to worry that their regular attenders are more honest than the rest of the population, they ought to worry why they are. For if it is because of the hidden influence of "common sense" Pelagianism, they should pause before they congratulate themselves: *c'est magnifique, mais ce n'est pas le Christianisme.*

A QUESTION OF HUMAN VALUES

10 December 1988

British society is becoming self-conscious about its "values", what they ought to be, whether they are in decline, whether anything can be done about it if they are, and whose fault it is anyway. Two instances of this preoccupation have just appeared in print: an article in the December edition of *The Director* by its deputy editor, Carol Kennedy; and the summary of a recent Ditchley Foundation conference by Tony Thomas, assistant editor of *The Economist*, published in last week's *The Tablet*.

Mrs Margaret Thatcher is invariably cited on both sides of the argument, as the best and worst thing that has ever happened to British values. Ms Kennedy's project was to interview more than a dozen men and women prominent in the law, business, the academic world and such spheres; and the Ditchley conference was attended by similar distinguished persons, some from abroad. In each case the natural point of focus seemed to be the impact of free market economics on traditional British morality and way of life; and there is clearly no consensus, except the simple one that things are changing.

Not everyone believes they are changing for the worse, and *The Director* found businessmen who disputed the more general view that business ethics has been a major casualty of the last decade. There have always been scoundrels, so their argument goes, and always will be; meanwhile "Thatcherism" has improved the nation's economic performance so the country can now afford to do what it could not otherwise have done, including such morally desirable objectives as looking after the less fortunate.

214

Some accept the latter but not the former: saying there has been a decline, but it is nothing to do with government policy. This shades into the view that the decline is connected with government policy, which is nevertheless right because things could not go on as they were. And to the left of that – left in the sense that that is the position Mr Neil Kinnock adopted in his "No number other than one" speech at the Labour Party Conference – is the view that the country's values are in decline precisely as a result of government policy. The most extreme view, only hinted at both in *The Tablet* and *The Director*, is that Thatcherism is the product and symptom of moral decline, not the cause.

The Government's view appears to be that there is indeed a decline, not, of course, caused by government policy; but that it is beyond the competence of governments, as such, to correct it. Religious institutions figure prominently among those regarded as competent and ought to be doing more. This is not, however, echoed in any of the views reported either in *The Tablet* or *The Director*, except for the remark reported in the former that in the United States "the Ten Commandments had become the Ten Suggestions".

The Government's hopes that the churches might lead a revival of national moral fibre is curiously paralleled in the Soviet Union, according to this year's BBC Reith Lecturer, Professor Geoffrey Hosking. He is not optimistic about the chances in Russia. And in Britain the churches know no better way of converting Britain back to Christianity than the one they have been trying, without too much success. If they have not yet succeeded in reversing their own downward trend, in numbers, they are hardly likely to succeed in reversing the nation's, in values.

There are more possibilities than those explored in *The Director* and *The Tablet* which could describe the fascinating relationship between Thatcherism and moral decline. One is that the nation votes for Margaret Thatcher because it perceives the moral decline, and sees her as part of the solution (even if she does not do so herself). Another is that there is a more fundamental shift, of which moral decline and Thatcher-

215

ism are both symptoms. And given that governments have to stand for election, there is bound to be some temptation to appeal to baser instincts, the "You've never had it so good' syndrome. But this Government did not invent it; nor are Opposition parties free from it.

What these two studies both lack is much in the way of remedy. The Ditchley participants seemed to be tending towards more government regulation to raise the standard of business ethics; and *The Director*'s leading figures had some expectations that education and communication might be the answer. The problem with the imposition of standards by statute is that all that is not illegal comes to be regarded as moral, and individual moral responsibility escapes out of the window. The problem with moral education is that somebody somewhere has to decide what standards are to be taught or communicated: education is a method, not a code.

One surprising omission among all these leaders of opinion is that no one suggested that good leadership and example were part of the remedy (though some thought bad leadership was part of the cause). That could also be why they omitted religion from their diagnoses and prescriptions. Their models of society and how it frames its values were largely mechanistic and impersonal, and generally also economic in thrust: as if an alteration in basic tax rates or the privatization of gas were crucial in determining whether people behaved morally or not. That is a surrender to behaviourism, to sociology and to Karl Marx. We can't help the way we are: it is someone else's fault. In a free market climate which is supposed to be all about choice, that is decidedly paradoxical.

And that could point to one other factor in the moral decline they were all trying to comment on, a factor also apparent in a lot of what was said about it: a note of fatalism. Fatalist philosophies are undoubtedly in vogue, whether by virtue of Freud, astrology or reincarnation; or the belief that "inevitable" economic trends determine public and private morality. If it is true, it gives the lie to religion. It is a pity they were not asked directly about that.

Taking a Charitable View

17 June 1989

The Government appears to have decided against immediate legislation to deprive such bodies as the Unification Church (the "Moonies") of the privileges of charitable status, in spite of pressure from backbench MPs to do so.

The Home Office White Paper on charity law published last month did not enter the difficult area of definition, but was mainly aimed at tightening up measures against fraud. Some MPs raised the omission with the Home Secretary, Mr Douglas Hurd, but he merely agreed to take into account views which had been expressed when legislation was being drafted. Further work on these more fundamental questions will be necessary before there is anything like a consensus, and it may well prove completely elusive.

It is clearly not acceptable to public opinion that an extreme cult or sect, operating in ways which are manifestly detrimental to the public interest, should nevertheless be entitled to the rich financial benefits of charitable status simply because they are, in the broadest terms, religious. A private member's resolution urging that the Moonies should be deprived of charitable status is currently on the agenda of the General Synod of the Church of England and when it comes forward for debate there is little doubt the general sentiment will receive overwhelming support.

But it is one thing to single out a particular religious body as undesirable and unworthy of the public support which charitable status implies; but quite another to frame a general law which could be trusted to separate the sheep from the goats. The present charity law, which dates back to the time of Elizabeth I, is based on the assumption that certain areas of activity are automatically deemed to be beneficial, and religion is one of them. In the sixteenth century, however, it was thought acceptable to ban religious bodies which were regarded as against the public (or state) interest, and to persecute those who held unapproved beliefs. Had the Moonies existed then, they would have been deprived of charitable status by being tied to a stake and burnt.

Those religious bodies and beliefs which were not illegal, namely those which could be accommodated within the comprehensiveness of the religion established by law, were taken to be for the public good. So in effect it was the Church of England, through its exercise of discipline over the religious life of the nation in the ecclesiastical courts, that decided which activities and bodies were to be allowed and therefore which were entitled to benefit from charitable status. The remainder were illegal.

If a religious activity was tolerated, it was assumed to be beneficial. But in the twentieth century all religious activity is tolerated unless it impinges on the criminal law; and therefore all religious activity is by the same token assumed by the law to be beneficial. To benefit from charitable status in the twentieth century, therefore, a body has only to show that it is working for the advancement of anything that could be called religion. There is no attempt at regulation.

In the present climate it is not conceivable that Parliament would pass a law listing those religions and religious bodies which it thought were for the public interest, and therefore should have charitable status. It is hardly less conceivable that Parliament would delegate such a tricky task to any other body, giving it statutory criteria to apply. Such criteria would in any case be impossible to frame. It does not follow, however, that such an exercise would necessarily be against the right to freedom of religion as protected by the European Convention of Human Rights. For religious groups not approved for the purposes of charitable status would still be free to operate at will. There is no requirement under the Human Rights Convention that religious bodies should be exempt from taxation, which is the principle material advantage of charitable status, nor that they should all be treated equally. Neither does English law insist that all religions have to be treated equally;

on the contrary the Church of England enjoys various privileges not granted to the other denominations and faiths.

The objections to the state regulation of religion lie elsewhere, and rest on the principle that one man's meat is another man's poison. In general there is a tendency in human nature to treat all religious beliefs, except one's own, as intellectually untenable and morally harmful. This shows itself in an extreme form when the belief in question demands a high degree of commitment and unusual forms of conduct. But it all depends where one stands. Devout Roman Catholic parents might well be delighted by a daughter's decision to enter a convent; a Free Presbyterian family would regard it as the worst disaster imaginable. The behaviour which would be regarded as correct by the Moonie parents of a Moonie child would outrage the staunch Church of England parents of a similar child.

The principal objection to the Unification Church, often heard also about other cults, concerns allegations of "brainwashing". Associated with it is the emotional and physical separation of an adolescent or young adult from the family. These factors combine to create the phenomenon of "deprogramming", a psychological technique designed to pressurize a cult member back to normality. Deprogramming is sometimes offered at considerable cost by so-called experts to distressed parents who understandably want their child returned to the bosom of the family.

There is a vast literature on the subject, particularly in America, where both these highly coloured expressions originate. But "brainwashing" has eluded clear scientific definition, and seems to refer to almost any sudden deep moral and ideological conversion of which the observer disapproves. It is based on the assumption that there is such a thing as a genuine religious conversion, and a false kind; and so there may be, but it has not proved possible to say exactly where the difference lies. Deprogramming, on the other hand, is often just as severe a psychological dislocation as the original conversion, and may indeed be closer to what is described by the word brainwashing. Such concepts rest on cultural assumptions of what is meant by religious normality, and these assumptions are relative. To make them the basis of legal distinctions between one religion or another is to turn them into absolutes, which is not a step a free and tolerant society should regard with equanimity.

AN ABSOLUTELY IMPOSSIBLE QUESTION:
Human embryos

12 August 1989

The Government's intention to introduce legislation concerning experiments on human embryos next session will revive an uncomfortable and confused public argument that last broke out after the publication of the Warnock report in 1984. It seemed to be a conflict between those who believe in the existence of moral absolutes – actions which are always wrong – and those who believe the rightness of an act will always depend on the circumstances. But it was not quite so simple.

The embryo issue is an offshoot of the more general abortion debate. In both cases the "absolutists" and the "relativists" exist in religious and secular clothes. Both positions can be traced back to largely religious roots, but are nowadays more often presented and supported as self-sufficient, even self-evident, and free of religious foundations.

Most people are absolutists on some issues, relativists on others, without any consciousness of philosophical inconsistency. The most useful argument about embryo research, therefore, is not which position is true and which false, but which principle should apply in this case. A further complication is that fashion in moral language has changed to the extent that both sides tend to translate their demands in terms of absolute rights "right to life", "woman's right to choose", and so on. It appears both sides are claiming to be absolutist, hoping to over-trump the other.

In a country equally influenced by Protestantism and Catholicism in the formation of its culture these two contemporary moral approaches can be traced back to one of these two sources. The common law, with its medieval origins, carries on the Catholic absolutist strand. Common sense, the practical judgement of ordinary people, is closer to the subjective moral intuition of Protestantism. Anglican ethics at its best has tried to do justice to both traditions; at its worst, it has had the worst of both worlds.

The relativist, common sense or Protestant approach accepts as a fact of life that there are certain circumstances in which it is necessary to make a choice between evils. Thus causing the death of a foetus is bad: insisting that a woman must bear a child after rape is bad; there is nothing to do but stand back, draw a deep breath, and choose whichever seems the lesser evil.

The absolutist, common law or Catholic approach asserts that it is never right to do evil that good may come of it: ends cannot justify means. So the good of sparing a woman the consequences of rape cannot be achieved by the evil of destroying the foetus she has conceived.

There are times when the rigour of the absolutist position is ameliorated by what is called the principle of double effect. It proposes that an evil secondary effect, provided it is not intended, can sometimes be excused for a greater good, the primary effect. Thus the unintentional but predictable killing of civilians in warfare is not murder. But deliberate killing, for instance driving civilians through a minefield to clear a path for troops, would be.

This is a case where almost everyone would claim to be an absolutist: no one would dare propose that ultimate victory, liberation from tyranny, even the closing down of a death camp, could justify such an atrocity. Almost everyone would be an absolutist, too, concerning the sexual abuse of children and the very concept of "abuse", suggesting that the immoral character of the act is innate, is a clue to its basis in the theory of natural law.

221

The distinctively Catholic concept of natural law was abandoned by the Protestant reformers following Luther, who denied that human reasoning alone could tell right from wrong. Furthermore moral theology in medieval Catholicism was preoccupied with the classification of various sins according to their gravity, and virtues according to their degree of merit. This arose out of the need to instruct priests in the conduct of the confessional and in the giving of appropriate penances, but was attacked by Luther as implying that salvation could be earned by personal effort. Following his principle of "salvation by faith alone" Luther taught that man's nature was so utterly depraved and corrupt that no good act could have merit in the eyes of God: all virtues scored zero, as did all vices. But Luther also believed that the righteous, once saved by faith alone, would henceforth be impelled to act righteously by a kind of instinct or intuition.

The natural law theory he rejected claimed not only that some acts were intrinsically wrong, but that the fact of their wrongness could be deduced intelligently by examining the act itself. Post-Lutheran Protestant moral theology, no longer able to find the source of the evil in the act itself, sought it instead in its consequences. Thus two acts could be compared according to their results, and a righteous man could be left to make the choice of the less harmful, the more "loving". But it is hard to see how anyone else could criticize such a subjective choice, while the natural law or absolutist approach offers an objective standard everyone can appeal to.

People no longer see themselves as beholden to medieval Catholicism or German Protestantism for the way they reach their moral conclusions: so they are free to decide which form of moral calculus is the more appropriate for analysing the morality of embryo experimentation.

In dealing with post-natal life, both the law and popular opinion still insist on an absolutist approach. One may not kill one's great aunt for her millions even to spend every penny on relieving famine in Ethiopia, although that may well be the lesser of two evils. But in dealing with the earlier stages of pre-natal life, popular opinion has tended towards relativism:

222

abortion up to a certain limit has become acceptable even to save a young woman's career. What has vanished, of course, is Luther's insistence on "salvation by faith alone" before making such decisions: nowadays everyone is presumed righteous.

At the heart of the annual Parliamentary argument about lowering the absolute 28-week limit on abortion is a very curious thing, therefore: it is about the stage in the pregnancy at which people want to switch from moral relativism to moral absolutism, from the Protestant track to the Catholic track, from "the lesser of two evils" to "the end never justifies the means". It will be even more curious if, as is by no means impossible, Parliament opts for moral absolutism in dealing with the first 14 days of foetal life, by banning all such experiments without exception.

NOT JUST BLACK AND WHITE

26 May 1990

Nothing will more undermine the efforts to make Britain a racially fair society than confusion between race, culture and religion. The two false categories responsible for the confusion are "ethnic" and "black", both American imports which do not work here. In Britain, the principal element in the definition of ethnicity is race – meaning in this context "non-white" – but language, country of national origin, social custom and religious belief are also embraced by the word.

In response to the influx of people from the West Indies and the Indian sub-continent it was deemed necessary in the 1970s to make it unlawful to stir up animosity against them, or to treat them individually less fairly than the indigenous white population. The focus was unmistakably on skin-colour; the moral argument was that it was outrageous to relegate a group of people to second-class status because of mere pigmentation.

In its American context, ethnicity refers not mainly to skin-colour, but to all the characteristics of the many cultural groups. Most of the American ethnic minorities are white Europeans; here, ethnicity is a euphemism for colour. But as talk of "ethnicity" has replaced talk about "race" the outlawing of racial discrimination has gradually been extended to all ethnic discrimination. This change of terms was originally intended to prevent circumvention of the discrimination laws by reference to related non-racial characteristics. It seemed necessary to make it unlawful to say "turban-wearers need not apply"; but this ignored the fact that turbans are worn for religious, not racial, reasons.

Those communities which derive from the Indian sub-continent define themselves under many headings. Religion would be one of the first, skin-colour one of the last. But discrimination strictly on the grounds of religion or culture is not illegal. So to avail themselves of anti-discrimination legislation, these groups had to make use of the law's definition of them according to skin-colour. The gradual substitution of ethnicity for race brought within the anti-discrimination laws matters which were much more important to them than skin-colour. In the process, however, the moral basis of the anti-discrimination legislation has been undermined.

All reasonable people accept that skin-colour is an accidental characteristic which ought not to be the basis for important decisions affecting individuals. But the other components in the ethnic package language in particular might well be proper grounds for discrimination, for they are similar to the reasons for choices ordinary people make every day, with no racial motivation. Members of ethnic minorities certainly think so themselves. It is perverse to treat such discrimination as morally or legally equivalent to colour discrimination, or to argue that anyone exercising a cultural preference is individually racist, or that society is thereby structurally racist.

The decent instincts of ordinary people are by no means the same as the judgements drawn from some tendentious ideological analyses of race relations. The analysts have devised a primary sociological determinant called "black" and invested it with elements of Marxist class-struggle. And although it has wide currency among non-Marxists, the concept is inexplicable without the ideological context, and probably in itself racist. Regarding as "black" someone with only one grandparent of African origin, for instance, is dangerously evocative of South African or Nazi doctrines of racial purity. Recruiting such people as automatic *ex officio* members of the struggling proletariat may be less offensive, but is no less questionable. Such classifications are dangerous whether they judge white or black to be beautiful. There can be no surprise if this ideological treatment of race relations finds deep structural white racism everywhere. Race is crucial, says the theory; everyone is a racist.

Since this is a Marxist analysis, it does not consider religion at all. Only recently and thanks largely, though unintentionally, to Salman Rushdie have people recognized the absurdity of treating British Muslims as if their primary characteristic were the similarity of their skin-colour to that of West Indians (a similarity apparent only to those with white skins), when British Muslims themselves insist that their determining characteristic is their faith. More and more Asians, Muslims and others, now reject the term "black".

"Black" was a white label, adopted by the people to whom it was applied. They did not realize its dangers, probably because the people applying the label seemed to be on their side. In the peculiar American context in which the concept first arose, pride in blackness was devised as an antidote to shame about blackness; but both attitudes assumed that skin-colour was the one crucial element of personal identity. So the American race relations problem was defined in a way which was inherently insoluble, and which made all attempted solutions likely to exacerbate it. Fortunately this is a mistake Britain can now avoid, for the conflict between Rushdie and the Muslim community has come just in time to explode the myths of British race relations ideology.

HOTBEDS OF HATRED

9 June 1990

No one seems to know how to make a bad person good. Many a parent of errant youth has agonized into the night, and many a theory has shaped world history according to the truth or otherwise of its answers. The Home Office is agonizing afresh over the problem in the wake of the Strangeways riot, as the inquiry under Lord Justice Woolf gradually turns into a practical and philosophical examination of the basis of British penal policy. The Woolf inquiry may become a landmark in social history, for by its attitudes towards its deviants and law-breakers, a society defines its attitudes towards itself. These attitudes are overdue for re-evaluation.

Britain imprisons a higher proportion of its population, in worse conditions, than almost any other country in Europe. It is not an attractive self-image. Public opinion is more vengeful and vindictive towards criminals than elsewhere, but this may not be because the British are a more unforgiving people by temperament – the evidence suggests otherwise – but because they know no alternative that works, and despair of finding one. The most primitive response to infringement of a social code is the infliction of suffering to gratify the baser instincts. People will always fall back on this if they lack faith in anything more sophisticated.

Penal policy reflects the moral philosophy on which the cohesion of the nation is founded. Unmistakably, most of the key elements in that philosophy as it has been received here from past generations come from the Christian doctrine of sin and redemption. Few races are as theologically illiterate as the British, and one of the consequences is that we have lost touch with the roots of our moral culture. If we cannot remember how it was supposed to work, we certainly cannot analyse and adapt it. But few nations can match Britain in thinking of the

226

past as a foreign country, and our abandonment of the old religious world-view goes a long way to explain this cultural bafflement.

The medieval system of justice, heavily reliant on the theology of scholasticism, believed that suffering balanced the scales of justice, so restoring the social equilibrium. This was the public dimension, the proper business of the state. Suffering was also thought to have redemptive qualities, as in the concept of penance, and this was the private dimension, the proper work of the church. The due suffering would, it was thought, not only balance the books, but reform the moral character of the culprit. Protestantism emphasized the idea that suffering would heighten the individual's awareness of his dependence on God, and this revelation of one's moral wretchedness was supposed to lead to radical conversion from sin. Thus it was appropriate to treat such people wretchedly, to bring home the lesson. Though now without the underlying Protestant theology of redemption, this approach to the treatment of prisoners still applies. Deliberate humiliation is as important a part of the present penal system as depriving people of liberty.

Strangeways, when built, exemplified the social theories of its time, heavily laced with Nonconformist puritanism. Those values have persisted: the ritual stripping of personal clothing, possessions and title conveys a powerful psychological message of worthlessness. Even the notorious practice of slopping out underlines the denial of dignity, and hence powerlessness, of the prisoner. The message he was once intended to draw from this treatment was that he is nothing because God is all. The message he now derives from it is that he is nothing, and that is all. It is a message of hopelessness.

Penal practice has also developed an *ad hoc* system of social control by means of rewards and punishments, so that good behaviour gains privileges, and ultimately, early release. Though it sounds Pavlovian, this system is designed to appeal to the prisoner's rational self-interest rather than his conditioned reflexes, and it stems from the need to contain and control an otherwise unmanageable community of prisoners. It owes little to any philosophical insight into the cultivation of virtue and suppression of vice, and even a model prisoner may leave prison more corrupted than when he entered it. Suffering can have a transforming power, but there is no simple connection between cause and effect. Humiliation is a well-known religious technique, for it can transform the personality, but equally it can destroy the personality altogether.

Penal policy should move in the other direction, based on realistic psychological theories, not reliant on theological premises no longer generally believed. Modern theory (and theology) concerning character development emphasizes the need to give people control over their lives, to reinforce rather than undermine personal dignity, so that the capacity to behave responsibly can grow. Those who are loved may learn to love; those denied love learn only how to hate.

The British penal system says very loudly and clearly that those who do time are outcasts from the human community and have given up the right to dignity. The new message should be the very opposite: that even those who have infringed grievously have not extinguished all that is of value in themselves. Above all, that small streak of human worth must be preserved and nurtured until it outweighs the rest. Those who have never experienced proper treatment before should experience it in prison. That way, now, lies redemption.

PEACE MEN IN WAR ZONE

11 August 1990

The day war broke out or shortly after, according to folk memory, people started flocking to church to pray for deliverance from perils. Yet this folk memory is a myth: the two world wars did more damage to church attendance than decades of peace damage from which the churches never recovered. At the end of the First World War, the churches engaged in a good deal of soul-searching over their performance. But it was not until 1978, in *The Church of England and the First World War* by Alan Wilkinson, that a comprehensive examination of the phenomenon appeared. Wilkinson, himself ordained, concluded that Christian teaching as presented in peacetime had been utterly inadequate to cope with the horrors of war, particularly after the decimation of Kitchener's "people's army" on the Somme.

For many, perhaps in a sense for the whole nation, the First World War was a decisive step away from Christianity, at least from its Edwardian certainties. People compared what they had seen and heard in church, at first or second hand, with what they had seen and heard on the battlefield or in the homes of widows and orphans, and they could not reconcile the two. Christianity and reality seemed to be mutually exclusive.

The horror of war was of course a deep shock to the whole culture of the nation, not just its religious dimension, and Wilkinson made a profound point about its impact on language. He referred to the "inhibition" others had noted about the use of expansive or eloquent language, which may have been a symptom of deep psychological disillusionment in the aftermath of war. As the inhibition deepened subsequently, "so it has now become very difficult to mint a convincing contemporary language to encompass love of country, religious belief or tragedy (for example); hence our problem in finding a genuine language for the liturgy or for translation of the Bible, and the tendency to fall back on an uneasy pastiche".

It would be wrong to single out the First World War as having a uniquely devastating effect on the religious view of the world, however, for the very different experience of the Second World War had a similar effect on church attendance and membership. The feeling of senselessness that gradually overtook the country after 1916 hardly surfaced during the Second World War, yet that conflict also saw a flight from religion. In both wars, church attendance was down from the outset, and not merely the result of war-weariness.

After each war there was some recovery by the churches,

but not nearly enough to make good the losses. And it is not irrelevant that service in the armed forces brought millions of men into contact with church chaplains and religious worship for the first time in their adult lives. Not for want of a captive audience did the church fail to make its mark. Nor was it a particularly Anglican failure. According to *Churches and Church-goers* by Currie, Gilbert and Horsley (published in 1977), which is still the only study of its kind, Nonconformist numbers were proportionately down.

Yet this backing away from religious practice in war may have been a profound tribute to Christianity, and to the moral integrity of the British. Though in both wars church leaders were emphatic in their support for the war effort, people knew in their heart of hearts that Christianity was a religion of peace. The pious patriotism of church sentiment between 1914 and 1918 did nothing to earn the public's lasting respect, though the same public might have been very angry if the churches had preached surrender.

Popular piety often exaggerated the idea of "gentle Jesus meek and mild", the almost androgynous Christ of parlour prints, but any honest reading cannot regard the New Testament as a manual of war. In wartime the churches find it extremely difficult to find anything to say that makes true Christian sense: they cannot advise turning the other cheek, letting the enemy in, which seems closest to their peacetime ethos; nor can they revise their image of Jesus by making him a machinegun-toting Rambo. So they cannot urge less killing and they cannot urge more killing. Although it makes no philosophical sense to say so, in war people prefer to think of Christianity as suspended for the duration, something to get back to when times are easier and life is less nasty. They are not taken in by churchmen who tell them nothing has changed, God loves them. In war, God is on trial, judgement suspended.

Those who take part in war, suffer war guilt. Killing the enemy they can accept as uncomfortably necessary, but to kill the enemy and then go to church for Christian worship is to make the discomfort that bit more acute. Some conflicts of conscience hurt too much. The nearest peacetime equivalent is a woman who has had an abortion. She may be utterly convinced it was necessary. She may be equally convinced it was wrong. Logic cannot help her; she does not ask that the contradictions be reconciled.

With rumours of war prowling the world once more, the churches would do well to acknowledge this psychopathology, and not rush in too fast with facile offers to heal it or facile prayers for peace. War is a human evil, when all the principles of morality are stood on their heads, when the purposes of honourable men are to take life rather than save it, to hurt rather than to heal. If it is not possible to say anything useful to them, it is wiser to say nothing.

GOING BY THE AQUINAS BOOK

3 November 1990

As armed force against Saddam Hussein looks increasingly likely, the question arises, would St Thomas Aquinas have approved? He it was who, in the thirteenth century, formulated the criteria for just wars that civilized nations everywhere have generally come to accept.

A dose of Aquinas's calm reasoning is needed as tensions arise within churches in Britain between those clamouring for some official church denunciation of war preparation and those less sure. The House of Bishops of the Church of England recently debated the issue but found itself so far from agreement that no statement was possible.

Both the *Church Times* and *The Methodist Recorder* lead their front pages this weekend with stories on this disarray, while in *The Tablet* Graham Greene and Bruce Kent skirmished with the military. The Bishop of Oxford, the Right Rev. Richard Harries, has emerged as Aquinas's standard-bearer with an article in *The Independent*, though his analysis was bettered by

Sir Arthur Hockaday, former permanent under-secretary in the Ministry of Defence, who applied the just-war doctrine line by line to the Gulf conflict in last week's *Tablet*.

Aquinas put forward three conditions for a war to be "just" (by which he meant justified). Subsequent commentators have expanded his third, that the intention of those waging war must be to promote good and avoid evil, into four supplementary conditions. In so far as there is Christian moral teaching on the issue (apart from an idealistic pacifism), church leaders need do no more than promote knowledge and understanding of these seven conditions. The fact that politicians and the military have turned to the UN charter and the Geneva conventions rather than theological textbooks makes no difference, for these are simply technical, legal versions of Aquinas's theology.

The first condition is that war must be waged by lawful authority: a private war can never be just. This implies that states must not act counter to the UN charter, by which they are lawfully bound. If the Security Council specifically forbade military action in the Gulf, for instance, Aquinas's first condition could not be met.

The second condition requires that those to be attacked must have done some wrong: there must be some "just cause". At least at face value this is clearly met in the Gulf case, though if Iraq's aggression against Kuwait were being treated differently from all other similar acts of aggression in the recent past merely because oil is involved, it could be argued there was a degree of bad faith in singling out Iraq.

The third condition, righteous intention, excludes bullying, hatred, cruelty, or a desire for revenge or domination, and implies that the motive for war must be the restoration of a just peace. A Gulf war fought to establish Anglo-American hegemony in the region, for instance, would not be righteous. Aquinas adds that it is legitimate to conceal one's military intentions from the enemy and that it is legitimate to fight on feast days (so Iraq could not count on a Christmas truce).

Aquinas was the founder of a whole school of philosophy based on the teaching of Aristotle that had been kept alive by Arab scholars. The first of the four subsequent conditions –

that war must be the last resort, when all other means for restoring justice have failed – is well represented in the section of the UN charter that says economic sanctions should be tried before military force is used. This applies in the case of the Gulf. Last resort can be the first resort, but only when no other remedies are available. And as Hockaday argues in *The Tablet*, such factors as the desert climate may legitimately affect considerations of last resort. Aquinas was a realist, and the last-resort principle does not mean waiting for ever, or even until after a favourable opportunity has passed.

To be "just", military action must be embarked upon with a reasonable prospect of success. Only those in command can judge such things, and it would be contrary to this condition for politicians to insist on action against the advice of their commanders, or for commanders to act prematurely to satisfy politicians (as generals have not infrequently asserted they have been obliged to do in the past).

A just action must discriminate between combatants and non-combatants, and this is the principle that has been used to call in issue the possibility of a nuclear war ever being a just war. It is allied to the principle of proportionality: the means chosen must be proportional to the evil being corrected. While this would rule out a major military campaign to redress a trivial wrong, any outrages against hostages committed by Iraq would weigh in the proportionality scales, justifying an attack sooner or on a greater scale.

The just-war principles of Thomas Aquinas are clearly relevant to the Gulf, and indeed the public debate in Britain about military action has so far been conducted in terms very close to those he laid down 700 years ago. But what is most arresting is that in the just-war section of his *Summa Theologiae* he deals with it under the heading of charity. For in Aquinas's teaching, to make war justly can be an act of love. It cannot be moral to hate an enemy, and every Iraqi death must be mourned as a tragedy. And that is the state of mind in which a Gulf war must be contemplated if it is to be just.

An Elite With No Answer

15 December 1990

Britain's commitment in the Gulf is second only to the American, and in Britain there is wider cross-party support. Opposition comes principally from the left of the Labour Party and from within the churches. And it is more the religious intelligentsia than the official religious leadership that is marching at the head of the peace column: the "religentsia", or at least a good part of it. The religentsia, it seems, would not fight for Queen and country, nor for the UN. Its attitude has had a striking influence on church leaders in Britain, who seem anxious not to defy too directly the pacifist intellectual consensus.

It is an elite group. Last month more than a hundred of its members signed a public anti-war declaration, and almost every one was a professor, a bishop, a religious superior, a theologian of known repute or something equivalent. They included the Bishop of Salisbury, the Right Rev. John Baker, the Bishop of Edinburgh, the Right Rev. Richard Holloway, and the Roman Catholic Bishop of Portsmouth, the Right Rev. Crispian Hollis – three of the leading churchmen of their generation. Even more remarkable was the intellectual shoddiness of the document they signed. It is so full of holes it is hardly worth tearing to pieces, though the Bishop of Oxford, the Right Rev. Richard Harries, duly performed the task in last week's *Tablet*. He concluded: "Sadly, this makes war more likely."

An unspecified "Arab opinion" floats into and out of the text, allegedly holding certain views or drawing certain conclusions unfavourable to the West. No undergraduate essay writer – and most of these people have marked a lot of undergraduate essays in their time – would be allowed to get away with so phoney a rhetorical device. The more serious bits of

the 800-word document skip over *non sequiturs* with a facility
Saddam Hussein himself would admire. The conclusion, not
surprisingly, neither follows from the premises nor is supported
by the argument, in so far as there is one. That conclusion,
equally not surprisingly, is against military action in the Gulf.
That may be right or wrong, and it is best to assume that the
case against a Gulf war is rather stronger than this one. But
why did anybody sign such a pathetic tissue?

Every one of the signatories could surely have done a first-
class job of it with a little effort. Bishop Harries, who accused
them of living in a fairy-tale world, must surely be right when
he remarked: "During the last decade some Christian churches
in Britain have been so opposed to Mrs Thatcher that many
Christians now have a knee-jerk hostility towards every government policy. Even stronger is the tide of anti-Americanism that
runs in the world . . . ". He might have added, too, a religious-
moral snobbery towards anything in uniform, anything military.
In other words, no project involving both the CIA and Mrs
Thatcher could possibly be honourable or noble, so please pass
the pen, we don't need to read the words. This is a classic
trahison des clercs. Needless to say, it has nothing to do with
Christianity, a religion whose ideals are pacifist but which lives
in the real world where ideals are sometimes out of reach.
Because of the human inclination to wickedness and the tendency for all power to corrupt, known in classical Christian
teaching as original sin, big countries will swallow small countries, tyrants will suppress human rights, minorities will be
persecuted, wars will break out, millions of innocent people
will die, for ever and ever.

Realizing that, and painfully aware of the failure of the
League of Nations over Ethiopia and Manchuria, Churchill,
Roosevelt and their colleagues devised the boldest remedy they
could think of, a new world order. Never again would Hitler
and his like be tolerated. Every nation was to be invited to
pledge itself to observe certain minimum standards of civilized
conduct, to abide by international law, to live in peace with its
neighbour, to lend its military strength to enforce these rules
if necessary, and to participate in the policy-making of a new

United Nations Organization. It was the very incarnation of the brotherhood of man.

This was something worth dying for. And if it was to work, real people would have to die for it. Deliberate willingness to sacrifice one's life for others and for the highest good is known in Christianity as martyrdom, the ultimate moral act. "Greater love hath no man . . . ". Every noble dream has a nightmare attached, and the UN has had its share. At last, however, after more than forty years of suspended animation, the real UN ideal lives again. A force of warriors has been assembled whose moral dignity comes not from the fact that they are prepared to go into battle to kill, but that they are prepared to go into battle to be killed, for a greater moral purpose than their own survival. Each must be praying that the bitter cup will pass him by, but they know it will not pass them all. They are entitled to know that the cause they might die for is the summit of human achievement so far, a vision of a lasting peace among the nations for the first time in history.

Meanwhile, the British religious elite, the religentsia, can only sneer that such delusions do not even warrant a serious and thoughtful answer.

Part Nine

RELIGION

IN A

SECULAR

SOCIETY

THE TRUE ART OF TEACHING RELIGION

24 September 1988

Religion continues to enjoy a unique status in British society, as is apparent from the boiling indignation on every page of *The Freethinker*, the journal of the National Secular Society. In particular, it has a guaranteed place on national radio and television, and a guaranteed place in the school curriculum. Two more powerful avenues of influence would be difficult to imagine. Its place in education has if anything been strengthened as a result of amendments to the 1988 Education Reform Act. And a threat to its special place on early Sunday evening television was beaten off last week by the Central Religious Advisory Committee of the BBC and IBA.

Yet it remains a paradox that the privileged access of Christianity in Britain to two such vital means of information and education has had so little apparent impact. Each generation is more secular than the last, each year's school leavers more dismissive of religion than the previous year's, and each opinion poll still records Christianity's "melancholy long withdrawing roar".

Those who defended religious education in the debates in the House of Lords this summer, and those who defend the privileged position of religious broadcasting, both sometimes give the impression that their efforts are vital to the very survival of religion in Britain. Yet in the United States, where religious television is almost universally appalling and religious education in state schools banned by law, the levels of religious belief and practice are far higher than in Britain. A lot of religious education in Britain is good, and a lot of religious broadcasting excellent, so this comparison is no indictment of the dedicated work of those engaged in them. But it does leave some awkward questions unanswered.

In both fields the prevailing professional assumption is that any form of "indoctrination" is wrong; no matter how personally committed the broadcasters and teachers might themselves be, they would regard it as an abuse to use their position to make converts. It is not their job to convince school children or television viewers that Christianity is true, they say. Their brief is limited to description and explanation.

They may be quite right to think so, and it may also be the case that any attempt by them to make converts would fail anyway. But to filter out from Christianity that essential element that demands a personal response is to change its nature: rather than an invitation to every individual to which the only possible answers are yes or no, it becomes an objective anthropological phenomenon to be discussed and analysed. It is about other people: it is never about oneself, never presented as if it should be.

It is religion as an anthropological phenomenon which is taught in schools and broadcast on television – an interesting one, no doubt, but with its central point missing. The problem is more acute in schools, where the natural question children must ask – what use is this to me? – is professionally off-limits for the teachers to answer. The standard statement is that Britain has a Christian tradition, and so any understanding of its culture requires some knowledge of it. But it is a thin reply, even if it is the only one possible in the circumstances. The unstated theory behind this approach is that even with the direct and immediate call to commitment and conversion which is at the heart of Christianity extracted, what is left is sufficient of an approximation to justify all the effort of teaching and broadcasting it, and still calling it "religion".

The dimension of personal involvement can be included later, if required, as a matter of personal choice: a sort of optional spiritual DIY add-on. And committed teachers and broadcasters may fervently wish that individuals will take that further step, and may even hope that they have prepared the way. But it is a hope that is contradicted by the evidence. In schools, far more are turned off than turned on. Television is another and more complicated matter, where the distancing is aggravated by the sterilizing artificiality of the medium itself; it can be turned off.

Only personal involvement can really make much sense of religion. From the outside, it is bound to seem absurd: and there really is no neutral ground to view it from. To be neutral is to refuse to respond: to refuse to respond is to deny that it is true. Without involvement, what remains is not an approximation that can be made good later, but a quite false version, something else altogether. It is entirely possible that too much clinical familiarity with that something else altogether, masquerading as an approximation, can have a severely repellent effect. It is the difference between a corpse and a living person: no one studying the former would claim to know the latter, nor regard the one as an approximation to the other.

Teachers and broadcasters come closest to success in this field when they are trying for it least, operating not in the name of religion at all but in the name of art, literature, poetry, music and drama. It is permissible then to do what religious teachers and broadcasters may not allow themselves to do, to reach out for that deep personal response which all true artists regard as the mark of their success. It is through such arts, too, that something of the nature of religious faith can sometimes be captured and conveyed: but it is a rare skill, not one to be commanded by advisory committees or Acts of Parliament. They can preserve and try to improve education and broadcasting which is "about" religion. The danger comes when that is confused with the real thing, as it usually is.

NO APOLOGY FOR TEACHING THE TRUTH

19 November 1988

A distinguished visiting churchman inquired of a young schoolboy which lessons he particularly liked, and was somewhat pleased to be told his favourite was RE – a crafty young man, perhaps. The visitor questioned him further: what in particular did he like most in Religious Education? He liked Bible stories. Which Bible stories did he like especially? He liked stories about Jesus. And so with mounting enthusiasm, the visitor pressed him once more: "The one about when he was a baby, about how he was found floating in a basket in the bulrushes."

One hopes the young man did not grow up to be a designer of Christmas cards. The sober truth from that story is that religious education has been universal in our schools, and compulsory by law, simultaneously with a quite colossal increase in ignorance about even the basic facts of Christianity. At least he had actually heard about the bulrushes.

There has been almost a Great Debate about religious education this year, as a result of the Education Reform Bill's progress through Parliament and the efforts, quite considerably successful, to influence its contents, in favour of the teaching of religion in schools. But the new Act happens to have arrived at a time when there has never been so much uncertainty and confusion about the aims and objects of religious education. Some of the more complacent assumptions of fifteen years ago have had to be abandoned, and not before time. Never has there been more need for some basic questioning in this area. The real Great Debate about religious education is still only just beginning.

Is it consistent to argue, as most religious educators do,

that religion is important; and at the same time to go on to say, as many of them would, that they are professionally indifferent to the success or failure, truth or untruth, of any and every particular religion? To put it in a nutshell: is religious education about other people, or is it about ourselves? Is it about formation: or is it merely about information?

There is an established, even establishment, orthodoxy in the world of religious education; and the time has come to challenge it. We cannot afford to make the mistake of thinking that just because RE has for so long been regarded as the Cinderella subject of the school curriculum, it is therefore not controversial. It is just about the most controversial subject there is.

Some of the disparagement of the present state of RE we heard in political circles this summer was quite simply buck-passing. The problem is a profound one, at the very heart of our whole culture, and therefore the responsibility of everyone. To blame teachers as if they were uniquely at fault is irresponsible. But it is equally a mistake to assume that the present state of RE is beyond criticism, that somehow the whole problem has been solved, and all that remains is to put more resources in, meaning more pay, more status, more staff, better training. That would be fine if we were sure what RE was supposed to be about. We are not sure: we cannot be sure. The present state of RE is not an educational Promised Land where all the difficulties have been solved. It is much more the reflection of a religiously confused society, which does not know what it wants its children to believe, and is therefore prepared to settle for the kind of RE which ducks that very question.

There is a key word in the educational theory of RE: "Indoctrination". Taken literally it means little more than the process of teaching – a doctrine, literally, is anything which is taught. But a whole generation of post-war educators adopted the idea of indoctrination in its new pejorative meaning as a kind of antithesis to all that properly civilizing education was about. It is a word to stop a conversation about educational theory and practice dead in its tracks.

What does it mean in RE? It refers to the teaching of

religious doctrine, not as part of a historical, comparative and anthropological study of what some people have believed somewhere at some time; but teaching it as truth. It is spoken, in educational circles, in tones of disgust. But indoctrination, shorn of its pejorative meaning, is still a useful idea in religious education. The use of the term as some kind of professional insult is surely an emotive recoil, not a worked-out philosophy of education. After all, no one would dream of calling the teaching of mathematics or geography indoctrination, just because what is taught is taught as the truth.

An RE teacher in a secular school in the state sector cannot call upon the ordinary authority of his status in the classroom in order to teach Christianity as true. For he has no mandate. Neither society in general, nor parents, in particular, would back him up. Or if they would, they have not yet said so. But the mandate does exist already in the large minority of schools, which wear a denominational label, the Church of England and Roman Catholic sectors. Indeed the very wearing of that label is authority enough. "This is a Church of England school", could quite properly be translated as "This is a school where Christianity is taught as true". No scandal would be given, nor any reasonable protests heard, nor any dissension caused in the church or in society, nor could any fair criticism be directed at such schools from within the educational world itself, if the church sector were to toughen its attitude to the teaching of RE out of all recognition, in this direction.

So far even inside the church school system, the cry "indoctrination" has warned everyone off. Let us call its bluff. The Church of England and the Roman Catholic Church, after all, both believe officially and without apology that the truths of the Christian faith are as true as the truths of science; and no less important in schools which bear the church's name, they can surely teach as true what they believe to be true. What else is the purpose of having them?

(An abridged version of the 1988 Hockerill Lecture entitled: "Time for a Fresh Vision", given at King's College London, 18 November 1988.)

STRIKING AT IGNORANCE

1 April 1989

Last October the Bishop of Salisbury, Dr John Baker, drew attention to the level of uncertainty and ignorance about the basics of Christianity among average churchgoers. His words need to be more heeded, for herein must lie a large part of the explanation for falling church attendance, the fuss the Bishop of Durham always causes when he sounds off, and even the general drift towards secularization of English morality and culture.

The Bishop of Durham always strikes a chord when he presents his anti-miraculous version of Christian doctrine, because there are countless members of the Church of England and countless more well-wishers and fellow-travellers for whom talk of miracles makes Christianity incredible. Englishmen do not like having to believe impossible things before breakfast: they would like to believe in Christianity but not if it puts itself out of reach. But there are also countless intelligent people, not excluding top scientists and philosophers and certainly including most of the bishops, who do not find miracles an intellectual affront to faith. It cannot be that they are more ignorant than those for whom these difficulties are so strong; it is more likely that they are less so. They probably know some theology, enough at least to know that traditional Christian doctrine falls into a coherent intellectual pattern whose various elements support each other, in a framework which makes the miraculous elements quite believable.

The Virgin Birth, for instance, is by no means just a stray idea which has wandered into Christianity from pagan cults, and which needs to be shooed away again. It is an element in the theology of the Trinity and of the Incarnation, where it performs an important supportive function for these keystones of orthodox Christian faith, and in return receives importance from them. It is virtually the case that given the truth of the doctrines of the Trinity and the Incarnation, if belief in the Virgin Birth did not exist it would have to be invented. It is a buttress against heresy.

No doubt for that reason the Bishop of Durham has always been careful never to attack the theological essence of the Virgin Birth and the Resurrection, whatever he might say about their interpretation as historical events. But it takes some theological sophistication to see the point of such nuances. To most people, he appears to be saying they are simply not true.

Dr Baker also remarked on that previous occasion that churches never go so quiet as when the vicar starts to explain a fundamental point to the children because the parents are also listening avidly, hoping to learn for themselves. And in his April newsletter to his diocese, the Archbishop of York, Dr John Habgood, stresses the importance of good preaching at ordinary Sunday services. "The art of the preacher is so to soak himself in the thought and themes of Scripture that he can use these to illuminate the lives of his hearers . . . ", he writes.

One ten-minute sermon a week is not a lot, however well it is done. Most of the congregation will have nothing much more than a distant memory of school RE lessons, to provide a background context to make sense of what they are hearing. And how much Christian doctrine is actually taught in such lessons in the average state school whether nominally a "C of E" school or not is open to question. One of the great historic mistakes of the Church of England and the Free Churches was to put their faith in the religious clauses of the 1944 Education Act, as the primary way of inculcating a basic knowledge of Christianity in the next generation.

If that is at the root of the ignorance to which Dr Baker was referring, it greatly strengthens the case for Mr Frank Field's new campaign to persuade church schools to opt out of the state system as a body, and take their destinies in their own hands. In his recent pamphlet, "Opting Out, An Opportunity for Church Schools" he writes: "As Christianity becomes a dying part of our culture, religious language becomes a barrier rather than a conveyor of meaning, and this loss of meaning results in even fewer people being able to understand what the Christian message is about." The recovery of that lost sense of meaning for religious language should be a primary aim for a new approach to religion in schools, he argues. He also advocates creating among the ranks of the parish clergy some with the specialist skills necessary for the conduct of worship and for teaching the faith in schools, as part-timers. There could be obstacles to this in the state sector, but none in an opted-out church sector. The possibility of some of the burden of teaching religion in schools being shifted to the parish clergy has been mooted before; but it would have to be very well prepared, with formal training and a proper system of qualifications.

Most Anglicans are still very shy of theology. It has a reputation for being as dry as dust. That is partly the fault of professional theologians, who have created all the usual obstacles to comprehension by which any specialist discipline preserves its mystique and intimidates the outsider. But a minimum level of theological literacy among the laity will become steadily more necessary as secular society drifts progressively away from its Christian moorings. Otherwise the Church of England's future will begin to look very dark indeed.

THE BARREN YEARS OF THE 1980s

3 June 1989

There are seven months to go before the end of the decade, and the 1980s have still not yet thrown up one interesting, original and powerful religious idea. Religion thrives on innovation and growth. And the statistics of church attendance continue their long decline, even though it is becoming fashionable for commentators to claim a new sense of spiritual interest in the population at large. But even the cults are not new any more.

The Billy Graham crusade, due to start in London later this month, is a modernized version of an idea which worked in the 1950s. The theology of liberation and the liturgical renewal movement emerged in the 1960s; feminist theology and women's ordination in the 1970s. They are all from the postwar agenda; and it has reached the bottom of the page.

The Bishop of Durham's ideas were already old-fashioned at the time he gave them a new lease of life, which may be why he was so taken aback by the reaction to them. Virtually all the religious controversies of this decade have consisted of a public scrap between theological ideas from previous decades. Even the famous 1980s row between church and government was a product of the 1960s and 1970s consensus thinking on the churches' part, with all the originality on the political side.

New ideas flourish because they catch the mood, which must be what is meant by the biblical phrase "reading the signs of the times" or the modern expression "an idea whose time has come". There is a full graveyard of ideas whose time had seemed to come and then went away again in the 1980s. As for the statistics, the Bishop of Hull, the Right Rev. Donald Snelgrove, has drawn attention in his June diocesan leaflet to what is surely not merely a local pattern when he laments the continual decline in confirmations in the archdiocese of York. "Our casualties are due to religion not reshaping or growing, to our worship lacking any sense of awe and mystery," he remarked. Perhaps the revival of awe and mystery is what the 1990s will be about; but it will still need that crucial undiscovered "idea" to make it happen.

The problem centres on the religious imagination, which is either fertile or not depending on a very peculiar combination of circumstances. In the church it has worked best when there was some external discipline over thought, but not too much; and enough freedom to move in, but with difficulty. The classic example of these optimum stress conditions in this century was the Second Vatican Council; and in the last 500 years, the Protestant Reformation. When anybody may say anything about anything, and no one much cares what they say, the religious imagination goes blank. So it does, too, when one wayward thought invites damnation or the torture chamber.

This is a flaw in every movement which seeks to liberate religion from the need for an objective point of reference, from doctrines and dogmas whose truth is in principle independent of one's opinion of them. It is an uncreative mental ambience in which to think: where there is no resistance to thinking, there is nothing against which the mind can push. In such a framework faith becomes a free-floating emotion with no particular shape, a fashionable and pedestrian "respect for the spiritual" which shuts out the question "the spiritual what, exactly?"

In spite of all the talk of a conservative backlash this lack of substance has been the flavour of the religious climate of the 1980s. The backlashers do not like to resist ideas with ideas but instead jockey for political leverage over their opponents. The Pope displaces progressive theologians from their teaching posts, but does not engage with them in debate; the synodical conservatives in England rally their troops through the division lobbies, but do not want to argue.

It is part of the flavour of the decade, equally, to lament the loss of a general sense of wonder, rather as the Bishop of Hull refers to the absence of awe and mystery in the church's worship. There has first to be a Something worth being awed by, however, and the church has gone shy of such Somethings. But this is a very concrete-minded age. What it can't grasp, it won't wonder at. Wonder is present in this interplay, in fact, but it is in the other direction: it is religion which is in awe of the mysteries of the modern world, not the modern world which is in awe of the mysteries of religion.

The secularism and scientism of the public culture and the private local culture of the churches have now moved apart to such an extent that there is a visible gap between them, and increasing difficulty in communicating across that gap. They are not even mutually hostile, in fact: each side yearns to move towards the other. Society senses the anguish of aimlessness and the disorder of ungrounded values without religion. On the other side religion offers just itself as if the medium was enough without a message, and the message might be laughed at. But religion does not start to be true or false, or useful, until it starts to say something. This it does not dare to do, because it fears rejection. So it offers itself as a sort of method, a kind of attitude, but without content or substance.

What has silenced new religious thinking in the 1980s, therefore, is this subtle sense of intimidation by the secular world and all its bright and brittle glamour. The present generation which ought to be doing the thinking has been struck dumb, its imagination swamped, by the astonishing technological revolution it has lived through, possibly the fastest and furthest rate of cultural change in one generation in all of human history.

When the next generation comes of age, intellectually, it will have known nothing but television, air travel, motorways, and computers, and find nothing intimidating in them because they are so ordinary. It will not be afraid of rejection, and it will not be shy of a firm religious idea or two. Then the mental engines should start to fire again.

THE LIBERAL PRESSGANG

16 June 1990

Few substances have such powerful emotional and ritual associations as blood, the sign of life itself. At the end of the third chapter of Leviticus, God solemnly commands his people never to let themselves drink blood, a command which throws into a more dramatic light the action of Jesus at the Last Supper, when he poured wine for his disciples and told them, "Drink all of you from this, for this is my blood . . . ".

A society which has grown indifferent to the power of blood shows itself indifferent to one of the most potent symbols of all. When that indifference is so assured that other people's deepest taboos are treated as little short of madness, a profound ugliness has crept in.

The word for it is bigotry. When a family of Jehovah's Witnesses is forced to flee abroad rather than allow a child to be subjected to a blood transfusion, a practice utterly forbidden by the tenets of their faith on the basis of the prohibition in Leviticus, Britain is caught in the act of blatant religious persecution.

Majorities convinced they are right are immensely dangerous; in this case the majority has, through the courts and the child protection laws, given itself the right to overrule the rights of a parent on a point of conscientious conviction. It is the majority's view that the point of conviction is not important, or not so important that it counts for very much. So a court may step in, declare the parents' conviction unreasonable, and replace them as parents, in effect, by its own so reasonable self.

But all religious convictions are in principle unreasonable, and so are many other cherished beliefs on which people are prepared to base their lives. Nobody, unless he is prepared to adopt for himself only those beliefs and practices which are supported by the majority, is safe from such bullying. For the real test is not reasonableness, but the opinion, reasonable or not, of the majority. One of the lessons of the controversy over *The Satanic Verses* is that majorities can be just as unreasonably intolerant as fundamentalists. Indeed, we have had to learn to speak of liberal or secular fundamentalism. Majorities pose as tolerant until they are challenged, then their bigotry is revealed.

Britain has yet to learn to live with a multicultural society. So far it has largely been assumed that the tolerance this demands will be begrudged only by a small minority, the obvious racists. This is a misreading both of the nature of tolerance and of the real implications of multiculturalism. Many of those who think they easily accept outside groups have not begun to think about the inevitable challenge to their own perceptions of right and justice.

Thus Asian immigrants must not be discriminated against

or insulted in the streets; but if they want to educate their daughters separately and differently from their sons, in accordance with their culture and beliefs, they must be stopped. Not all racists are blatantly so. Liberal fundamentalists cannot understand that many Asian immigrants want to uphold their basic religious laws even at the cost of insult and discrimination.

A society needs laws which none can break with impunity. Even if his religion says he has to – although in practice no religion does – a father may not sell his daughter into slavery or prostitution. The rules imposed by criminal sanction represent the basic values of that society, which is entitled to insist that those not prepared to keep them should live elsewhere.

There would be no point in making a child a ward of court if the judge himself were a Jehovah's Witness and the court were committed to upholding the beliefs of that group. When the American Mormons found that their beliefs were regarded as criminal, they decided to start a society of their own, and did so in Utah. As, much earlier, did the Puritans who crossed the Atlantic. Multiculturalism has far deeper roots in America than here.

Criminal law represents the relationship between the individual and the state (prosecution is always in the name of public authority, usually the Crown), but civil law regulates the relationship between individuals, for which the state also makes rules. In civil actions, which are essentially actions between private individuals, a different standard, far more sensitive to a diversity of values, ought to apply. Parental rights are a matter for civil law. In reality, however, wardship proceedings to gain control of a child in order to grant consent to medical treatment, though civil in character, have trespassed into the area which ought to be reserved for the criminal law.

This could not happen in a country with a bill of rights, which would require a clear and deliberate decision by Parliament to make a law dealing with consent to blood transfusion when parental religious conviction forbids it. Only Parliament can adjudicate when basic rights conflict. At present the courts do not recognize religious rights as such at all.

The more sinister problem, peculiarly British, is the way

indifference to religion is turning into contempt for it. This is a movement away from tolerance. To understand and respect the beliefs of another, it is necessary, at least to a degree, to have a religious imagination. The retreat from religion, which began as tepid lapsing from the practices of the Church of England, is gradually passing through indifference into insolence: if God exists, it is necessary to disinvent him.

In Search of the New Age

25 November 1989

It often happens that new ideas become important just because important people say they are important. So far, it seems, no member of the British Government has yet uttered the words "New Age" in public. The Archbishop of Canterbury, Dr Robert Runcie, certainly now has; and so it will only be a matter of time before a Minister does too – perhaps Christopher Patten, the nearest to a New Ageist in the present administration.

The New Age movement, Dr Runcie told a conference recently, is hard to define and "that is what makes it so important for us to take it seriously". It is, so to speak, an idea whose time has come precisely because people are looking for things difficult to define. It refers to a ground swell, an uncentralized movement of many diverse constituents, which seeks to reunite the spiritual and the natural order which hard science and soft secularism have put asunder. The name itself is Californian (of course) but there is no head office: a New Ageist is simply someone who looks at reality in a certain way and reacts a certain way. It has echoes of the mystical fringe of the 'sixties hippy movement, and the title itself refers to the astrological progression, associated with the start of the third millennium, from Pisces to Aquarius. But astrology is not compulsory; nor in fact is anything except a certain outlook.

What interested Dr Runcie about it was its religious aspect, and the nagging thought that New Age thinking corresponded better to the spiritual needs of the present generation than orthodox Christianity could hope to do. His advice to the church was to adopt the New Age agenda for itself, if not its answers; and on Thursday in Strasbourg he could be heard following his own advice. In a speech to European Parliamentarians he urged the extension of the well-known Christian coupling of "justice and peace", a phrase he attributed to the Second Vatican Council, into a trinity: justice, peace, and the "integrity of creation".

The New Age is undoubtedly green. It shares the contemporary perception of Planet Earth as a small and fragile globe which is mankind's one precarious home in the entire universe. The concept of Gaia, invented by Professor James Lovelock to describe the unity, interdependence and equilibrium of the planetary eco-system, offers New Ageism the beginnings of a theology once Gaia is made to sound (contrary to Lovelock's intention) like a mother goddess who is divine protectress of all living things. Many agnostics are more unhappy with monotheism than with all other theisms, and eco-pantheism has a lot which could appeal to them even if it leads a few to Stonehenge in mid-summer. The British are particularly prone to the idea that God inhabits nature. Blake, an early prophet of the New Age, had Christ "walking on England's pastures green" and studies of spontaneous religious experience have shown that they are often triggered by scenes of great natural beauty. Nature can still conjure awe where formal worship fails.

Apart from Blake, the New Age's patron saint would have to be St Francis, not for his love of landscape but his teaching that all life is sacred. The New Age covers animal rights (whatever that might mean), herbal remedies and health foods, cottage industry like pottery, and a general dislike of high science, new technology and factory farming. The New Age even has a psychology of its own, stressing personal fulfilment and open and free relationships, though it has no distinctive sexual connotation. Anything goes, so long as it is "holistic".

It is too disorganized to be a cult; but still too close to the mood of the times to be ignored. If those commentators are right who see a growing appetite for a return of the spiritual and a hunger for values, the New Age could well win the jackpot. This would not be without political significance, for one of the few agreed doctrines of the New Age is that "sufficient is enough", that the endless pursuit of economic growth or personal wealth is not only spiritually ignoble but harmful to the planet and everything dependent on it. Needless to say New Age is the product of a certain level of prosperity and security: it is definitely bourgeois, yet fits badly with Thatcherism. The opposite of the New Age is the Yuppie, until the Yuppie sheds his Porsche and turns evergreen.

The New Age movement is consciously millenarian, both in the literal sense that it sees the year 2000 as a watershed and in the apocalyptic sense that it fears the possibility of mass destruction by the ruination of the planet. It is ready and waiting, therefore, to step into the shoes of CND and to appeal to the same idealism. And as in that case, the fear it raises is realistic enough.

Not all of this need worry organized religion in Britain, particularly if it follows Dr Runcie's advice and embraces the better bits. There is a significant part of the New Age spectrum which is Christian already (though the stress on salvation by organic food rather than by faith worries Evangelicals). Catholic thinkers like Schumacher, Barbara Ward (the late Lady Jackson), and Teilhard de Chardin have all contributed, wittingly or not, to the philosophy of the New Age. Buddhism is even closer in spirit. There is nevertheless a tendency, which the Archbishop of Canterbury identified in his recent speech, for the New Age to treat all religions as equivalently true, even as needing to be synthesized into a new whole. That is what happens whenever religions are recruited to some other cause than their own, not treated as ends in themselves but as spiritual support for some other vision. Ideology always corrupts theology.

The New Age is only secondarily religious, seeking to borrow religion to fill its own gaps. It would be good for the spread of New Age ideas, but bad for religion itself, if the attempt were successful. But the colonization of ideas could just as well happen in reverse. It would be good for organized religion if it could learn from the New Age movement a relevant and pressing concern for the "integrity of creation", thereby correcting one of its own most serious oversights; and at the same time good for Planet Earth to be befriended by such powerful forces just when it needs friends most.

THE SIN OF SIMON MAGUS

6 January 1990

A survey into church-going habits of Canadian Anglicans last year made the revealing discovery that the one word that summed it all up was "consumerism". The average church-goer saw himself as a consumer of religion, the survey concluded, much as he might consume goods and services of other more material kinds.

This is a fascinating flash of illumination on the whole state and status of religion in modern Western secular multi-cultural democracies. A consumer is someone who pays his money and takes his choice. Religiously, he stands in a supermarket of ideas, beliefs and observances, taking down from the shelf what appeals to him. He is not necessarily selective, adopting a "pick'n'mix" approach to religion, for he may only have popped in for one loaf of bread. But the basis of his relationship to the goods he buys is specific and contractual. He buys what he wants, and consumes it. If it does not please him, he does not buy it again. This is too close to the truth to be comfortable, and not just for Canadians and not just for Anglicans. Regardless of political or religious preferences, this is the free market applied where it does not belong.

The difficulty for religious organizations in the West is that however much they may dislike this as a true picture of what actually happens, there seems to be almost no escape from it. If every other department of life has become consumer-oriented, then that sets the cultural expectations for the whole. Canadian Anglicans certainly did not learn from their church to regard religion as something to be bought and consumed, even less from their Bibles. They learnt it in their high streets and televisions, and took it with them into church.

It has all the warning markings of a half-truth. People must be free to choose their own fundamental beliefs. If the state is not to be allowed to impose them, individuals must conduct the search themselves, and choose from what is available however they wish. But the Canadian survey implied that this attitude of consumerism applied not just to basic choices but to the whole religious life. It was also how the respondents reacted to the church at a more routine and mundane level.

They shopped around, until they found what they wanted in the type and style of services. They went to church when they felt it was what they needed to do. The focus was all the time on the autonomous individual, the choice-making consumer, who selected in the area of religion what he felt would meet his immediate needs or wants, just as he might select a new car, with or without ashtrays and power-steering. And of course, as an honest man, he will willingly pay for the goods and services he consumes.

The implication was that the church had to respond like a good retailer, adapting the products on sale to suit the market. No doubt product loyalty can be built up by good sales technique, and the gentle knocking of rival firms and wares. But product loyalty would have replaced true commitment. Should religion be so careless of market forces as to demand things rather than offer them, for instance to act in such a way as to make people less rather than more comfortable, then the logic of competition would assert itself and people would look elsewhere for their instant spiritual satisfactions.

While true enough to modern life, this is a ghastly parody of religion. The danger to the church is that it will fall into the consumerist trap, and play the game of best-buys, special offers, this week's new model, and the "Good Church Guide" – every bishop with his sell-by date, every prayer book with its shelf-life. And the ideal consumer will be the Woody Allen character who shops around and tries everything, until he finds something he likes, at a fair price. A consumer-oriented attitude would not do so much harm if it was confined to the supply of religious superficialities, such as the choice of hymns or a preference for guitars over plainsong. But the warning in the Canadian survey was that it can go deeper, and that religion itself was beginning to be treated as if it was a piece of personal property or service, chosen according to the same criteria as other things to be bought, with value for money as the only true test. Religion was becoming judged as if it was a financial and contractual relationship.

If this represents the ultimate danger, it also suggests a possible point of recovery. The language of contract and covenant is not absent from the Bible, though only by the shallowest of analogies is it a financial one. The deal on offer is that in return for a commitment from His people, God will be faithful. Furthermore there is a profound biblical analogy between this and a marriage contract. The debts and duties incurred in such a contract are not, however, to be settled by money. Economists and lawyers have come to treat contracts as binding agreements to do something, on the one side, in return for a cash payment, on the other. That is the consumerist reduction. But a contract can just as well be a binding commitment to do something by one party, in return for a binding commitment to do something else, by the other – without either action having a cash equivalent or being thought capable of having one. In marriage the commitment is to the three traditional Augustinian "goods", fidelity, permanence, and child-bearing, the first two of which at least are enshrined in common law as the basis of the definition of the state of matrimony, while the third is heavily implied.

To reduce the obligations of one side of the relationship to the payment of money, while the other side still delivers the goods, is called prostitution. In religion it is the traffic in sacred things, called simony after Simon the Magician who offered to buy the power of the Holy Spirit. At least the sin of religious consumerism now has a name; and it always helps to name the sin.

BACK-TO-FONT REASONING

14 July 1990

Christenings remain an important social and ceremonial part of the British way of life. A large proportion of the population turns to the Church of England to provide them, as it does for wedding and funeral services, so giving the church a constituency that other parts of its ministrations cannot reach.

Nobody in the church begrudges a church funeral, it seems, no matter how immoral or unbelieving the occupant of the coffin may have been. Except for the divorced, the clergy of the established church are obliged to marry anyone who meets the minimal legal requirements which say nothing about believing anything in particular about marriage or religion and no fuss is made about that either. But christenings, which the church prefers to call baptisms, have become deeply controversial. This is a service the church is in the process of withdrawing from the general community. For a few moments at least, the York meeting of the General Synod last weekend looked about to embark on legislation to ban "indiscriminate" baptism, confining it to those who take it seriously as a rite of Christian initiation. Parents would have been required to make a solemn promise that they were willing and able to raise their child in the Christian faith, which, by implication, would have restricted christenings to the families of those who are regular members of local congregations.

But before battle had been properly joined, the synod was told that a report on the wider issues was almost ready for publication, and so was persuaded to take the matter no further for the time being. Yet the debate and the proposed legislation were signs of growing pressure within the church to put a stop to indiscriminate baptism. Sooner rather than later, that pressure will prevail. Already fewer than half the number of newly-born children are baptized into the Church of England. Indiscriminate baptism is an embarrassment because it amounts to a public admission by the church that an important religious service may properly be used for purely social and conventional purposes by those who regard its religious content as meaningless. Many vicars refuse to officiate at christenings for non-believing families, and their refusal provokes many a storm in parish teacups.

This is partly the church's own fault. The traditional doctrine of baptism has become meaningless for many inside the church too. There is general agreement only that baptism is a ceremony marking entry into the visible community of the church (which is why so much weight is placed on the importance of parents being regular worshippers). The traditional view was that baptism is far more profound and significant, but it reflected beliefs that are now thoroughly out of fashion. For to believe in the traditional view, it was first necessary to believe in hell, damnation and the devil, in heaven and salvation, and in Christ's atoning sacrifice for sin. Those who still talk like that except as a metaphor for life's hard knocks are deemed to be such dyed-in-the-wool conservatives that they are right off the Anglican scale.

Traditionally, baptism was a washing away of original sin, a passage from spiritual death to spiritual life. The unbaptized did not go to heaven when they died, for they were still enslaved to Satan. Baptism was a permanent mark on the soul, showing which were God's own, even as the Israelites marked with blood the immunity of their homes from plague before the exodus from Egypt. To die unbaptized was a fearful thing. To be baptized was to join Christian civilization.

Such deep feelings linger long, particularly in the rural areas of England and in the rural subconscious of the townsfolk. But they get little support from churchmen, who are inclined to treat them as superstitious. And they do dwindle into superstition when such notions are no longer related to Christian doctrine: not to have a child baptized, it is still widely believed, is to invite bad luck. This is folk religion because the church has moved away from what it originally taught about baptism, while ordinary people have hung on to it in a half-remembered and less-than-half-understood form. But they remember that baptism is a sacrament, while the church now remembers it only as a symbol.

Baptism is more than, even other than, the recruitment of a new member to the local parish church. Taken as merely that, it is meaningless, for no baby or small child can make a lifetime's religious commitment, least of all by the proxy voice of adult parents and godparents. The informed answer to a clergyman who refuses to allow a baptism unless the parents and godparents truly believe the words they have to say is to ask him whether he truly believes them himself. Does he, for instance, believe in the devil?

If traditional doctrine no longer meets the need, the answer is not to translate it into a merely sociological phenomenon that drains away the sacramental richness. That merely throws the font-water out with the baby. The answer is to dig deeper into the sources of doctrine, to find those levels of resonance which were always present but went unheard. Only by recovering a meaning for baptism more momentous than a scout's promise, more profound than putting a child's name down for Eton, will the church know what it is doing and what it ought to be doing. Meanwhile, indiscriminate baptism is as good a policy as any.

Part Ten

ISLAM

AND

CHRISTIANITY

WHY ISLAM IS NOW INFLAMED

15 February 1989

In the eyes of fellow Muslims, apostasy from his faith is the most serious crime a Muslim can commit. The second most serious crime is to insult the prophet Muhammad. Put them together and they constitute the sort of challenge which will drive fanatical Muslims to extremes. It is an affront which even moderates are not allowed to ignore.

There is nothing so surprising, therefore, in the international Muslim protest over Salman Rushdie's *The Satanic Verses*. Under Muslim law an apostate should be put to death; it is a matter of honour that any slight on the honour of Muhammad must be avenged. And before the West gets too high and mighty about it, it needs the salutary reminder that the history of Christianity has been through such phases too.

The outlook of Islam in the twentieth century is not so different from that of Christianity in the thirteenth or fourteenth. Indeed, many scholars regard Islam as going through a period in many respects analogous to Europe's own medieval era. The dates fit this analogy: Islam is approximately 600 years younger than Christianity, and is now beginning its fifteenth century. The fate of a European author who insulted the honour and chastity of Christ 600 years ago does not bear thinking about.

The analogy breaks down, however, once the situation of Islam is seen not in isolation but in the context of its relationship with the West. For most of their history Christian Europe and the Muslim Arab and Turkish empires have existed in a state of tension, if not of war for territory and dominance. On both sides this long struggle was always seen as having strong religious overtones. The Crusades were religious, not political, wars, fought with Christian passion for the honour of Christ in no way less intense than the fanaticism now associated with Ayatollah Khomeini in defence of the honour of Muhammad.

The last phase was that of European colonial expansion, including the final defeat this century of the Ottoman Empire. Tens of millions of Muslims found themselves colonial subjects of one or other of the Western European colonial empires, in the Middle East, Asia and Africa. Islam was further humiliated by having to suffer the activities of Christian missionaries, protected by the colonial powers, attempting to induce Muslims to commit the ultimate sin of apostasy.

Now we have a phase of renewed independence and revival as Muslims, their colonial status thrown off, search for their own authentic expression of Islamic statehood. It is proving a difficult rebirth. In almost every variety of Islam – and there are many – factions have arisen which insist on the restoration of complete purity of faith, and the expulsion from their culture of every trace of infidel, meaning Western, influence. In the Muslim minorities in the West, especially Britain, it is an impossible dream, though bodies such as the Union of Muslim Organisations have campaigned tirelessly for some parts of their culture, particularly religious and family law, to be insulated from Western influence.

Islam is based on a fusion of the public and the private, the spiritual and the temporal, and it knows not the meaning of the common Western term "secular" except as one more pernicious Western influence. Muslims are united in the view that the Western secular culture represents the degradation of Western Christianity; and so it comes about quite inevitably that the autonomy of secular life, regarded in the West as an achievement of civilization, is to a Muslim no more than an abomination. So no purely "secular" argument, for instance in support of Rushdie's freedom of speech or Penguin Books' right to publish what they like, gains the slightest respect from a Muslim in his own terms. The most he might concede is that

Muslims have to follow the rules of co-existence in majority non-Muslim communities. Even that is only a temporary phase, as it is a cardinal principle of Islam that one day the whole world will accept the truth and bow the knee to Allah.

To a Muslim, Muhammad is an intimate and revered friend, closer to him than his own brother. The relationship is in some respects even more intimate than the Christian's relationship with Christ. Gai Eaton, a noted English Muslim scholar, described yesterday how he had seen a poor and ignorant Muslim man quietly sobbing his heart out, having heard of *The Satanic Verses*. "He was not about to kill anybody," Eaton remarked, "or make any fuss. He was just distraught." Rushdie knew what he was doing, Eaton believes. "He knew just where to put the knife in. But I have my doubts whether he knew the danger he was putting himself in."

Muslim leaders in Britain have been taken aback by the hostile reactions to their protests, particularly the notorious book-burning episode in Bradford – they do not have the racial memory of Nazi book-burning, and they have learnt a hurried lesson. But they defend it as a lawful demonstration of their community's anger, which, if not vented by such a dramatic ritual, could have turned a lot nastier.

It is vital now that moderate leaders in the one million-strong British Muslim community should retain control, and not see it pass to the more fanatical elements with all the incalculable consequences that could follow for inter-community relations. But to demonstrate their leadership they must also, without hesitation, repudiate Khomeini's "holy war" on Rushdie, and rebuff the Ayatollah (and the wilder spirits in their own community) on the grounds that British Muslims are peace-loving and law-abiding. And it is not Muslim law they must abide by in this case, but British law. Those are the terms on which they came here. And that is what it means to be Muslim but also to be British.

MAKING PEACE WITH MUSLIMS

———•◆•———

25 February 1989

Even if the law of blasphemy were to be expanded to cover non-Christian religions, it is hard to imagine an English jury convicting Salman Rushdie for his *The Satanic Verses*. It is too subtle and theological an assault to expect a jury of passengers on the Clapham omnibus to take the true measure of it. Blasphemy is a very slippery concept. That does not make the libel any less pernicious, and may indeed make it more so. As well as feeling that their deepest religious feelings have been affronted, Muslims in Britain at least also feel the frustration of not being understood and supported by the larger community. An acquittal after a blasphemy trial would, from that point of view, have made a bad matter worse.

Because few non-Muslims have been able to grasp why Rushdie's obscure and surrealist parody on the life of Muhammad has offended them so much, there has been a profound failure of empathy in the majority British response to their protests. And thanks to the Ayatollah Khomeini's death threats, British Muslims also find themselves branded as alien extremists and fanatics. The worst thing that could happen to them now would be for some Iranian agent or British Muslim hothead to succeed in carrying out the Ayatollah's sentence. The entire community of one million or more Muslims would find British society as a whole, with whom their relationship is in any case not yet comfortable, turning its back on them in cold hostility.

The presence of Muslims in Britain in such numbers had, even before this crisis, already begun to resemble a monumental and somewhat precarious experiment in community tolerance which will call upon the very best qualities of both communities if it is not to end in tears. So far the Rushdie affair has brought out the worst qualities on both sides, and in that respect at

268

least it may truly be described as satanic. But agreement would go no further than that. The devil, in non-Muslim eyes, is the Ayatollah; in Muslim eyes, Rushdie. The two views could not be further apart.

There is, nevertheless, still time for conciliation. The state of British law on religious defamation is far from satisfactory, and it needs urgently to be reformulated. To do so quite deliberately as a result of *The Satanic Verses* furore would be a fair and British response. But neither the widening of the present criminal law of blasphemy, nor such formulae in substitution as have been canvassed, nor any law aimed only at preventing threats to public order, will meet the case. A better answer would be to proceed by analogy with the law of libel with its test of "hatred, ridicule and contempt"; and to make an exception to the general principle that it is not possible to libel the dead by deeming, for legal purposes, the revered founders of major religions to be still alive as their followers do in fact believe they are.

Such a law would have to name them; and clearly Jesus Christ and the Prophet Muhammad would be at the top of the list. And such a law would meet the need far better than the concept of blasphemy, for it would redress the offence where the real sting lies, namely the imputation of sexual impurity or other dishonour, against such persons as Christ or Muhammad. As to the prosecutor, it should be the Attorney General. As to the penalty, it should be a fine and confiscation of the offending material. And as to the jury: it could readily grasp the concept of the libel of a supposedly living person, simply by asking itself how it would find if the person were alive now, and a holy and revered member of society now.

God is above being insulted. So, in truth, are Christ and Muhammad. But because their followers feel so personally close to them – a feeling properly described as love – any insult to their name or honour is a wound to a followers' deepest feelings for which the law ought to offer a remedy. If a physical wound is a criminal assault, an emotional and spiritual wound should be too. The analogy with libel is entirely appropriate, for the sort of slurs that most defame the living also most defame the dead. For Christians, Christ is not dead; for Muslims, nor is Muhammad. Blasphemy, on the other hand, is either too abstract or too subjective a concept.

Such a move to calm Muslim feelings would bind the Muslim community more closely into British society, which is the only way it is ever going to prosper. But it must look to its own state of health as well. The outside manipulation of Muslim affairs in Britain, including the funding of rival British groups by rival Arab nations, is one of the most dangerous features of the British Muslim scene.

The role of Arab ambassadors as trustees and patrons of important British Muslim institutions should end, and the Regent's Park Mosque and Islamic Centre, originally founded as a gesture of British goodwill, should revert to home Muslim control. The flow of imams into Britain from abroad is a further channel of manipulation and confusion; it is in everyone's interests that the spiritual leaders of British mosques should know and thoroughly understand British society and culture – they should not have arrived yesterday via Heathrow.

Instead the presence of such outside influence and leadership is a barrier to the proper development of an indigenous British Muslim leadership, and in the longer term, a truly British Muslim culture and spirituality. That may suit foreign interests, but it suits neither Britain as a nation nor the mass of British Muslims. They are being held back in a state of dependence, and it must sadly be added, of ignorance. And if this essential transition from outside dependence is costly and painful, the British community at large has so much at stake in its success it should be wise enough to lend its aid in every way possible. How British Islam takes its shape in the future is a matter for British Islam alone to decide, not for the rest of Britain; but nor is it the proper business of Iranian ayatollahs, Pakistani political parties, Arab oil-rich princes, or Colonel Gadaffi.

Inquest on the Enlightenment

---

25 March 1989

The Rushdie affair caught Western culture off-guard. For years those who like to think about the past and future of civilizations had been thinking serious thoughts more troubled than before, but academically and without a sense of urgency. Was religion over? Or was it the Enlightenment which was over? Was the light of Western civilization beginning to dim, and if so which candles were they that had gone out? It was a good subject for a learned paper.

But suddenly the Enlightenment and religion were in deadly collision – not with the gently decadent Christianity of the West but with fundamentalist Islam of the East – and everyone's gut reaction was straight from Voltaire. But the stirring slogans from the start of that new movement in human consciousness look less confident two centuries later, when the ideas sound like clichés and no one would defend to the death the Nazis' right to drive six million Jews, with campaigns of words as much as with gangs of thugs, into the gas chambers.

There is perhaps no more serious topic to talk about than this. The Enlightenment fed so many tributaries into politics, philosophy, morality, literature and almost every other working of the modern mind that if indeed it is now a spoilt and stagnant source, those who have lived by its banks must start to think about a move to somewhere more fertile.

The Enlightenment's old enemy was dogmatic religious faith, so-called superstition. It is still around unvanquished, and has learnt a few good tricks from the battle, even absorbing into its own system some of the Enlightenment's best achievements. "Human rights" is virtually a dogma of the Roman Catholic Church, for Archbishop Lefebrve was excommunicated for denying it, thereby completing one of the great circu-

271

lar ironies of Christian history. Voltaire should have been alive to marvel at it.

The inquest on the Enlightenment has already begun, perhaps indecently as it cannot yet be said for certain that there is a corpse. It has begun under the unlikely auspices of the British Council of Churches, but it is rapidly drifting into a movement of its own with secular as well as religious input. In fact those churches cannot be excluded from the list of all those other fruits of the Enlightenment, for their temper, if not their doctrine, is modern liberal Protestantism, an inconceivable school of theology without the Age of Reason. An examination of religion is not a bad place to start an examination of the Enlightenment, as Karl Marx almost said.

Clustering round the first theological project in this movement are growing groups of scientists, doctors, historians, educationalists and similar disciplines. Although the phenomenon started in Britain it has grown tentacles in Europe, north and south America, even, it is said, in Korea. Its seminal work was "The Other Side of 1984" by Bishop Lesslie Newbigin, which was commissioned by the council of churches in 1982 as not much more than a shot in the dark. But he hit his target squarely, and in terms which did not demand either a commitment against the Enlightenment or a commitment to dogmatic religion in order to join the conversation. The broader movement has hardly got a name, though the core project has set up shop under the somewhat limp signboard "The Gospel and Our Culture".

A turn-off or not, the name does nevertheless point to a key concept in post-post-Enlightenment study: that it is impossible even to begin the exercise from an intellectual position entirely within the culture of the post-Enlightenment era: there has to be one foot, or at least a toe or two, planted on something right outside the system. Otherwise, as one critic has commented, it is like trying to move a bus while sitting inside it.

During previous phases of the interchange between religion and Western culture, it was the culture which judged religion, and under such judgement religion sheepishly backed away from those parts of its belief which were most at risk from

Enlightenment ridicule. Miracles and resurrections were particularly ridiculous, so they had to be "reinterpreted" in a language intelligible to modern sensibility. In this new phase, however, there is no longer such a mood of philosophical intimidation. Dogma is no longer a dirty word, not least because one of Newbigin's achievements was to demonstrate how the apparently self-contained ideas of post-Enlightenment science and philosophy were in reality far from self-evident or objectively provable, but were themselves riddled with dogma. He didn't invent the point, for this is a movement with several begetters, but he focused it.

If science and secular philosophy rest on assumptions no more nor less secure than religious faith and of the same dogmatic character, then one of the key illusions of the Enlightenment has been shattered and religion need no longer cringe in the corner. It is a basic shift of perception. Before, the teachings of the Enlightenment were "true", in the sense of being the furthest point yet reached in mankind's quest to understand reality; and religion was an atavistic philosophical or sociological phenomenon which that "truth" had somehow to analyse and explain. Now, it is the teachings of religion – in this case the Christian religion – which are awarded the status of a prior truth, and the culture gathered round the Enlightenment which is the phenomenon to be analysed and explained.

The most subtle insult to the Enlightenment is the recent trend to apply the insights of so-called "missiology" to it. For many years European churches with missions in Africa and Asia had been worried about the impact of Christianity on culture. They worried about preserving Christianity from contamination by local pagan cults; gradually they also realized that the Christianity they were implanting was infiltrated by European cultural assumptions which were also not "part of the Gospel" itself. These were the distortions that missiologists tried to identify and eliminate; and they concluded that there were good things and bad things in the local "native" culture, some to be rejected and some to be converted into an emerging indigenous version of Christianity, that was genuinely African or Asian yet still genuinely Christian.

It is part of the new missiological thinking to see the Enlightenment as no more than the equivalent local native culture of Europe, even to see in it equivalents to the magical cults, witch-doctors and superstitions that the first Christian missionaries found in Africa. They too are therefore subject to rejection or conversion. But that is far from treating it as the leading edge of mankind's objective search for truth. And, it must be admitted, this is to see it not so differently from the way that Muslims see it – though with more love, less incomprehension and disgust.

A VERY BRITISH LESSON MUSLIMS MUST LEARN

8 July 1989

The arousal of anger in the Muslim community over *The Satanic Verses* affair presents Muslims themselves, the Government, and society at large with a critical turning point in the development of community relations in Britain. There is no apparent precedent for a government minister to write a long and reasoned open letter to leaders of a religious community in Britain, as Mr John Patten, Minister of State at the Home Office, did this week. But nor is there a precedent for the delicate and precarious situation which now exists.

The presence of a million or more Muslims in Britain does not by itself represent a radical threat to social stability. But when this million or more are largely concentrated in certain areas of half a dozen large towns and cities; and when they are being mobilized to demand, in return for their peace, terms which the majority just will not concede, then real danger looms.

What triggered Mr Patten's letter was a meeting he

attended the week before between the Home Secretary, Mr Douglas Hurd, and a deputation of Muslims organized by the Union of Muslim Organizations. His response shows evidence of much careful thought by the Home Office. What is lacking from his letter, perhaps necessarily, is any recognition of the extent to which the Muslim position flows strongly and naturally from the teachings of the Koran itself.

He speaks throughout of the Government's goodwill towards British Muslims, and of their right to remain faithful to their beliefs as members of a plural society. But the Home Office must know that some of their beliefs, at least at face value, are not compatible with a plural society: Islam does not know how to exist as a minority culture. For it is not just a set of private individual principles and beliefs. Islam is a social creed above all, a radically different way of organizing society as a whole. The nearest many British Muslims have got to reconciling themselves to life in Britain is to try to draw a line right round their community, to create an island inside the line in which Islamic law can be applied and Islamic customs preserved. It is only a sophisticated minority which has already grasped that British society and British law could never accommodate such opting out, and that this cannot be what is meant by multi-culturalism.

The Union of Muslim Organizations, which on this occasion echoed the views of most Muslims in Britain even if it does not always do so, itself freely uses the rhetoric of multi-culturalism. It told the Home Secretary that Muslims wished to "play their full role within the mainstream of life in this country while retaining their religious and cultural identity". But its practical demands do not fit this pattern of mutual tolerance and state neutrality – it wants a Bill of Rights for Muslims in Britain, changes in the blasphemy law so that *The Satanic Verses* can be prosecuted, the recognition by English law that Muslim family life must be governed by Islamic law, separate state-funded Muslim schools, and so on.

Mr Patten tactfully but firmly resisted every one of these claims. He did not spell it out, but beneath the exquisite courtesy of his letter lies a hard saying: the very presence of Muslims in Britain can only be on terms which are acceptable to the majority. What he did not like to tell them was that they can declare war on the values of British society; they can even make living in Britain in the next twenty years a disagreeable experience for everyone; they can fulfil Mr Enoch Powell's horrific prophecies – but they misjudge Britain if they think they can greatly change it towards their own ideals.

The common Muslim perception of Britain – as a society which has gone soft and lost its way, which is therefore likely to give way to any demand which is pressed forthrightly enough – is dangerously misleading: the white tribes of Britain can be every bit as stubborn and intransigent, and no less forceful in defence of their beliefs, as the brown tribes. But it would be a disaster if they insisted on putting this to the test; and that is where the real peril lies in *The Satanic Verses* affair. It has not become a best seller beause hundreds of thousands of people want to explore the wilder shores of modern English literature. It is bought as a gesture against Muslim book-burning, and each demonstration seen on television will sell a thousand copies more, stoking up another kind of fire.

Every other religious minority in Britain has eventually found that the only way of securing its position is by compromise. The logical result of a refusal to compromise is separatism, as in Northern Ireland; and hence violence too, as in Northern Ireland. The burning of books leads inexorably to the burning of bookshops: talk of killing leads to actual killing.

In the short term the Government has a difficult calculation to make. It may hope that by firmness of intention expressed in quiet and reasonable words, as in Mr Patten's letter, Britain's Muslims will quickly realize that they are a resistable force colliding with an immovable object. But it is a British habit always to understate the strength of British resolve, which is often mistaken for its opposite. It is a mistake which urgently needs to be corrected. "Death to Rushdie" may be an equivalent degree of overstatement.

It would be a salutary lesson, nevertheless, if anyone found parading such a placard, and anyone circulating or encouraging such criminal sentiments, was taken at his word and arrested for incitement to murder. The immediate consequences could be unpleasant, even including the risk of riot. But the painful shock of such a confrontation may regrettably be necessary before the British Muslim community is brought face to face with the reality that tolerance and compromise, even over fundamentals, are a fundamental requirement of life in Britain. And that they have no other option.

RUSHDIE TO THE RESCUE

29 December 1990

Salman Rushdie's conflict with the Muslim world was indeed a family quarrel, as he called it yesterday in *The Times*. As a Muslim problem it has found a Muslim solution: Mr Rushdie's return to the faith into which he was born. In a conflict between Muslim demands and those of secular western society, however, there is a danger of this Muslim solution being used as bad example. Not all conflicts between Muslims and others can be resolved by the others becoming Muslims. There must be other answers too.

The paradox of Islam is that it knows how to treat minorities – its record of toleration is, in the long term, better than Christianity's – but it does not know how to be a minority.

In principle, Islam makes no distinction between church and state, between temporal and spiritual. The ability to make that distinction has been valuable in helping Christianity to adjust to pluralism, although it has exaggerated a tendency to mind-body dualism which was innate in Christianity. But the rules of Islam, the *sharia*, are also the rules by which an ideal Muslim society should be governed, so such a society is by definition a theocracy, and there is no material-spiritual dichotomy in its ideology. Here the Muslim world divides into two. The fundamentalists for whom an uncritically literal application of the *sharia* is the only option are bound to find living in the West almost intolerable. In Britain, their response has been to try to create a Muslim state within a state that is outside British society and law, part instead of the Muslim "nation", the *umma*, where the *sharia* can be applied.

There have been demands for a special Muslim family law, under which an area of personal life would be roped off from state legislation and left to the religious authorities. Though fundamentalist, its supporters are by no means all fanatics: many are quite prepared to argue the toss with the legislators and meanwhile abide by state law. The model for their Muslim family law is the way the Koran grants an equivalent dispensation to Christians and Jews living in Muslim societies, allowing them to marry, bury and worship according to their own creeds, though not to proselytize.

The more Westernized Muslim approach approximates to the Christian church-state distinction, rendering unto Caesar the things that are Caesar's. This technically imperfect way of being a Muslim is possible because of the temperate attitude within most of Islam towards those of its members who live less than perfect Muslim lives. It is tolerant of short-falling, and therefore can tolerate those for whom the *sharia* is little more than a historic memory or an infinitely postponed goal. These Westernized Muslims say, at least in private, that the *sharia* was not written for a world of motorcars and television, and certainly not for secular pluralist democracies. The notion of a special family law for Muslims implies a degree of compulsion by the religious authorities, a prospect that many Muslims living in the West do not find inviting.

Among those with this more Western Muslim approach, probably an emerging majority, the Rushdie affair has caused deep embarrassment and profound misgivings, for it has been handled by the fundamentalists so as to coerce not only Mr Rushdie but them too. They have been put under notice that Western freedom of speech does not apply to them should they ever dare question their faith publicly. As a Muslim, Mr Rushdie could do much to help them by accepting moderate Muslim demands but refusing to bow to the extremists. Very few Muslims in Britain have any time for the ayatollahs of Iran, though until now it has been hard for them to say so. They would welcome such a stand.

The false fundamentalist image of Islam projected in the West obscures the degree of clear-sighted wisdom among the great majority of its members and their leaders, who are not remotely fanatical nor ready to turn their backs on the real achievements of western civilization. Christianity went through the eighteenth-century Enlightenment as a trauma; but Islam, by and large, would have found it quite congenial. Its recent contact with the West, including the Rushdie affair itself, has been an Enlightenment experience two centuries late. Only the real fundamentalists insist that Islam has nothing to learn, as it knows everything already. The rest will want to know what the Rushdie affair has to teach them.

What it teaches is that a secular pluralist state like Britain, far from being indifferent to religion, is prepared to defend literally to the death the right to religious freedom of absolutely anybody – a left-wing ex-Muslim Indian or anyone else, whatever the merits of his case. Relations between states will be broken off, even wars will be fought, before those obligations are broken. Muslims should admire such resolution: it matches their own. They need to be able to incorporate into the Islamic tradition of religious tolerance the western (and by no means un-Islamic) principle that to compel a man against his conscience, or to punish him for his religious thought, is one of the most abhorrent of crimes. Once past that watershed, Islam has a healthy future as a western religion. If not, it has no future here at all.

Part Eleven

THE IMAGINARY BATTLE: FAITH AND SCIENCE

Re-enter the Divine Creator

27 June 1988

Astronomers, nuclear physicists and mathematicians have been somewhat taken aback by new evidence that suggests the universe had a divine creator. The evidence comes in the form of what is called the "anthropic" theory or principle, which relies on fairly precise calculations of the probability that complex life forms would eventually emerge somewhere in the cosmos.

Before the calculations became possible as a result of recent nuclear and astronomical discoveries, it formed one of the background truisms of scientific thought that life appeared without any great mystery surrounding it, because the probability was not far sort of certainty and therefore no other explanation was necessary. The universe could have begun any old how it liked, and after enough millions of years, there would be life.

But the actual probability, it has been worked out, appears to be so amazingly small that the hypothesis of divine creation has to be taken quite seriously. Professor Stephen Hawking, Lucasian professor of mathematics at Cambridge, describes in his book *A Brief History of Time* how the latest discoveries and theories about the origin of the universe may point to an act of God, though he is at pains to explore alternatives.

"The laws of science as we know them at present", he writes, "contain many fundamental numbers, like the size of the electric charge of the electron and the ratio of the masses of the proton and the electron. We cannot at the moment at least predict the values of these numbers from theory – we have to find them by observation.

"It may be that one day we shall discover a complete unified theory that predicts them all, but it is also possible that some of them vary from universe to universe or within a single universe.

"The remarkable fact is that the values of these numbers seem to have been very finely adjusted to make possible the development of life. For example, if the electric charge of the electron had been only slightly different, stars would either have been unable to burn hydrogen and helium, or else they would not have exploded . . . It seems clear that there are relatively few ranges of values for the numbers that would allow for the development of any form of intelligent life. Most sets of value would give rise to universes that, although they might have been very beautiful, would contain no one able to wonder at the beauty."

And later he says: "The initial rate of expansion would have had to be chosen very precisely for the rate of expansion still to be so close to the critical rate needed to avoid recollapse. This means that the initial state of the universe must have been very carefully chosen indeed if the hot big bang model was correct right back to the beginning of time. It would be very difficult to explain why the universe should have begun in just this way, except as the act of a God who intended to create beings like us."

Professor Hawking is one of the world's leading experts on "black holes", the strangest bodies in the entire universe where time stands still and the laws of science break down. His own thinking is moving towards a model of the universe which, in spite of the dominance of the big bang theory in modern cosmology, had no beginning or end, being finite but without boundaries in space-time. Such a model has no need of an original moment of creation finely tuned towards the ultimate emergence of intelligent life, and therefore could dispense with the "God hypothesis", but it has one drawback: its time-scale is based on the square root of minus one, which does not exist.

This imaginary idea, known to mathematicians by the letter

i, has proved extremely useful in simplifying and solving various problems in physics and engineering, by allowing the pretence that there is a number which, multiplied by itself, gives a negative result. To be useful, of course, the imaginary number i cannot appear on the bottom line; it has to be eliminated from the equations in the course of the working out. There is a parallel to i in the way Professor Hawking uses the hypothesis called "God", something which enables the analysis to proceed towards a bottom line when it would otherwise get stuck. In fact God and i have a peculiar symmetry in his theory of a finite universe without space-time boundaries, for the two possible solutions he discusses to the fundamental shape and origin of the universe seem to contain either imaginary time using i, or God; but not both.

But human consciousness exists in, and is only aware of, "real" time; and Hawking is going a bit far when he suggests time is nothing more than an element in a scientific theory, and "a scientific theory is just a mathematical model . . . it exists only in our minds". It leads him to state: "It is meaningless to ask which is real, 'real' or imaginary time?"

If the human mind is left to make the choice between these hypotheses, an uncreated universe using i or a created universe using God, it will choose that which corresponds to its experience of time as real: and perhaps conclude, on the back of the anthropic theory: *cogito ergo deus est.*

From his closing paragraphs it is possible to discern a different cry for help from modern philosophers in the navigation of such difficult waters. But as he points out, it is an Aristotle or Kant we need, not Wittgenstein.

SCIENCE VINDICATES THE
DOUBTING BISHOPS

29 September 1988

All the leaks and indications point to the same conclusion: the Vatican is about to announce the discrediting of the Shroud of Turin. Carbon 14 tests performed by three independent laboratories appear to show beyond argument that the garment dates not from the first century AD but the Middle Ages; as evidence of the Resurrection of Christ it is worthless.

So perhaps the atheists were right all along, and the Roman Catholic Church can console itself that it never made the mistake of guaranteeing the shroud's authenticity. But right at the end of its career as "the most sacred object in Christendom", the shroud has vindicated two churchmen in particular, both bishops of Troyes, who denounced it as a trick when it first appeared. The second, Bishop Pierre d'Arcis, even named the guilty man. The story of the shroud thus ends as a tribute to the integrity of these two obscure medieval ecclesiastics who refused to bow to popular superstition and who, 630 years later, deserve belated recognition.

The shroud became an object of veneration thanks to the dean of a collegiate college in Lirey, who saw a chance to make a fast franc by exploiting the late medieval passion for holy objects, miracles and instant religious ecstasy.

The good Bishop d'Arcis even defined the one objection which has always been the most telling Christian case against the shroud: "Many theologians and other wise men declared that this could not be the real shroud of Our Lord having the Saviour's likeness thus imprinted upon it, since the Holy Gospel made no mention of any such imprint while, if it had been true, it was quite unlikely that the holy evangelists would have omitted to record it . . . ". Clearly it was the bishop's faith

286

in the reliability of the Gospels which told him the shroud could not be what it was said to be.

The controversy surrounding the shroud has always been about faith. It was in the late nineteenth century, when the dominance of science had begun to challenge the religious view of the world in popular culture, that the shroud was taken up as the proof "modern man" was looking for. The excitement was increased when photography, then still one of the miracles of science, was first used to explore the mystery, revealing that the image of a corpse could be seen clearly when the shroud was viewed as in a negative.

Since then, the whole armoury of science has been turned on this piece of old linen, culminating in the ultimate test, Carbon 14. The study of the shroud even has its own name – sindonology, from the Greek *sindon*, fine cloth.

There have always been two sorts of sindonological sceptic, both of whom will now be feeling quietly satisfied. The first group is made up of those who reject in principle the claims of religion altogether, particularly anything magical or miraculous. Had the shroud been shown to be from the first century, they would by no means have surrendered their case, though it would have been dealt a heavy blow. They would have said that if the shroud was not a fourteenth-century fake, then it was a first-century fake; or, if it were a real burial cloth, it could have come from anywhere. Finally they might have fallen back on atheist dogma: God does not exist, *ergo*, the shroud cannot be genuine, regardless.

The second group of sceptics have doubted the authenticity of the shroud for theological reasons. The scriptural case against it is a strong one, from the story of Christ's treatment of St Thomas, who demanded to be given proof that he could see and touch, to St Paul's assertion that acceptance of the Resurrection was the result of faith. The argument that the Gospels would have mentioned a surviving burial cloth, particularly one with all the signs of the Crucifixion on it, is also overwhelming, though hardly one an atheist would want to adopt.

What sort of God would leave this sort of evidence lying

around, waiting for twentieth-century science to be invented to prove it was genuine? It would be a God who shared modern man's conviction that science is the ultimate criterion of truth, and modern man's confidence that this is an age entitled to privileged aids to belief. There would have been no point in God "creating" the shroud in the first place, or in ensuring that it survived 2,000 years, unless sooner or later it was to be vindicated.

FOCUSING ON THEISM

21 January 1989

If each generation reacts against the fashions of its predecessor, the time may have come for a review of the supposed conflict between science and religion, but with a quite different outcome from that taken for granted thirty years ago. For instance, there is a growing defensiveness about those who call up science in support of atheism, and new confidence in those who deny such a link – or even treat it as so out of date as to need no answer.

An article written by Dr Jacob Bronowski in 1952 is reprinted in the latest edition of *The Listener*, as part of the celebration of its diamond jubilee. The serene confidence of its faith in science is, by 1989 standards, quite startling: science, he said, will one day look right into man, and thereby create values and discover virtues. Having banished God from the physical world, science would ultimately banish Him from the moral world too. It is not the sort of thing scientists say today. God is back on their agenda, even in the physical sciences.

Bronowski also wrote of a fear of science, which suggests the presence of an overwhelming, mysterious and irresistible power, almost Godlike in its dreadful potency. There is no such mood today. Science is more familiar and domesticated, more interesting than wonderful, slightly suspect, definitely not terrifying.

In terms of mood and tone, a booklet on science and religion just published by the Methodist Church is no less revealing. Called boldly "God of Science, God of Faith", it lacks the defensiveness of tone on the part of religion that would have been automatic a decade or two ago, and speaks in relaxed and confident terms of a new harmony between science and religion, as if that was the only intelligent view a reasonable modern mind could entertain. There is little doubt Dr Bronowski thought he occupied the intellectual high ground in 1952; but it has moved.

There were scientists among Bronowski's contemporaries who were religious believers, just as there are scientists who are atheists thirty years on. Somewhere in between, however, the burden of proof seems to have become reversed. That may be no more than the pendulum of intellectual fashion; but it may also be because religion now unexpectedly holds a scientific trump card in its own hand, the overwhelming evidence from the frontiers of scientific discovery pointing to intelligent design in the Universe. The Methodist scientists take it all in their stride: so simple, so obvious – what can the fuss have been about?

The irony is that the defenders of religion, when religion was on the defensive, were wont to deny that science had anything useful to say about the truth of religion, perhaps to hold at bay what science did actually seem to be saying. Science seemed to be saying that the notion of an intelligent creator had at last been mown down by Occam's Razor – was a hypothesis, in short, for which there was no need. Theism was just a personal taste, and the resort of those without the courage to face the world as it really was.

That is not what science says now. The Anthropic Principle has thrown a gigantic metaphysical spanner into the argument. It is virtually a Copernican revolution in reverse. The principle, which is not seriously contested though differently interpreted, states that the balance of various fundamental quantities and forces in the universe, from the sub-atomic to the astronomical, is so astonishingly precise that they cannot have happened by accident. What has been discovered is that from the first instant after the Big Bang, the scientific laws, ratios and constants of nature had to be arranged with hair's breadth accuracy to produce a universe in which life, and ultimately human intelligence, was possible (and even inevitable). Had there been the slightest deviation from these settings, it could not have happened. So the odds against the universe being "human-friendly" by accident were literally astronomical, one with dozens of noughts. That is where the word anthropic comes from.

It was as if, from the first moment of its existence, the universe "knew" what it had to do and where it was going. The question "Who told it?" is perhaps not a scientific question at all, but it is difficult to get very far in a scientific discussion of the Anthropic Principle without at least a passing reference to God.

The old image of the universe was one where life and everything just happened, and there was no significant connection between its early state and the complexity of structure that eventually emerged. Plank's famous Constant, the speed of light, the ratio of the mass of a neutron to the mass of an electron, and all sorts of other values fixed for all time from a micro-second after the beginning of existence, could have been this, that, or the other, and it would still have developed roughly the way it did. Even the hypothesis of an initial Big Bang was controversial, for it was thought the universe might well have been infinitely old.

But it now seems beyond dispute that these fundamental quantities had to be exactly what they actually were, with a margin of error so tiny as to be negligible. There was indeed a cosmic starting point, and nothing was left to chance. It is no exaggeration to say that the universe, in its first micro-second of existence, was programmed to produce Mozart and every lesser mortal, however long it took. Again the question is unavoidable, "Programmed by whom or what?"

No such argument can ever be conclusive, and the Anthropic Principle stops just short of knock-down proof. For there could have been millions and millions of different universes created, each with different settings of the fundamental ratios and constants, so many in fact that one with the right set was eventually bound to turn up by sheer chance. We just happened to be the lucky ones. But there is no evidence for such a theory whatever. On the other hand the evidence for the truth of the Anthropic Principle and what it points to is of such an order of certainty that in any other sphere of science, it would be regarded as settled.

To insist otherwise is like insisting that Shakespeare was not written by Shakespeare because it might have been written by a billion monkeys sitting at a billion keyboards for a billion years, typing at random. So it might. But the sight of scientific atheists clutching at such desperate straws has put new spring in the step of the theists. For the first time in more than a hundred years they no longer feel the need to apologize for their beliefs. Perhaps they should apologize for their apologies.

THE BATTLE THAT NEVER HAPPENED

17 February 1990

The intellectual route to religious faith is not the most common one; but the belief that such a route is not possible has had a powerful influence in the opposite direction. Faith has become an irrational "leap in the dark" in the face of all the evidence to the contrary, so intelligent and honest people feel they are being asked to suspend their intelligence and honesty, a price many of them will not pay. The belief arises from a supposed conflict between science and religion which science is perceived to have won, once and for all. This perception is "so obvious, so familiar, so pervasive and so respectable that even to contemplate its refutation might be held to be folly, if not sacrilege".

This is how Professor Colin Russell, Professor of the History of Science and Technology at the Open University, described the present state of affairs in a paper which was republished last year in the first edition of a new journal, *Science and Christian Belief.* His business is that of a historian, examining and correcting the record; he is not concerned to refight the "science versus religion" battle in order to show that the wrong side won. His conclusion is much more remarkable – that there never was such a battle. Instead there was a deliberate plot to pretend there was, in order to claim that science had emerged triumphant. It was a campaign of black propaganda and misinformation on a vast scale, and at the heart of it was the great Thomas Huxley FRS, known for his pugnacious manner as a controversialist as "Darwin's bulldog".

Professor Russell was making visible, albeit to a select audience, a revision of history which he believes has now become generally accepted by professional historians as the only possible view once the evidence is investigated. It is that Huxley and his associates were engaged in a "hearts and minds" campaign of literally cosmic proportions, to undermine and displace the pre-eminent role of Christianity in Victorian society with something closer to their own agnostic and anti-clerical prejudices. Like all good historians, Russell dislikes conspiracy theories, but this one seems to stand up to the most sceptical scrutiny.

Huxley was seeking the transfer of power and influence not from religion as such to science as such, but from the church and churchmen to an equivalent corpus of scientists like himself. It was about power rather than about truth. He did have some facts on his side, particularly the celebrated debate about Darwin between himself and Bishop Samuel Wilberforce; but he built this into a famous myth as an archetypal confrontation between the two forces: science based on truth, and religion based on dogma and superstition. This is how it is still commonly remembered today. And it was not so much that Wilberforce was wrong, but that the affair could be used to represent religion as doing what Huxley wanted people to believe it had always done, trying to resist the honest discoveries of science because they were a threat to its own nonsense. There were many other such myths invented for the same purpose – that the clergy had opposed the use of chloroform in childbirth, that Galileo had been tortured by the church, that the church opposed the introduction of modern sanitation, that Calvin condemned Copernicus, and so on.

It is less well known that Huxley was equally at war with a whole generation of first-rank Cambridge physicists, such as Lord Kelvin and J. C. Maxwell; and his own scientific first principles now sound as primitive as Wilberforce's naive creationism. The advantage was that they were easily grasped by non-scientists, not that they were true; and therefore they were well chosen to serve the purposes of his campaign. It was the supreme battle for cultural ascendancy and philosophical hegemony in the late Victorian era. His myths and legends eventually became the sort of truths that "every schoolboy knows", and his fundamental invention that there was a battle and that science won it has passed into the collective subconscious all over the world.

As Professor Russell tells it, Huxley's originally more innocent purpose was to encourage the advancement of science in a very unfriendly cultural climate not caused by the hostility of religion but of ordinary people. Some of his associates had other ulterior purposes such as enmity to Roman Catholicism, particularly in Ireland, or opposition to the church school system.

Huxley's strategy was not merely the public discrediting of religion, but the substitution of science, or what he called "Nature", almost as an alternative deity. There was talk of the "priesthood of science" and of "the church scientific", with Huxley as "the Bishop" and a parallel Sunday school system was set up to spread the message (and occasionally sing a "Hymn to Creation"). The Natural History Museum in London was consciously designed as "Nature's cathedral".

Behind this propaganda war was a group of Huxley's friends – almost all, like him, senior Fellows of the Royal Society –

who met regularly in private in what they called their "X-Club". At its peak of influence, the X-Club virtually ran British science (except for Cambridge physics). But Professor Russell believes it fell short of a single grand conspiracy, for while each member was encouraged and inspired by the others, each pursued his objectives in his own way. Some of them even rewrote history in order to show that the progress of civilization had been a constant battle between scientific enlightenment and religious darkness, inventing illustrations where necessary.

Huxley's own greatest propaganda manoeuvre was to have Darwin buried in Westminster Abbey – to the dismay of his family, who wanted him buried where he had lived. It created a shrine, symbolic of the final triumph of science, in the very heart of the enemy's territory. Huxley's role was to trumpet abroad in every way possible the fact that he had taken on and vanquished religion; and he repeated it so often that people finally believed it. "So prevalent has this idea become in popular culture that it is now a staple theme for the media, where its dramatic potential has long been recognized and exploited to the full," Russell observes, concluding: "In their bitter battles for scientific hegemony the Victorian scientific naturalists fought largely in vain. But in establishing their myth of an enduring conflict between science and religion, they were successful beyond their wildest expectations."

It would be dishonourable of religion to start an opposite black propaganda campaign, to reverse the effect Huxley spent his life's work to achieve, to pretend there is a new conflict between science and religion from which religion has this time come out on top. For the reality is more prosaic: there is not now, and never was, any conflict of principle at all. It was a methodically cultivated Victorian myth which virtually everyone still believes to be true.

Part Twelve

PROFILES

RIGHT MAN, WRONG TIME?
The Archbishop of Canterbury, Dr Robert Runcie

<hr>

14 July 1988

The Most Reverend and Right Honourable Robert Runcie MC, Primate of All England and Metropolitan of Canterbury, once had the indignity to be described by Clive James as "an anodyne divine who'll put unction in your function". James was right, but not entirely in the way he meant. Dr Runcie is a soother away of pain – an anodyne; he is a godly and learned man – a divine. And the supplementary definition of unction in the Concise Oxford Dictionary "a sympathetic quality in words or tone caused by deep religious or other emotion" describes his style perfectly. He is affectionate, decent, loyal, amusing, sentimental and industrious. He is even a great Archbishop of Canterbury, or as great as the age will allow.

Yet he is a failure at his job, though such is the impossible nature of it that success would elude even a saint with genius. He may be presiding over a Church of England in the early stages of breaking up, and over an Anglican Communion in the later stages of the same, but there is almost nothing he can do about it. He movingly quoted and endorsed at the General Synod last week the remarks of Archbishop Frederick Temple that he could imagine nothing worse than a Church of England divided, a far worse fate than a Church of England disestablished. And the synod promptly did the very thing he was pleading with it not to do – by no means the first time it has heard and then ignored him.

The obvious but great mistake in assessing Runcie is to make comparisons between his office and some other, supposedly similar, such as that of a president, prime minister or pope. They all have the power to make things happen or to stop them. Those pulling this way and that need them on their side, and so must persuade them or give way. But hardly anyone needs to persuade an Archbishop of Canterbury, for he has so little power. And thus there is no point in kicking him either. The late Dr Gareth Bennett's famous Crockford's preface attack on Runcie last December, for lacking decisiveness and always going with the crowd, was unjust because these very qualities are part of the job specification. If the church wants firm leadership, it had better first learn some of the necessary conditions of leadability, and create a position from which it can be led. It is not the position currently occupied by the tall and amiable man from Lancashire. He is just the fall-guy, an Americanism all the more appropriate in view of what is likely to happen to him shortly at American hands.

The archbishop was described by his biographer Margaret Duggan as temperamentally a conservative, intellectually a liberal. This is the key to understanding this complex, intelligent and likeable man. When the emotional and intellectual forces in his personality are aligned, he is as formidable as any churchman of his generation; but when they are opposed he is almost visibly unmanned.

Once, as Bishop of St Albans, he had proposed an amendment which the General Synod had debated, and so swayed was he by the strength of the case on either side that he admitted half way through his speech that he did not know whether to press on or withdraw. There was an interval of amused silence, as the synod waited to see if he could commit himself. He could not, and left it to the synod to choose, siding, just as Bennett unkindly charged a decade later, with the majority whichever way it went. One senses that what was made manifest on that occasion has happened many times in private, before or since.

What pains the church just now is the ordination of women: in the Church of England, to the priesthood; in the Anglican Communion, to the episcopate. On the former, at least, Runcie has declared himself intellectually convinced; where he stands on the latter we will know in a week or two. And in a church where intellectual conviction is regarded as the only sort that counts, Runcie is therefore now seen to be unmistakably on the side of women priests. He is a man of strong temperament, however, and his temperament is nothing like as convinced as his intellect. He has run out of arguments; but now he smells danger.

It would be revealing to know what his private thoughts and feelings were at the time Terry Waite set out on his last journey to Beirut. Waite and he were not, by all accounts, getting on too well at the time. It is likely Runcie allowed himself to be persuaded to let Waite go against the advice of his instincts, again smelling danger but having run out of arguments. The archbishop had a bad year last year, inevitably blaming himself for the misjudgement, and for a while went off to Oxford for a rest. He gave all the signs of a man who needed a long conversation with himself, to struggle through a difficult private conflict.

This year he is back in better form, half way through a critical year. Because an Archbishop of Canterbury is *ex officio* the senior among all the bishops and archbishops of the twenty-seven provinces of the Anglican Communion, it falls to him to try to hold the Anglican Communion together, a job no one else could hope to do. That an Archbishop of Canterbury has such a role is one of the few things it can be certain the rest of the Anglican Communion agrees upon. The last Lambeth Conference, to which by custom all diocesan bishops of the Anglican worldwide family are invited each decade, fell just ten years ago; so it was Runcie's task to call another. And now the four hundred-plus bishops and their numerous wives and advisers are due to arrive at the university campus just outside Canterbury this Saturday. Runcie knows it could be the show-down, the last in the long procession of Lambeth Conferences which started with a meeting, at the request of the Canadian bishops, in 1867.

Like the office of Archbishop of Canterbury itself, the meetings have been important but not powerful; a Lambeth Conference is technically no more than a consultation between equal and autonomous parts, in effect separate churches of the Anglican Communion. What has united them in the past unites them less and less as the years go by, those same fundamentals of historic Anglicanism whose demise so grieved Bennett. Just as the Church of England has moved on from the Thirty-nine Articles and the 1662 Book of Common Prayer, relegating them to a place of honour in its museum of doctrinal history, so have the other churches. The influence of English and an English way of looking at things has also declined, and this will be the first Lambeth Conference at which simultaneous translation into other languages has had to be provided.

Out of this Runcie has to extract something like common ground, something more than a brief warm glow of episcopal fellowship, strong enough to hold worldwide Anglicanism together for another ten years. Yet many of the bishops are coming to Canterbury to do bitter battle. For some, continued association with the Anglican Communion is only acceptable provided women bishops are acceptable to it, at the very least on a "live and let live" basis. For others, little short of a permanent ban on women bishops throughout the Anglican Communion will keep them in.

The 1978 Lambeth Conference, after much agonized debate, reached a "live and let live" compromise on the ordination of women to the priesthood, mainly because it was an innovation that could be kept out of sight and far away. But the formula barely managed to persuade such opponents as the Bishop of Truro (now the Bishop of London, Dr Graham Leonard) that this would do; and for such as him, agreement this time to the consecration of women bishops certainly will not. But the Americans, who regard women bishops as the natural and logical next step after women priests, do not accept that the Lambeth Conference has any authority to stop them. They come to Canterbury to convert, not to be converted. As an advance gesture of their militancy, some forty of them have already announced that they will play no part in Church of England services while they are here, as a protest against the English all-male priesthood.

It will be sad for Runcie if these irresistible forces and immovable objects collide before his very eyes; but it will not be his fault. He can only really be judged, in such a desperate case, by how well he handles the damage limitation afterwards. And in that respect, he is the right man in the right place at the right time, precisely because of those qualities which Clive James was so rude about. For at this ecclesiastical function there will be plenty of pain to try to soothe away, by a sympathetic quality of words from a godly and learned leader. And the more he follows his temperament rather than his intellect, the better he will do it.

MILESTONE ON THE PAPAL PATH
Pope John Paul II

17 September 1988

Pope John Paul II has returned to the headlines from which he is never long absent, demonstrating again his unique ability to attract attention wherever he goes and whatever he does. Next month he celebrates the tenth anniversary of his election, and there is little sign that age or ill health will prevent him eventually celebrating his twentieth.

His eventful tour of southern Africa may well turn out to be an excellent preparation for the official visit he has said he wants to make in due course to South Africa itself, now the ice has been broken by his unscheduled diversion to Johannesburg. But more than one undemocratic regime has welcomed the Pope in the hope that he would add lustre to its image, only to see him undermine its position once he was there. He would be bound to take with him a very large hammer and many nails, and drive them loudly into the coffin of apartheid.

The Pope is most commonly categorized in Britain as a

conservative, largely because of the things he stands for in the area of personal and sexual morality. He is strict on contraception, abortion, homosexuality and divorce; and under his leadership the Vatican has been trying to weed out clergy who publicly oppose that position. In British experience, figures in public life holding such traditional moral views are also likely to be right-wing on political matters, but such generalizations break down in the case of the quite different background of a Polish Pope, who therefore manages to be, in Western terms, both right-wing and left-wing simultaneously. Politically he is liberal or even radical by Western standards. His repeated stress is on the upholding of human rights, which he has made the central plank of the Vatican's international policy.

When he became Pope, the first non-Italian since the Middle Ages, the changes initiated by the Second Vatican Council, which ended thirteen years earlier, were still somewhat precarious, and there had been a visible weakening of the position of the papacy during the latter years of Pope Paul VI. It was widely felt that the theological thrust of the council required some further reduction in the papacy's central power, in order to make more room for conciliarity, collegiality and delegation in decision-making. The challenge facing the new Pope was to reconcile these two apparently opposite needs: to strengthen the role of the papacy again, while at the same time letting the influence of the council continue to exert itself in loosening up the church's structure.

His famous papal visits represent the solution he had found to these apparently contradictory requirements. That to southern Africa is his thirty-ninth; and he has used it once again both to draw attention to the importance of his office, and to confirm and fortify the leadership of local church hierarchies. He can thus emphasize both the variety and the unity of the church by giving it a mobile centre, one not exclusively Italian but common property. And while taking himself as its centre out to the dispersed church, he has also brought that to the centre by internationalizing the Vatican Curia and the college of cardinals as never before. It is one more example for church historians of the way theology can be shaped by technology, in this case the technology of international air travel and of mass communications.

The papacy under Pope John Paul II has been dominated by his travels, and by the corresponding media coverage they generate. Had he never set foot beyond his diocese he would have enjoyed only a fraction of the fame and prestige he actually has, though in Rome itself there is some impatience with his many absences abroad. But the long-term effect will be to alter fundamentally the basic understanding of authority in the church, as it becomes much more to do with influence than with power. Once more the pen is proving mightier than the sword, for a persuasive papal speech from a rostrum in Harare is mightier than any canon law instruction issued from Rome.

At the start of his reign the Second Vatican Council and what it was seen to stand for was still regarded as a rather tentative and progressive version of Catholicism, the shape of things to come rather than the way they were. In ten years it has developed to the point where Vatican II is now the only official version, an umbrella under which conservatives as well as progressives both have to shelter. The excommunication of Archbishop Marcel Lefebvre earlier this year was symbolic of the change, and of the paradox which it has produced, for here was the traditional smack of discipline being applied against those who refused to accept the need for change.

There is a further paradox in his ten years' reign, which may point to where the actual limits of papal authority really lie in the present day. The conservative morality preached by the Pope, always stressed during his visits, has, in fact, had little apparent effect in changing moral behaviour. He has failed to find the right wavelength for communicating his teaching to modern audiences all over the world, and his reign has seen liberalizing legislation on contraception, divorce and abortion passed or consolidated in many traditionally Catholic countries, usually in the face of strong church opposition.

This is a tide the Pope has been unable to turn; yet surprisingly the effort does not seem to have damaged his prestige. In contributing to his public portrait of a man with firm principles, it may even have enhanced it. But the Pope's insistence

303

that his is the only acceptable Catholic view of marriage, sexuality and related issues has persuaded many of the church's best thinkers that it would be more productive for them to turn their attention to other safer areas. The pressing need at the start of Pope John Paul II's reign was for new Catholic thinking on sex and marriage: and it remains no less a need ten years on.

A MISSION TO COMMUNICATE
The Most Rev. Robert Eames

29 September 1988

It is a measure of the parochialism of the English that they paid little attention to Ulster's leading Protestant churchman until this summer. Then suddenly he was being spoken of in London as a future Archbishop of Canterbury, just as he was being promoted into the front line as an ecclesiastical trouble-shooter. The Prime Minister, it is said, has her eye on him.

But the Primate of All Ireland and Archbishop of Armagh, Dr Robert (Robin) Eames, is already a key figure in the convoluted and agonizing life of his native land. There he is becoming something like the one-eyed man in the kingdom of the blind, in the unique position of being respected and listened to both by Margaret Thatcher and by Charles Haughey. It would be sad to see him plucked from there merely to raise the tone of the otherwise unexciting line-up of possible successors to Dr Robert Runcie. Northern Ireland needs a good leader even more than the Church of England does, particularly one with connections like these. For the moment he is fully briefed on both, trying to heave Anglicanism out of the scrum it has stumbled into over women priests and bishops, and trying to steer the Irish towards the calmer waters of peace and reconciliation. He was a lawyer by training, and rugby and sailing are his sports.

The suspicion that his destiny might be leading him towards Anglicanism's primary see seems to be based on the glowing opinion they have of him at 10 Downing Street, where leading Anglican clergymen are not usually spoken of in terms of admiration, and where the ecclesiastically minded are already browsing through the field against the day that the present incumbent of Lambeth Palace, Dr Runcie, has had enough.

Dr Runcie says his diary is full for the rest of this year and all of the next, which is another way of saying his successor is not going to be the currently obvious man, the Archbishop of York, Dr John Habgood, who, at 63, would be just about too old by 1990. Senior churchmen are well aware of how much they can influence their succession simply by the date on which they choose to retire. On the other hand, Robin Eames (as he prefers to be known) is still only 51. Dr Runcie likes him a lot, and gave him a key job at the Lambeth Conference. Afterwards he respected his judgement enough to ask him to handle the hottest potato in Christendom at the moment: the international Anglican crisis over women bishops. Eames, if he makes a good fist of it, will be a hero throughout the Anglican Communion, in which case, if the next Archbishop of Canterbury is not going to the English, he will be an Ulsterman. It could end in tears for Ulster, however, for Eames is now beginning to provide the sort of moderating statesmanship rising above party and almost above politics for which the province has been crying out for more than a generation.

The bitter in-fighting of Anglican church politics would seem like a holiday to a man who helped families put their loved-ones' names to bits of mangled bodies round the Enniskillen memorial last November. Even for a man who had already written a book on suffering, it was one of his most severe tests. And this week he buried his fifty-fourth victim of the troubles, a young man from a local church family shot by the IRA.

In an interview with *The Times* this week, he said he was now bent on persuading the present Unionist leadership in

Northern Ireland that they were standing on the brink of an abyss. There just had to be movement. Someone had to introduce someone to someone, for the sort of conversation that has never happened in Ireland before; and Eames is that first someone, an opener of doors. He knows Margaret Thatcher fairly well, he knows Charles Haughey even better; he knows the chief constable, the cardinal, the Orange lodges, the SDLP, and even some names better not mentioned. Almost everyone likes him. He does not know Ian Paisley, who has called him "politically naive", but people in England forget that Presbyterians and the Church of Ireland are the Sunni and Shia of Protestantism, and are only on the same side in Northern Ireland by historical accident.

Eames describes himself as a catalyst rather than a leader of opinion. He explains people to each other, explains the Catholics to the Protestants and vice versa, explains Unionism to Dublin, explains the Anglo-Irish Agreement to the Unionists, Unionist objections to the British Government. He will not even talk about who he has been connecting to whom most recently, for the story is still too hot. But if the Irish problem can be solved by introductions, he is the man to do it. He is said to be gifted with a particular sensitivity, the ability to pick up what people are really trying to say behind their words. And it is no surprise that his recipe for bringing the Anglican Communion through its present crisis includes "more communication".

But it is hard to pin him down with an opinion of his own, even to define who he is. Is he an Irishman? There was a long pause, so long that he broke the silence by remarking on it, wondering why such a question should be so difficult. "I am an Ulsterman," he eventually said, admitting that was no answer. In fact Eames comes from a Dublin Protestant family, more Methodist than Anglican until his father changed, and he presides over a church that has refused to accept the Irish border in its own affairs, while staunchly in favour of it politically.

Eames senses a vocation ahead for the Church of Ireland, as a *via media* in Irish affairs, using to best advantage its composite character as a church which is, in theory, both Catholic and Protestant, from north and south. He has never expressed an opinion on long-term reunification "and I never will", he adds; and he calls himself an agnostic on the Anglo-Irish Agreement (though not on the need for long-term reconciliation). But he also says he can see the agreement's faults and prefers to regard it as a step to something else. It happens to be the sort of approach that gives the least offence to as many factions as possible, and seems to be the sort of thing Mrs Thatcher is ready to listen to as well; and in Eames's case it also happens to be what he really thinks. Critical new moves, about which he knows much more than he is prepared to say, are to be revealed in November, he said, and both governments have to recognize some of the lessons of the past. "I am encouraged to believe that will happen."

He admits, too, that the Protestant record in Ireland is somewhat less than glorious, and that for years they never gave a thought to the troubles they were storing up for the future. There is a specially productive relationship opening up between him and the Roman Catholic bishop in Belfast, Monsignor Cahal Daly, who is himself one of the best things to have happened to Northern Ireland for a long time.

Yet, for all this, Eames has not changed sides, for he insists "there is legitimacy in the Protestant case. Many Protestants feel their case has not been fairly understood, and this is part of their frustration. People are inclined, worldwide, to give the impression that they see only the Nationalist side. There is legitimacy in the Protestant case . . . " But it was characteristic of him to add, after further thought, " . . . just as there is legitimacy in the Nationalist case".

He is an orthodox man in doctrine, conservative in worship and good with people, particularly children and clergymen. People open up to him; he knows how to listen. He also has that vital ingredient of modern churchmanship: a pleasing television manner.

There is almost no staff with the job, just a part-time secretary or two, and he works until the small hours and rises early. If he has a weakness it is in formal theology, although it has yet to be demonstrated that theology, at least in Northern Ireland, is part of the solution rather than part of the problem.

MAKING SENSE OF A PREACHER MAN
Billy Graham

1 June 1989

The Billy Graham phenomenon is back in town; and so is the man, offering to make sense of life. Posters have been appearing all over London displaying various combinations of the letters "LIFE.", with the challenge: "Can you make sense of it?" As the opening of his public campaign draws near, they are being replaced with another poster, showing not the answer to the riddle but the man who knows what the answer is, the doyen of American evangelists himself.

The campaign has cost upwards of half a million pounds, and is said to be based on extensive research among 25 to 34-year-olds. It is an expensive and brave attempt at what is probably a hopeless task, for this age group is the most secular section of the population in the most secular city in one of the most secular nations of Europe. The advertising agency which did the market research, Foote Cone and Belding, said it found that the name of Billy Graham was still recognized as someone with something to say; and it also found that people were looking for a deeper philosophy of life. That is the gap in the market – but can they hope to fill it?

In fact, Billy Graham is not so much a purveyor of a philosophy of life as an extraordinarily gifted preacher. His message is less complicated. What he demands of people is an action: they are to get up out of their seats, pass to the front of the arena, and give their names to a steward. This will be sent to their local church, of whatever denomination they select, and in due course they may expect to be invited to a meeting in that church. It may lead them to the meaning of life, eventually, but the first objective is to get their names and addresses.

At Upton Park, Crystal Palace and Earls Court from the middle of this month that is the invitation he will throw out to them as he has done countless times before all over the world. He was raised in the American revivalist tradition, which has always attached the utmost importance to the single act of standing up and coming forward, regarding it as the very moment a sinner is saved. But Billy Graham, perhaps alone of all the famous evangelists of this century, has transcended that tradition just as he has transcended the narrow Carolina Calvinism of his youth. Nowadays, middle-of-the-road Anglicans and sometimes even Roman Catholics support his preaching crusades, although they do not necessarily share the belief that salvation can happen in one electric instant.

Billy Graham was seventy last November, and when he was last seen preaching in Britain, in 1984, he was no longer the young man who could set a football stadium alight with his passion. His mature technique, less entreating and more reasoning, is no less persuasive and for a London audience may even be more so, as the English tend to like their religion served cool. So "Isn't it time you gave Christianity a closer look?" is probably more likely to work than "Open your hearts to Jesus!"

But there is another good reason for going to Upton Park, Crystal Palace or Earls Court which does not seem to have occurred to his advertising agency: the man is a legend in his own lifetime if anyone ever was, and this may well be London's last chance to see him in action. This is the man who has supped with presidents in the White House and world leaders everywhere, who has been for almost a generation the unofficial grand chaplain to a succession of American administrations, and far closer to them in friendship and influence than any Archbishop of Canterbury ever achieved in Downing Street.

No breath of scandal has ever tainted Graham's image. He draws an annual salary of only $59,000, and has been devotedly married to his wife, Ruth, since 1943. They have five children. He has avoided the money-talk, the vulgarity and hyperbole, which has made so much American evangelism unexportable and, in English eyes, even ludicrous. He has kept that distinctive style of small-town wholesome innocence and very American charm, and it hard to believe a cynical word ever passed his lips. If he has a besetting sin, it is that he trusts people too much, and takes too many things at face value. And he likes being liked; he has that sharp American appetite for affection and acceptance. In fact he is impossible to dislike, being open, generous and friendly, the very essence of the "nice guy".

Some have even seen Billy Frank Graham as almost an icon of America, an archetype of all the finest things that the country stood for, and for a long part of his career he seemed to make the easy equation of Christianity with traditional American values. He once described his image of Jesus as "the most perfectly developed physical specimen in the history of the world", suggesting some sort of all-American athlete. Indeed he added on that occasion: "He would have been one of the great athletes of all time. Every inch a man!" As his biographer, Marshall Frady, remarked in *Billy Graham, a Parable of American Righteousness*: "On the whole, Jesus emerges in Graham's perception of him as a figure remarkably not unlike Graham himself." It was, Frady added, a perception many of his adoring public fully shared. But if Frady meant to insinuate that there is nothing more to Graham that conceit, he was wrong. Graham's faith in Christ is profound, and as he has got older, seems to have grown even deeper.

But only slowly has he learnt to talk of himself as a Christian first, American patriot second. He was once much more inclined than he is now to offer America leadership in the thin borderline between religious morality and politics, and there is a whole series of markedly right-wing utterances to his name from that earlier stage. His politics were distinctly apocalyptic, and he was a heavy hammer of the American bogey of communism, which he called a conspiracy by Satan. He was fond of predicting that the Cold War would soon give way to a hot one, thereby ushering in the end of the world; it certainly injected adrenalin into his sermons.

He was, by all accounts, quite shattered by Richard Nixon's Watergate disgrace, and struggled for a long time with a sense of betrayal – Nixon had been a particularly close friend. It was that which seemed to be the watershed, turning him away in disgust from the unclean temporal world towards the purely spiritual. It destroyed his taste for politics. What he will not do in London, for sure, is to offer any thoughts on the grumbling tensions between the Church and the present Government. No one who asks him about Margaret Thatcher will get much more than a tribute to her graciousness last time they met. But he will say, because he will have been advised by his British church hosts to do so and because it has become part of his theology in recent years, that Christians cannot ignore the injustices of the world, and faith without works is dead. For Billy Graham, the meaning of life has become a little more complicated, a little less easily reduced to the small-town Bible-belt certainties of the 1940s and 1950s and the secure world of born-again individualism.

The British churches use him largely for his pulling-power, and the crucial decisions about his campaigns here are made by committees of local churchmen, who plan both the preparation and the follow-up. Although the Billy Graham Evangelistic Association itself takes a back seat, Graham, with disarming humility, has no quarrel with the arrangement. He is, in other words, a performer; and public preaching is an art he has long perfected. But he is also completely committed to the product of which he is the master salesman as he was once totally committed to the brush company whose wares he once sold door to door. (It is not an unkind comparison, as he has suggested it himself.)

He is surprisingly sensitive and vulnerable, and intelligent enough to be aware that among the sceptical intelligentsia his name is something of a joke. Frady reported Graham once told him: "Whenever I enter a restaurant now, any public place, I can see the mockery in their eyes. I can see the hostility. I can see people punch, nudge each other, whispering among themselves, 'watch out, here comes Billy Graham, be careful, don't get converted'." Poignantly, Frady said, he added: "I'll be very happy when my time comes to go to heaven."

LEAD, KINDLY LIGHT, AMID THE ENCIRCLING GLOOM
Cardinal Newman

3 February 1990

There is probably only one Victorian Englishman of whom it may safely be said that his influence has even now not reached its peak. John Henry Newman was born on 21 February 1801 and died on 11 August 1890. This is his centenary year, and the two dates have made a useful bracket for a sort of Newman season or festival all over Britain. His two Oxford colleges, Oriel and Trinity, anticipated the first date by inaugurating a series of weekly lectures in his honour last month. The Chancellor of Oxford, Lord Jenkins of Hillhead, is to conclude the series appropriately with a lecture expounding one of Newman's most celebrated and civilized works, *The Idea of a University*, on 27 February, followed by a dinner at Trinity. Birmingham, to which Newman moved after Oxford, is having a civic dinner in his honour; and all the other institutions with which he was connected, or which claim some association, are similarly arranging their events. The National Portrait Gallery is staging a Newman exhibition.

The Idea of a University remains the classic statement of the case for liberal education as good in itself, thereby investing Newman with the posthumous status of a controversialist in the contemporary debate about the meaning and purpose of the academic life. He was a controversialist throughout his longer career; nor is this the first time his voice has been heard arguing from the grave. The Archbishop of Canterbury, Dr

Robert Runcie, who has two Newman services to preach at this year, recently declared that some of Newman's questions, especially on the development of doctrine in the Christian Church, were still waiting to be taken seriously and the time had come to face them. The *Essay on the Development of Christian Doctrine* is a uniquely ecumenical work, Newman having started it as an Anglican and completed it as a Roman Catholic.

It is an extraordinary man indeed who is still writing the agenda a century after his death. Newman certainly wrote the agenda of the Second Vatican Council from the grave, changing the whole direction in which the Roman Catholic Church was moving with consequences which will last for centuries yet. Cardinal Manning, his slight friend and strong foe, regarded Newman's "old Anglican, patristic, literary, Oxford tone" as inimical to the triumphal intolerance of the dominant mood of Catholicism of the late nineteenth century, and events a hundred years later showed how accurate his misgivings were. Vatican II, more than one Pope has since remarked, was "Newman's Council".

Before the Council his writings were the inspiration for a whole generation of Catholic theologians struggling to uncoil themselves from the strangulations of scholasticism, and because he had been made a cardinal as a personal tribute by Pope Leo XIII, Newman was an unimpeachable foundation for them to build on. Through him, some distinctively English thoughts and ideas, not least the primacy of conscience before authority and all else, have gained a universal Catholic circulation. Meanwhile the full impact of his *Consulting the Faithful on Matters of Doctrine* still lies in the future, and is not without relevance to the unresolved dispute over contraception.

He was a particularly English cardinal, and it was in a particularly English way that he got his red hat. Members of the aristocracy, including the then Duke of Norfolk, used their influence. The novelist A. N. Wilson has said of Newman that he was the only Victorian intellectual of the first rank who had not been disabused of Christian faith by the theories of Charles Darwin; and Newman himself said he was happy to "go the whole hog" with Darwin's hypothesis of natural selection. But

313

far from this marking his surrender to scepticism, he promptly set about another of his great works, his *Grammar of Assent*, to vindicate religious faith before the challenge of science and agnosticism. It too is ripe for revival, for these issues still perplex. It is a philosophical masterpiece in the area of epistemology (how one knows what one knows) which is again becoming a fashionable and fertile field of philosophical inquiry.

He was above all a churchman and theologian, though in the nineteenth century circles of expertise were not so discrete as today – he was also a friend of Gladstone, a violinist, a regular butt of Punch cartoons, and a grand master of English prose. Apart from his immense theological output and a vast correspondence, he founded two religious houses and a public school, and a university (in Dublin); he wrote one of the best autobiographies in the English language, *Apologia Pro Vita Sua*, two novels, a violin sonata, and various poems, of which his *Dream of Gerontius* has entered the standard choral repertoire; and from it comes the hymn "Praise to the Holiest in the Height", still a popular favourite with Sunday congregations, as is his "Lead Kindly Light".

If he was a genius of sorts, was he also a saint? Of a sort, perhaps he was. There is an official "cause" in his name before the tribunals of Rome, and no lack of goodwill towards it in the highest places. His intemperate quarrel with the London Oratorians and his cynical view of Manning might suggest he had unsaintly moral faults; or might merely suggest that they were insufferable. Some who met him late in life had a distinct impression that they were in the presence of a saint. He wrote of himself: "I have nothing of a saint about me as everyone knows . . . I have no tendency to be a saint . . . saints are not literary men, they do not love the classics, they do not write tales." But there is a characteristic touch of irony about that disavowal. It would certainly need the Vatican dicasteries to apply a more than usually broadminded test of sainthood, for him to qualify. It is as a result of Vatican II, and therefore partly due to Newman himself, that such an intelligent adjustment of the criteria can even be contemplated.

He could even be the first ecumenical saint, though not

yet. Before his death most Anglicans had begun to forgive him his defection. There is a whole party of Anglicanism still busy, the Anglo-Catholic party, which owes its existence as much to him as to anyone; and there is no party of Anglicanism which has not felt his influence to some degree (and Newman never completely stopped being an evangelical, whatever his formal allegiance).

Dr Runcie seems minded to deepen his effect on the Church of England even further. It has been a little slow to recognize his real greatness, perhaps because it is only recently that Anglicans have felt free to appropriate for themselves the glories of his post-Anglican career. It is significant that Anglicans who have looked into the Catholic Newman say they find a great deal that is recognizable and familiar, very Anglican in temper. In this ecumenical age the Church of England is beginning to think it can rightly feel proud of having produced such a giant rather than sorry it could not hold on to him – as proud as Oxford manifestly is.

If he deserved to be a cardinal then, for services rendered then, he surely no less deserves to be a saint now, for services rendered since; and no doubt, also, for services still to come. It would be timely, in this Newman centenary season, for there to be some sign of progress towards his canonization, in the Roman Catholic Church; and some sign of enthusiasm for the prospect, in the Church of England.

THE FORTHRIGHT COCKNEY WHO DID THE LAMBETH LEAPFROG
Dr George Carey

26 July 1990

The entire Church of England will have caught its breath yesterday at the unexpected announcement of a new Primate of All England, and especially at the man appointed. George Carey was never a safe and soft candidate, not a grey man of grey opinions, not what you get if you add all the bishops together and divide by 43.

This is an exciting appointment, bold and even risky. It provides a chance – perhaps the last chance – for the Church of England to do something different and thereby to break out of its gentle downwards spiral. One of the youngest and most junior of the bishops, almost untested in high office, has leapfrogged the entire roomful of his elders and betters.

But his promotion is not the result of political acceptability. The prime minister has endorsed a man not afraid to use the leftwards-leaning language of deprivation and social justice. The church, he has said, cannot stand aloof from human pain and misery. The Gospel has political significance."We have a duty to represent the oppressed and deprived, and to care about moral issues and values." So "Carey bashes Thatcher" headlines should not be ruled out.

When members of the General Synod took part in a private poll earlier this month, the Bishop of Bath and Wells came eighth with only five first preferences, equal with such wildcard names as Archbishop Desmond Tutu and Bishop Richard Holloway of Edinburgh. How the Crown Appointments Commission came to a decision so quickly – most churchmen did not expect it before Christmas – is a story its members are sworn never to tell.

Dr Carey is of the Evangelical camp, part of the church's Protestant wing, and by common consent its turn had come for more seats at the top table. The theological colleges, including the one Dr Carey used to run in Bristol, are said to be bulging with them. He was nowhere near the Evangelicals' first choice, however. His commitment to unity with Roman Catholicism is not quite to their taste. He is an intellectual and a theologian, which is a further reason for their not being quite sure he is "sound" on the simple fundamentals of the Evangelical creed. Yet there is logic to the Carey appointment. His studious mind will make him attractive to some who favoured the Archbishop of York – the bench of bishops' leading intellectual – to succeed Dr Runcie. Dr Carey is no less clever, but he is not so sceptically inclined, and favours intellectual rigour. He is more a man to take on the theological liberals at the highest philosophical level.

Dr Carey's Roman Catholic sympathies will make him attractive to those who favoured Bishop David Sheppard, a pioneer of ecumenical work in Liverpool. His working-class origins – he is technically a cockney, son of a hospital porter in the East End – will make him more than attractive to those who believe the church's most important work in the present day is its *Faith in the City* commitment to the inner cities. Under his vigorous leadership his diocese has raised more than £500,000 for the inner cities, exceeding its target and impressing the administrators of the Church Urban Fund with his dedication to their cause. He also showed he has a lot of energy.

Dr Carey's Evangelical background still breaks through in his style of public speaking and preaching, in a characteristic willingness to talk of the Gospels as a call, of Jesus as the man who calls, of religion as an intensely personal, warm and intimate meeting of the soul with its maker demanding a radical change of life. Middle and high Anglicans tend to be shy of such direct, even emotional, use of religious language. Dr Carey is not.

In January, all the major churches are due to launch a "decade of evangelism", initially conceived by the Pope. An Evangelical appointment for Canterbury is therefore appropriate, more so if the new archbishop can work with the other churches on a level of partnership and respect, without the notorious "effortless Anglican superiority" which so offends non-Anglican churchmen. On both counts, Dr Carey is the man.

In choosing him, Mrs Thatcher's known impatience with theological and moral woolliness in the church will have been a factor. It is a premise of later Thatcherism that Britain badly needs an injection of "values", both to humanize the otherwise harsh impact of free-market policies and to keep the peace in the streets. Dr Carey is not reluctant to speak in such terms, and has sometimes echoed her thinking in referring to the importance of family life. On moral issues he is a conservative, with views on abortion, homosexuality and divorce which would not be out of place in the Vatican. But his views on the ordination of women would be, and he once uttered an outspoken rebuke for papal teaching on contraception. He is by no means an "on the one hand, on the other hand" Anglican.

Dr Carey upset opponents of the ordination of women in his diocese by asking them to consider whether they had a future in a church with women priests. Anglo-Catholics in Bath and Wells sought to make a *cause célèbre* out of it, saying he was trying to persecute them out of the church, which he had to deny. Although sympathetic to Roman Catholicism, he does not seem to have much patience with Anglo-Catholicism in the Church of England, particularly disliking that flavour associated with misogyny and homosexuality. Some Anglo-Catholics will not be delighted with yesterday's news.

Dr Carey fits nobody's mould as a typical Anglican bishop, not least because of his East End origins. And it is not hard to find the explanation of some of his present concerns in his early experiences as an elementary schoolboy and RAF conscript. One in particular is worth remembering. At the end of his preface to *The Meeting of Waters*, in which he displayed a knowledge of Roman Catholic theology rare for any Anglican, let alone an Evangelical, Dr Carey let slip a glimpse of the personal.

"I wish my father were able to read this book," he wrote, "because I think he would have been pleased. He was a hospital porter, and had a very special colleague who was a black Roman Catholic Christian. Both of them were outstanding witnesses in their work. One day his friend said to him: 'It grieves me we cannot meet as Christians round the Table of the Lord down here, but, you know, one day we'll meet around the Lord in glory'."

COMPASSION AND MERCY
Archbishop Derek Worlock

22 December 1990

Roman Catholicism in England and Wales was not in great shape in 1965. It was suspicious of other churches and of secular society and trapped in a ghetto by out-of-date rules and customs. It was about to experience the impact of the Second Vatican Council, which ended that year and which might have torn it to bits. English Catholicism from 1850 to 1965 represented the triumph of Cardinals Wiseman and Manning and the eclipse of Cardinal Newman, the triumph of the ultramontane model of Catholicism over the conciliar.

A quarter of a century later the church is hardly recognizable. Catholic churchmen all over the world envy the quality of its ecumenical relations, its unity of mind and purpose, its quiet liberality, its subtle grasp of church-state relations, its commitment to a faith that is both entirely orthodox and smoothly adaptable. While the Catholic church elsewhere is in a state of upheaval, the English branch just gets on with its job. It has become the church of Newman.

319

The explanation of this turnaround lies in personalities more than in policies, in so far as the two can be separated. The character of the English Catholic church changed with the character of the English Catholic churchman. Cardinal John Heenan was a key transitional figure, and his successor, Cardinal Basil Hume, confirmed the transition. Behind the scenes, credit must go to the apostolic delegate (later nuncio) for many of those years, Archbishop Bruno Heim. But more than any of them, the story of those twenty-five years is the story of Archbishop Derek Worlock, who last night celebrated in Liverpool the silver jubilee of his consecration as a bishop.

His background is unusual for a Catholic priest of his generation (he was 70 this year), in that his father was a local agent for the Conservative party in Hampshire, his mother a suffragette. Soon after ordination, he was chosen as a private secretary by Cardinal Griffin, the first of three such posts under successive cardinals in twenty years. Then Worlock had a spell in Stepney as a parish priest before his appointment as Bishop of Portsmouth in 1965. It was his attendance throughout the Second Vatican Council in Rome (from 1962 to 1965), as a consultant and finally as a member, which transformed his career. He was totally convinced by the council, and above all he understood it. The council wrote the agenda through which international Catholicism has been working ever since, and his position has given him enormous authority to shape events.

At this distance one can forget how remarkable the Second Vatican Council was: like a mighty battleship at full speed in a storm, turning through 180 degrees. A lot of the deck damage has still not been repaired, and many of the crew were washed overboard, never to return. But at last the vessel was heading towards the future rather than the past. There are no charts of such waters, but the documents and decrees of the council, still almost as fresh as they were thirty years ago, lay down the broad principles of navigation. Derek Worlock has proved himself the master navigator.

Outside the Catholic church he is best known for his unique relationship with his Liverpool opposite number, the Right Rev. David Sheppard, now the outstanding bishop on the Anglican

bench. In no other city in Britain have the two leading churchmen (not to mention their partner, the Methodist Dr John
Newton) even remotely comparable civic weight and prestige.
In their time, Liverpool, the most self-destructive of cities,
has been through every kind of agony and anguish short of
earthquake, and at each turn of the knife "Derek and David"
have been at the city's bedside together, pastors nursing it
through. But in the long list of disasters – Toxteth, Heysel,
Hillsborough, municipal bankruptcy, the worst unemployment
and some of the worst housing in England – there is no mention
of inter-faith rioting, no overspill from Belfast, even in the one
place in England where bitter Protestant-Catholic communal
tension was once endemic.

This does not begin to measure Derek Worlock's contribution, however, for much of it has been hidden even from
ordinary Catholics in the pews. He has been vice-president of
the Roman Catholic Bishops' Conference since shortly after
going to Liverpool, and the one man above all on whom Cardinal Hume relies. He has raised the National Conference of
Priests to maturity, while never letting it become the defiant
opposition to the hierarchy it might easily have been. He has
spent countless committee hours holding the organized laity in
dialogue, not least through the potentially explosive conflict
after *Humanae Vitae* in 1968. His words then that birth control
was "not the acid test of Christianity" have held that dispute
in check in England ever since. And he was one of the chief
architects, perhaps the master builder, of the Inter-Church
Process and of the successor bodies to the British Council of
Churches that came into being earlier this year. Suffice to say
that without him, all this would have fallen through. Yet he has
never been physically strong, nor free of illness.

Pope John Paul II may or may not have thought of it already,
but Archbishop Derek Worlock is one of the few Catholic
church leaders alive today who, on the merits of personal
service to the church (rather than *ex officio* position), have
earned the ultimate earthly recognition a pope can bestow.
After twenty-five years, Archbishop Worlock fully deserves a
red hat.

Part Thirteen

OBLIQUE
VIEWS

MISCELLANEOUS

LAMBETH CONFERENCE DIARY

30 July 1988

It is typical of the Archbishop of Canterbury to begin his speeches with a self-deprecatory story, though he admits he had wondered whether the English sense of humour would baffle the largely non-English audience at the Lambeth Conference. He need not have worried – they have laughed well enough, though it is not known how well his light-hearted touches translate into Swahili, one of the four non-European languages available in simultaneous translation.

Dr Runcie's device has been copied by others. The Archbishop of Adelaide, the Most Rev. Keith Rayner, recalled a misreporting of the 1958 conference: that they had resolved to have a meeting with the Deity in 1963 (a misprint for "laity"). The saving grace of Anglican bishops is that they do not take themselves too seriously. It is the least fanatical of religions, hence one of the most civilized.

The story told to the bishops by Dr Owen Chadwick was a true one. In 1908 the bishops went on pilgrimage by boat to the Holy Land, but the organizers misjudged the tide. To get to one particular holy place on time, therefore, they had to jump overboard and wade through waist-high water to the shore. "I find that story characteristic of the Anglican Communion, but also very edifying," he remarked. To be characteristic of the present conference, it is waist-high paper that they would have to wade through.

The conference is not what it sounds like: lots of bishops in one large room continuously debating. That happens next week; and they have all been given cushions by the Mothers' Union to ease the hardness of the plastic chairs. They have been in small discussion groups so far, or most of them have. One English bishop confessed to me that he had brought with him the complete works of Evelyn Waugh, and found the temptation to slip quietly back to his room for a further read got the better of him more than once. "More amusing than the conference", he explained.

Many bishops have their wives with them, and some have taken to wearing mufti on the Canterbury campus: perhaps that makes it easier to get away with a spot of truancy. If they look scruffy enough they might even pass for journalists, who are not allowed into the group meetings. But at least we haven't had to spend two weeks living in student bedrooms, as they have. While the bishops have better halves, we reporters have better quarters.

The only organized joke of the conference so far was the cricket match, which was rained off after 15 overs, thus depriving us of the chance to write that "Vespers stopped play". Deacon Sheila McLachlan, who opened the batting for Canterbury Diocese against the Archbishop of Canterbury's XI, was out fourth ball. The *Church Times* described her brief performance as "courageous", which counts as Anglican self-depreciation with irony – Miss McLachlan was also the *Church Times* cricket correspondent for the occasion.

One man having a particularly good Lambeth Conference is the cheerful Primate of All Ireland, Archbishop Robin Eames of Armagh. He has been given a key role concerning the vexed, if rather abstract, question of authority in the Anglican Communion. Under this heading, one of the issues being raised concerns the future leadership of the Communion itself – should it remain with the Archbishop of Canterbury after Dr Runcie retires, and should a non-Englishman be given a go at it next time? The problem with the latter is the oath of allegiance new archbishops have to take to the British Crown. It has occurred to some that this would be no problem if he was from Northern Ireland, though it is not yet clear whether Dr Eames is up to umpiring the 1998 Lambeth Conference cricket match. No doubt 10 Downing Street will check that out: there is surely a script for *Yes, Minister* here.

What has bothered the conference most is someone who does not actually yet exist, the first Anglican woman bishop. Dr John Spong of Newark, New Jersey, is foremost in insisting that she must, or else; and Dr Graham Leonard of London, that she must not, ditto. They are two ends of the spectrum at Canterbury but they have also been seen dining together and, it is said, have had a quiet drink in Dr Spong's room. Whatever happened to *odium theologicum*?

One of the original 11 women priests in America, the Rev. Betty Bone Schiess, who has been at Canterbury, has disclosed that she started legal action against the bishops at one point of her campaign. She was nominated as a woman bishop as far back as 1982, for Central New York, and is a hot tip to be the first to be elected after Lambeth. "It is the threat of lawsuits rather than the Holy Spirit which is moving the bishops along effectively," she is quoted as saying.

In a sense, the entire Lambeth Conference is about her, which is no small achievement. I bet she drinks Carling Black Label.

A UNIQUE VEHICLE TO PROMOTE UNITY

11 February 1989

Large and diffuse institutions such as the churches depend for their vitality and cohesion on the wide circulation of ideas and information. Without it they would wither. Yet their principal channels of internal communication are in virtually every case in the hands of lay people, and what is more, outside any official ecclesiastical control. The *Church Times*, which it is said may shortly change hands, is a classic example. Without its detailed reporting of the General Synod, that body would quickly become so isolated from the church at large as to make its role impossible. But the "official" church has no control over it whatsoever: it is strictly a private enterprise. The same is true of the *Church Times*'s Anglican sister, the *Church of England Newspaper*.

Nor is this confined to the Anglican community. In the Roman Catholic Church in England, often said to be dominated by its clergy, the organs of mass communication are all in lay hands, and all outside the church's official jurisdiction. Neither Cardinal Hume nor the Pope himself could command even an inch of space in *The Universe*, the *Catholic Herald* or *The Tablet*, if lay editors appointed by lay boards chose not to give them any. Although *The Universe* recently passed into the ownership of the Catholic hierarchy, which many lay Catholics thought a dangerous move, there is an elaborate structure of boards and trustees to provide a barrier against clerical interference and to guarantee its continuing independence. The *Methodist Recorder* and the *Baptist Times* enjoy similar independence of church authority.

Their role in the interstices of church life is by no means confined to communication with lay people. There can be few vicarages, presbyteries or manses in Britain which take no church paper, or which indeed do not rely on one for vital information. These papers assume their role with impressive seriousness. Throughout Christendom the cry is heard that the church laity must be involved and trusted as never before. Although this suggests an official image of a lay person as an overgrown child needing to be helped into its spiritual adolescence, in the church papers the laity have been taking the lead for years, unaware of any need for an invitation from on high.

The Universe, for instance, has just launched a regular supplement, *New Creation*, in which lay people address the difficult questions of faith with the utmost maturity, with not a glance in the direction of "Father" for permission. Judging from the Catholic section of the church press, and entirely contrary to the stereotype, the Catholic laity emerge as less rather than more dependent on their professional clergy than any other. *The Tablet*, for instance, enjoys immense prestige, both internationally and in other denominations. It is entirely in lay hands; and often severe in its criticism of the way the professionals run the church.

These papers are without exception characteristically English in the sceptical and detached attitude they take to the churches' official leaderships. They oppose, on occasion; but they are never anything but a "loyal opposition". They reflect the English climate of freedom of speech, which requires an almost instinctive knowledge of the outer limits of intelligent dissent. Some of the controversies on the letters page of the *Church Times*, for instance, are vitriolic to a degree. Beneath the surface of them all, however, is a common language of goals and values that makes them all recognizably Anglican, however much they may denounce each other as traitors to the cause.

There is no ecclesiastical "media culture" or ethos in England, no distinct community of specialist journalists, no society or association to which they all belong. Their various editors and journalists meet each other almost never. If the *Church Times*'s approach to the Church of England is much the same as the *Catholic Herald*'s approach to the Roman Catholic Church, this can only be because they are both part of English culture at large, not some special ecclesiastical sub-section of it. And the proof of that would be the *Jewish Chronicle*, again lay controlled, which approaches the Jewish establishment with exactly the same tone of sympathetic scepticism.

But outside the churches themselves, the church press receives almost no attention; and by the secular press they are usually dismissed as objects of amusement. Yet a leader in the *Church Times* probably carries more weight in the affairs of the nation than any in *New Statesman and Society* or the *Spectator*. These papers are also neglected by non-specialist advertisers, even though their circulations are respectable – probably totally a quarter of a million a week combined – and their readers are above average in prosperity, education, and commitment to the publication of their choice.

There is also a long tradition in the church press of ignoring all the other church papers; they are amazingly jealous of their separate identities and cussedly unco-operative with each other. And just as they are insular as newspapers, so they are in their denominational bias. The *Church Times* would look for an Anglican angle even in the assassination of a Pope, probably concentrating its coverage on a message of condolence from the Archbishop of Canterbury. The *Universe* would do no better in the other direction.

So no one who relied only on a church paper would get a fair impression of any other church; and would be likely to conclude that his was the only one around. Perhaps the ecumenical spirit of the age is still only skin deep; and perhaps the church press knows its readers well enough to give them what they want – a strictly one-denominational diet. But some of the evidence points the other way. Virtually all the papers, even the *Baptist Times*, treat Christian unity in their opinion columns as one of the major issues of the day. They have yet to obey their own editorials, however, and take the opportunity which is uniquely theirs to break down the barriers of ignorance and misunderstanding which are as potent an anti-ecumenical force as any doctrinal disagreement.

THE BISHOP'S EMPTY BELIEF

27 March 1989

It is not at all clear what the Bishop of Durham, the Right Rev. David Jenkins, really does believe. For a man who likes to think of himself as on a crusade to clarify and update the Christian faith, he can be remarkably obscure. For instance he said on television yesterday, sticking fairly close to the sort of language he has used before, that he did not think the Resurrection of Jesus Christ was a "physical resurrection" but a "spiritual resurrection", and yet a "real resurrection".

For most people a real resurrection means a physical one. It means, in short, that the Tomb in the Garden was really empty – perhaps one has to add for the sake of clarity in this context – physically rather than spiritually empty. As in his television interview, Bishop Jenkins likes to emphasize that the important thing was the conviction of the disciples that there had been a resurrection. So it is their "experience" of this conviction, and of the transformation it produced in them, that mattered.

But it surely also matters whether they were liars. The Gospel record is quite clear that what they claimed to have experienced was an objective phenomenon. The tomb was empty; Jesus was somewhere else. It was because they believed the evidence of their own eyes that this produced a transformation and gave rise to an inner conviction. That, at least, is how the Gospel tells it. What is the point of the story of Doubting Thomas otherwise? He did not believe them when they told him they had seen the risen Lord. So when Christ appeared to him too, he was allowed to feel as well as see; and blessed are those, we are told, who have neither felt nor seen, yet believe.

Bishop Jenkins has it differently: he has them experiencing a conviction that Christ had risen, while knowing full well that the body was still cold in the tomb. The experience must have been "more than encountering a ghost" and "more than the revival of a corpse", which is his way of contemptuously dismissing what he thinks orthodox believers believe, though with a careless use of language – he can only mean "other than" in both cases.

Disbelievers do of course agree with Bishop Jenkins that the Gospel narrative of the Resurrection evidence is not true. But it must be somewhat exasperating to have him on their side, for he insists that he does believe in the Resurrection in his own way which he usually insists is the only possible way in spite of rejecting the evidence. The real mystery is why he stops where he does. For the only source he has for the infor-

331

mation that there was an Easter transformation in the disciples, an inner conviction arising from some nameless "experience", is that same Gospel narrative.

The same objection applies to his celebrated doubts about the Virginal Conception. The source for that is the source for everything we know about Jesus's birth. The bishop must have a method by which he can tell which bits of the New Testament are meant be believed and which bits are not; and it appears to be his conviction that the record can be relied upon except in so far as it involves miracles. For those, he has decided, are beyond the credibility of modern, sensible and sophisticated minds.

Why he is so down on miracles he did once venture to explain. He summarized all the worst cases of evil in the world. Then he summarized the faith in a god of miracles as faith in a god who would step in and fix things or stop things, if asked properly. That sort of god could stop all the evil in the world in an instant, but chose not to. He could not, therefore, be a good god, but was indeed "the very devil". Thus did the Bishop of Durham solve, at a stroke, one of the profound mysteries of religious faith with his own simple knock-down proof that miracles do not happen.

So if there is a miracle in the story, as there certainly is at the heart of the Resurrection, he reinterprets it as an allegory pointing to a change in mental attitudes. Not the least of the confusion he causes, however, is because of his insistence that such changes can be called real miracles, and the experience that brought them about a real Resurrection. To understand the Bishop of Durham one needs a glossary, otherwise any discussion with him is totally at cross-purposes.

To understand the Bishop of Durham one also needs to bear in mind a tale from his childhood. Young David loved circuses. One bank holiday a circus came to Bromley, where he lived, but the price of admission, even for youngsters, was half a crown. And David had no money.

He prayed and prayed, convinced that half a crown would materialize by means of a miracle – the Jenkins family was a pious one, the father being a Nonconformist clergyman. Every

332

time he dipped his hand into the back pocket of his school trousers he felt to see if the coin had come, and it had not. And the end of the circus drew nigh. Meanwhile, Mrs Jenkins said to her husband, all unknown to the boy David, how nice it would be if their son could indulge his passion for circuses. And so, just at the point when David was becoming convinced that prayer was a waste of time, there was no God after all, etc. etc., Mr Jenkins gave him the money and all was well. And that, for David Jenkins, now Bishop of Durham, is what miracles are really like. God answers prayers not by materializing things as if by laser beams, but by suggesting ideas to people. For instance, the idea of the Resurrection.

The Archbishop of Canterbury, Dr Robert Runcie, on the other hand, does believe in miracles. He said so again yesterday. When these matters were put to the test in the Anglican House of Bishops not so long ago, the great majority sided with Dr Runcie against Bishop Jenkins. It is hard not to conclude, therefore, that Bishop Jenkins must think most of his fellow bishops are stupid, or devil-worshippers. But it is his own position which does not make sense. Perhaps a man so muddled is no great danger to the faith; but he hardly enhances the Church of England's reputation for being clear about what it stands for.

JERUSALEM CHAMBER BEGETS ECUMENICAL, BRITISH BIBLE

24 June 1989

"Whatever happens we have got the Jerusalem Chamber and they have not" may sum up the thoughts of the Oxford and Cambridge University Presses, as they contemplate their imminent and risky launch of a new product on to the highly competitive and already saturated Bible market.

The Jerusalem Chamber in the shadow of Westminster Abbey is famous, among many things, for being the place from which the Authorized Version of the Bible was produced under King James I. When the successors of those revisers and translators undertook the production of the New English Bible after the war, they also used the Jerusalem Chamber for their meetings. On Thursday yet another Bible committee held its final meeting in the Jerusalem Chamber, to review preparations for the launch of their Revised English Bible, a thorough reworking of the New English Bible which is being published jointly by the two university presses in September. Bible publishing is very big business indeed, and this is an ambitious project, designed to supplant all other Bibles as brand leader, in quality if not in quantity.

It is also unique, being the only version in English which is really and truly ecumenical, really and truly British. Among the sponsoring bodies are the Church of England, the Church of Scotland, the Baptist Union, the Methodists, the Salvation Army and the Roman Catholic Church in England, Wales, Scotland and Ireland. To have a representative of the Irish Roman Catholic hierarchy sitting down with Scottish Presbyterian Bible scholars in the Jerusalem Chamber in London, and furthermore to have them all agree on a version they will all take equal responsibility for, is something of a landmark not only in Bible-publishing but in church relations generally.

It does not follow, however, that the REB will automatically be approved for liturgical use in the Roman Catholic Church, which is one of the biggest prizes. The Jerusalem Bible continues to have that corner to itself, but the REB is obviously going to mount a serious challenge to it. The Jerusalem Bible was originally a work of French scholarship, though the "new" version was an English revision of an English translation.

Aside from its place of publication being the two senior English universities, it would in fact be more accurate to call it the New British Bible rather than English, except the Irish might object; and perhaps more accurate still to call it Scottish. The original NEB project, from which the REB derives, resulted from an initiative of the Church of Scotland, when it was found that servicemen returning from the war complained that they did not get on well with the archaic language of the Authorized or Revised Standard Version they had encountered in the Forces. And the director of the project, Professor William McHardy, is a Scotsman: he served also on the translation panel of the original New English Bible, and was therefore a crucial link between the two versions.

But perhaps the title refers to the language rather than country of origin, in which case it ought to be known internationally as the "English-English Bible" to differentiate from American versions such as the Good News Bible and the New International Version, Anglicized though they have been.

The language question is crucial. The Good News and the NIV Bibles went for the common touch, which makes them more suitable for schools but less so for formal public worship. There has been a conscious attempt, including the seeking of advice from the late Philip Larkin, to enhance the literary and poetic quality of the text of this version, and to make it read worthily in public. It prefers precision to popularity, and employs a wider vocabulary than the Good News and NIV, including the use of a few words which are mildly archaic.

The precision in the use of words was in evidence even at Thursday's meeting, when the textual debate turned on the exact meaning of a publicity hand-out rather than words from the Bible itself. It was not accurate, one Bible scholar pointed out, to describe it as a "completely new" translation, because it was only a revision of an earlier one. It was duly explained to him that publisher's hype and biblical criticism are not on the same planet.

There was also some hopeful talk of television and radio publicity, and the committee chairman, Lord Coggan, hoped they had not forgotten "the Third Programme", the pre-revision name for Radio Three. An approach was suggested to Sue Lawley, in the hope that she might allow the Bible that she hypothetically presented to every victim of Desert Island Discs to be a Revised English Bible. And Oxford University Press said it had indeed made the suggestion already.

That this is to be a good Third Programme–Desert Island Discs kind of Bible is clear enough, and apart from the New Jerusalem Bible it should have the market to itself. Both adopt the fashionable "inclusive language" approach, avoiding the use of male nouns to refer to both males and females, which that section of the population is more sensitive about. It is, in these respects, slightly "up-market" in its appeal; but it could hardly be otherwise if it is to stand as a permanent memorial to the best of British Bible scholarship and the best of modern English usage.

Whether it has the merit to become such a memorial only the public will say, in the end. But it will need exposure for it to be put to the test, and the churches which have supported the exercise owe it that. Total sales of Bibles in Britain continue to run at the phenomenal rate of about a million a year, and are increasing. It would be shocking if there was no room for at least one modern fully British-born-and-bred Bible in that market.

Is it Simply a Matter of Style?

5 August 1989

The Right Rev. Richard Rutt, Bishop of Leicester, has declared war on lordly ecclesiastical titles, saying that to treat Christian ministers as "a higher class of being" is to create an unnecessary barrier.

Archdeacons, he irreverently states in his diocesan journal *News and Views*, "are lovable but hardly venerable" which may not be wholly true in his own city, as the Archdeacon of Leicester is venerable enough to be a hot tip for the see of Truro. But perhaps there is an argument for changing "the Ven. David Silk" into "the Lov. David Silk", as a preliminary to him being made Right Lovable west of the Tamar.

Meanwhile the title Reverend is being quietly squeezed out in his diocese . . . just as women, now admitted to Holy Orders as ordained deacons, have achieved the right to use it. But Bishop Rutt's titular reductionism may at least be in time to stop the spread of the rough Americanism "Reverend Bloggs," to which female diaconal ordination has unintentionally contributed because of the difficulty of choosing between the Rev. Miss, Mrs or Ms. Whether Reverend Bloggs is dreadful and Bishop Rutt is not is another question. "The deacons ordained this summer are doubtless proudly putting 'reverend' in front of their names, presumably hoping that they will one day be revered for their holiness and wisdom," Mr Rutt goes on. But he has a pious eye for the spiritual paradox: "if they ever achieve holiness and wisdom they won't want to be revered."

It is a right reverend can of worms the bishop has opened, nevertheless. By his logic MPs should stop calling each other "the honourable member", except perhaps as a Parliamentary irony; and royalty might have to review their titular usage of majesty and highness. As the Parliamentary example demonstrates clearly enough, however, such courtesies are directed at the office not the bearer of it; and at the standards of behaviour expected, not necessarily those observed.

If the subtlety of this distinction is lost on the general public, and that is no doubt Bishop Rutt's feeling, then all those who use such honorific titles are being generally regarded in all innocence as pretentious hypocrites – mere humble aspirers after virtue and honour though they may really be. So perhaps the need is for a better set of titles for the clergy, which corresponds to the true humility of their spiritual condition (graded according to status), such as Sinner Silk, Even Greater Sinner Rutt, and for the archbishop, perhaps, Worse Than You Can Imagine Sinner Runcie.

The only existing clerical title which really fits this alternative approach is the Pope's, "Servant of the servants of God", though the other of his titles, "Vicar of Jesus Christ", "Prince of the Apostles", "Supreme Pastor", and the preliminary "His Holiness", all tend to undermine the humbler message. Mere "Mr Pope", on the other hand, sounds like a Paisleyism.

Without help from the Bishop of Leicester, fashion has already changed concerning modes of address. The pseudo-aristocratic is out, with one unfortunate exception. It is uncommon but not yet rare to hear an English archbishop addressed as if he was a duke, "Your grace"; more uncommon and indeed rare for an English bishop nowadays to be called "My Lord" except by his wife when he is behind with the washing up; and Cardinal Hume has never yet been known to insist on the attribution of eminence to which he is entitled by custom, nor the Prince Bishop of Durham his princeliness. It is a pity Bishop Rutt is in no position to wage a campaign against the least elegant of modern clerical titles, monsignor, which is a foreign and feudal mode of address – it means simply "My Lord" – that has somehow persuaded itself it is a title of rank somewhere around the level of Chief Petty Officer.

But titles and modes of address are all of a one with such other accidentals as appearance, especially in this case the standard uniform of the clergy – about the only bit of which is really still standard is the Roman collar. Like the title "Father" it crossed the Channel in the nineteenth century, but while it has been almost universally adopted in the Church of England and most of the Free Churches, Father, away from its original Roman Catholic home, still has a self-conscious flavour when Anglicans use it.

The main body of English clergy which eschews the ring of white round the neck is the Evangelical one. But there is a pleasing irony in such abstention, if they think they are thereby consciously avoiding papist neckware out of dislike for papist doctrine. For the Roman Catholic clergy on the Continent have themselves moved away from the Roman usage, collarwise, and look en masse for all the world like Evangelical Anglicans or car salesmen.

And the other Anglican sartorial shift of the late 1980s, a gradual move away from episcopal purple towards nondescript black, is also in imitation of a Roman trend, for it is no longer possible to distinguish at a glance a Roman Catholic bishop from a Roman Catholic priest. Not surprisingly, the leading edge of this new fashion in Anglicanism is the Anglo-Catholic one. Indeed, some Anglo-Catholic bishops have been seen in natty collar-and-tie, jumping a whole stage in the process. The Methodist clergy, incidentally, like their Roman collars broad, as do Scottish Presbyterians, and they have scarcely even begun to imitate the tiny square of front-of-the-neck white which is the latest trendy modification higher up the churchmanship register. It is said to have the advantage that spares can be cut from the plastic of a washing-up liquid bottle.

Taken with the Bishop of Leicester's campaign against titles and the general shift away from gushful and awed modes of address, however, such changes amount to a gradual winding down of the pomp and circumstance of the church, and the slow dissolving of surface distinctions between the clergy and the laity. That is obviously what the clergy want, or they would not be doing it. Their judgement, presumably, is that that is what the laity want too. Or it may indicate more radical anxieties that the real place where the action is nowadays is the lay place, without benefit of clergy, and to get as close as possible to where that action is, the old truth still applies: when in Rome, do as the Romans do. But not quite. If Bishop Rutt wants to try for the big one, Eminentissimo and Reverendissimo Signori Cardinali awaits him.

FAITHS THAT SHOULD FIGHT

21 April 1990

Ask a typical Anglican churchman about disestablishment of the Church of England and he will be quick on the draw with a well-rehearsed knock-down argument: "People want things the way they are."

While few people in Britain now go to church, the majority seem to think religion is still quite a good thing, and that to have a church upheld and protected by law is to make a constitutional statement in favour of religion on behalf of society and the state. Disestablishment is therefore conceived as anti-religious. There is also a general state of neurotic national guilt about the neglect, or rejection, of religion; maintaining an established church helps to soften the sting. It indicates that somewhere in us still lurks a respect for higher things, even if we want no part in them ourselves, particularly on Sundays. It is nevertheless comforting to pass a church and to feel in some remote way that its air of obscure goodness rubs off on us and that it exists because we condescend to let it do so.

A different argument is often heard from the unestablished religions. The Free churches such as the Methodists and Baptists, the Roman Catholics and non-Christian communities such as the Jews all long ago accepted the establishment of the Church of England with varying degrees of enthusiasm or acquiescence. This sentiment springs from a deep neurosis of insecurity. At various times, the Free churches, the Catholics and the Jews have all experienced some hostility. The Free churches have suffered explicit exclusion and humiliation, manifested sometimes as rampant religious snobbery, at other times as a thousand tiny pin-pricks of condescension, rejection and discrimination. Catholicism was persecuted almost out of sight until Irish reinforcements arrived in the last century and deep in the psyche of the average middle-ranking Catholic churchman is still the shadow of a fear that the Gordon Riots might start again tomorrow if he does not watch his step. Most British Jews have also experienced their share of persecution, though not mostly at British hands. But subconscious fears have no great respect for nationality and antisemitism is not unknown in Britain either.

All three groups display symptoms of an unhealthy and sycophantic gratitude to Anglican England. It is the gratitude of the victim to the bully after he stops his bullying. A condition of being excused further bullying is to have to deny that it ever happened. In the case of religion, the formula to be consented to is that England has always been a remarkably tolerant society, unlike those foreign blighters everywhere else. Have not the English even stopped burning effigies of the Pope on 5 November – almost?

None of this is the present Church of England's fault, for the modern Anglican churchman is full of ecumenical love without even a trace of that "effortless Anglican superiority" which marked his predecessors. To be approved of ecumenically by him and his official state church is to be allowed to bask in legitimacy.

The non-established religions would be much more honest, and much more psychologically healthy, if they had the courage to admit openly that the establishment of the Church of England offends them deeply, and is quite incompatible with the basic principles of parliamentary democracy. It would be as healthy for the Church of England to have to face the accusation of past bullying; then ecumenism would begin to mean something real. The Church of England would begin to see which of its present attitudes are still insufferable, and which part of its present identity is still being maintained at the expense of other people's rights and pride.

The real governing body of the Church of England is not the General Synod but the Crown in Parliament. Parliament is supposed to represent all the people, of every persuasion and none. The Queen is head of state of Anglicans and non-Anglicans alike. Non-Anglicans actually make up the majority of the citizens of the United Kingdom. Though few of them recognize the fact, they are still not full citizens, for the Crown and Parliament have functions, relating to the Church of England, which do not and cannot concern them. These areas are marked: "Keep off, Anglicans only."

It would be possible for all these non-Anglicans to assert their democratic constitutional rights by seizing the reins in Parliament, to insist that it was their Parliament too and was no longer going to be used by one group to give special status to its own sectarian purposes. But that would be to cross an emotional and intellectual picket line, to say things which, for various unhealthy reasons, cannot be said, no matter how true and obvious they may be. At the back of their minds is the secret fear that the exclusion and bullying could start again.

By this feature of the constitution, non-Anglicans are, in effect, rendered foreigners in their own country, implicitly told they do not quite fully belong. When they were timidly grateful to be allowed to belong at all, they were not going to put their precarious safety in jeopardy by complaining. But it is coming to the point when they must claim back their full citizenship; and it will not be right or good for the Church of England to stand in their way.